3 Dec
£37-50

The Establishment of Modern English Prose in the Reformation and the Enlightenment

Ian Robinson traces the legacy of prose writing as an art form that was theorised in a manner quite distinct from verse. Robinson argues that the sentence is a stylistic as well as a grammatical conception. Engaging with the work of the great prose writers in English, Robinson provides a bold reappraisal of this literary form, combining literary criticism with linguistic and textual analysis. He shows that the formal construct of the sentence itself is historically conditioned and no older than the post-medieval world. The relationship between rhetorical style and literary meaning, Robinson argues, is at the heart of the way we understand the external world.

Ian Robinson was formerly senior lecturer at the University of Wales, Swansea. He is the author of *Chaucer's Prosody*, *Chaucer and the English Tradition*, *The Survival of English*, *The New Grammarians' Funeral*, *Prayers for the New Babel*, and *Swift: Madness and Art*.

The Establishment of Modern English Prose in the Reformation and the Enlightenment

Ian Robinson

CAMBRIDGE
UNIVERSITY PRESS

PUBLISHED BY THE PRESS SYNDICATE OF THE UNIVERSITY OF CAMBRIDGE
The Pitt Building, Trumpington Street, Cambridge CB2 1RP, United Kingdom

CAMBRIDGE UNIVERSITY PRESS
The Edinburgh Building, Cambridge CB2 2RU, United Kingdom
40 West 20th Street, New York, NY 10011–4211, USA
10 Stamford Road, Oakleigh, Melbourne 3166, Australia

First published 1998

Printed and bound in Great Britain by
Biddles Ltd, Guildford and King's Lynn

Typeset in Plantin 10/12 pt [CE]

A catalogue record for this book is available from the British Library

Library of Congress cataloguing in publication data
Robinson, Ian, 1944–
The establishment of modern English prose in the reformation and the
Enlightenment / Ian Robinson.
    p. cm.
Includes bibliographical references.
ISBN 0 521 48088 4 hardback
1. English prose literature – Middle English, 1100–1500 – History and criticism.
2. English prose literature – Early modern, 1500–1700 – History and criticism.
3. English prose literature – 18th century – History and criticism.
4. English language – Rhetoric. 5. English language – Style. I. Title.
PR751.R63 1998
828'.08–DC21 97-35275 CIP

ISBN 0 521 48088 4 hardback

To the Prayer Book Society of England

Contents

Acknowledgements

This book mentions a number of matters one too easily takes for granted, so I begin with the manuscript and rare book services at Cambridge University Library and the British Library. The delights of a reader's ticket—to be able to fill in a simple form and half an hour later be handling priceless and often very beautiful manuscripts! Mrs Gill Cannell, Assistant Librarian of the Parker Library at Corpus Christi College, Cambridge, and the librarians of Emmanuel College, Cambridge, were especially helpful. I am grateful to the Cost Centre Managers at University College, Swansea for never questioning the large number of inter-library-loan requests I made, and to Miss Pember for tracking so many of them down.

My subject does not belong to any very well-defined category, and I was particularly glad when I was able to find anyone to discuss it with. Professor John Stevens, who supervised my first piece of research, was helpfully perceptive about the early stages of this one. At Swansea, my colleague David Parry was steadily interested and encouraging for several years. I am grateful to some correspondents mentioned below, for answering a curious question; in particular to Duke Maskell, with whom more than anybody I have discussed the book. I am grateful for conversations with Roger Elliott and Howard Mounce. Dr L. R. Leavis put me on to the work of Geoffrey Nunberg, which otherwise I might well have overlooked. The late Geoffrey Strickland also brought a number of relevant essays to my attention, as well as showing a keen and intelligent interest. I had looked forward to showing him the finished product.

The readers for Cambridge University Press really helped with the work. Their detailed and very painstaking criticisms were invaluable, but my main gratitude is for their intelligent understanding.

Some parts have appeared at earlier stages of their development in *The Pelican Guide to English Literature, The Cambridge Quarterly, Faith and Worship*, and *Medieval History*, and I am grateful to the respective editors

viii

for their interest, in particular Mr Arthur Capey, whose unfinished book *Translation* vs *Paraphrase* is a *desideratum* on a related theme.

I am grateful to University College, Swansea for two Research Support Fund grants that made it easier for me to get in some days at some of the Cambridge libraries and the British Library, and for a sabbatical term (Lent, 1995).

Some of the preliminary work that, metamorphosed, has found its way into this book, was done as long ago as 1977–8, when I was fortunate enough to hold a Leverhulme Fellowship. The bulk of that year's work has still to appear, in the book to which this one is pointing, *The Possibility of the Tragic English Novel*, but I am glad of the chance of a preliminary expression of gratitude to the Leverhulme Trustees.

Note on texts

It is sometimes important to my argument for the original punctuation of texts to be quoted. This means, for medieval and early Renascence texts, that most modern editions are unusable. Even in the case of scrupulously scholarly editions one has to watch out. The only twentieth-century collection I know of medieval texts about punctuation does not reproduce their punctuation, and in the act of quoting one source strictly ordering any transcriber to keep the punctuation, replaces it with modern punctuation:

Iste est liber lectionarius ordinis fratrum predicatorum diligenter compilatus et correctus et punctatus et uersiculatus. Nullus addat, uel mutet, uel minuat, uel subtrahat aliquid transcribendo.

This book, the lectionary of the order of preaching friars, has been diligently compiled and corrected and punctuated and divided into verses. Let nobody add, or change, or truncate or take away anything in transcribing.[1]

The promisingly titled collection *Caxton's Own Prose* does not take Caxton's own punctuation to be part of Caxton's own prose, and discards it.[2] The publications of the indispensable Early English Text Society (EETS) have varied very much, even in recent years. The editor of the Old English Orosius tells us that 'the punctuation, including capitals, has been modernized throughout.'[3] When I was looking for perfectly ordinary medieval prose, cookery books looked a safe bet, but the editors of *Curye on Inglysch* say, not very prominently, 'Punctuation is also purely editorial.'[4] Texts published in the 1990s sometimes still offer editorial punctuation. So I have been all the more grateful for the texts that do follow the original punctuation, in the case of the EETS for instance the series of editions of individual manuscripts of the *Ancrene*

[1] Hubert, *Corpus Stigmatologicum Minus*, p. 140, citing 'Rome Sainte Sabine' f. 142 r. a, which I have been unable to check.
[2] William Caxton, *Caxton's Own Prose*, ed. N. F. Blake, 1973.
[3] *The Old English Orosius*, ed. Janet Bately, EETS SS 6, Oxford, 1980, p. cxvii.
[4] *Curye on Inglysch*, ed. Constance B. Hieatt and Sharon Butler, EETS SS 8, Oxford, 1985, p. 34.

Wisse. I have taken the word of reputable editions that claim to reproduce sources exactly. These are not always recent. The idiosyncratic series of reprints put out by Edward Arber from 1868 onwards is still serviceable. Naturally I have gone to originals when I have had time and opportunity, and have done what I can with facsimiles and with the frontispiece photographs of manuscripts with which editors often garnish their heavily edited texts.

This is not, however, a work of palaeographical research (for which go to Parkes, *Pause and Effect*), and I have aimed only at the degree of authenticity necessary for my argument. To represent medieval punctuation marks in print has meant some conventionalization. The various heights of the *punctus,* three in number in classical theory and early medieval practice, appear to be reduced to two in the late medieval manuscripts I quote, and I have recorded them all as either on the line at the position of our full point, or raised like our decimal for the *distinctio* and *media distinctio.* The *punctus circumflexus* is rare in the texts quoted, though in some distinguishable from the *punctus interrogativus* and signifying a different intonation; both are conventionalized into our question mark, which they often resemble (*?*). The *punctus versus* is so close in shape to the modern semi-colon that I have represented it by the latter (*;*). These two marks are printed in italics, to remind us that they are different from their modern descendants. The punctus, especially the *subdistinctio* on the line, is usually much closer to our comma than to our full stop; on the other hand the *;* was a big boundary, marking the end of a period. The virgule is represented by the modern /, which is more definite than many of the hairline ascenders used by medieval scribes but not actively misleading. The only common medieval mark unknown to the modern world, the *punctus elevatus,* appears as itself *⸗*, its unfamiliarity being quite an advantage. All paragraph marks are shown as ¶ though they are of very various shapes in manuscripts and sometimes divide periods rather than paragraphs, and all the symbols that could be represented by modern ampersands are so represented. No effort has been made to represent the colours of punctuation marks.

Manuscript abbreviations have been silently expanded, which involved some discretion or guesswork. The runic characters have been transliterated, *eth* and *thorn* into *th, wynn* into *w* and *yok* into *y, g, gh, w* or *z* as appropriate, which last occasionally involves challengeable editorial decisions. I have not tried to reproduce the lineation of prose manuscripts (which has occasionally made virgules appear rather strangely at the beginnings of lines) or variable spaces between words, though both have been noted if relevant. Medieval *litterae notabiliores* may be anywhere from about the same size as what we call lower case to very big, and they have been conventionalized as our capital size.

Unless reported as edited, texts are otherwise meant to follow sources in spelling, capitalization and punctuation.

Greek quotations are transliterated into roman type, without accents. I am sorry if this is a barbarity; it is done for the sake of readers who may not know Greek but can take an etymological point.

Prosodic marks: ´ marks a syllable more stressed, ˘ a syllable less stressed than others within a defined context, and ˋ a syllable less stressed than ´ but more than ˘ . Some reasons for putting it this way are given below. | division between feet.

Preface

Archbishop Thomas Cranmer's work on liturgy created a new English prose, which was much changed in the time of Dryden. I only have to support this thesis and to make some suggestions about why it is worth considering. We shall have to go perhaps surprisingly far afield for both.

A book centring on Cranmer that has to bring in prose rhythm, the history of the sentence, and the question how style implies world, may seem both ambitiously vague and to belong to that irritating kind which begins by asserting that its subject cannot be understood without prior treatment of other matters, to which the author forthwith turns, or, worse, refers you to other authors for. Limitations of space, I state frankly, have made me postpone the treatment of some questions about rhythm to a companion volume in progress; further, I shall sometimes just give page references to other works of mine rather than repeat arguments. I do intend, however, to show the coherence of a range of topics by treating them all at once. Literary criticism, I believe, should just get on with it. If I can show why this is not practicable here much of my work is done.

The topic itself arose because it turned out that the book I was trying to write, *The Possibility of the Tragic English Novel*, demanded the present discussions. Not to belittle them unduly, I should say that the bye-products, as well as a few additions to previous scholarship I have made along the way, will include a new slant on fiction, the re-editing of most medieval and many Renascence texts, and renewed attention to the topic of prose rhythm almost universally neglected for three quarters of a century. The main aim, however, is fusion. Persist past the contents page and you will see that the links make the point of the whole; which is an example of what I mean by *rhythm*.

Here or there I have probably been anticipated. If so, I shall be grateful for the proof that I have not been as lonely as I thought. Far be it from me to invoke the one and only hackneyed quotation from Donatus. One thing I do know for sure is that my field is a mine-field, and that after my best efforts specialists on one part or another of it will find omissions, mistakes and misunderstandings left in my text. I shall be duly grateful for corrections. The assembly of some different kinds of solid evidence does, however, establish the thesis stated above.

Trying to fuse a number of matters, I had some trouble with the title. My first choice, *Cranmer's Sentences*, was overruled. My second has been used already. Maurice Merleau-Ponty did not finish that most interesting book or choose its title, but the copyright laws prevent me from re-using *La Prose du Monde*. The title I have settled for is meant to suggest that there *is* a subject. What to put where must, however, be a question.

All things considered, we had better begin with sentences and their punctuation, because sentences are where both modern prose and the modern world start. The immediate surprise, I hope, is the limitation to 'modern'.

The only 'A'-level paper I ever marked had this rubric:

All questions require answers in continuous English prose. Candidates are reminded that, as part of the marking criteria, they will be assessed on their ability to organise and present information, ideas, descriptions and arguments clearly and logically, taking into account use of English grammar, punctuation and spelling.[1]

'Continuous English prose', 'information . . . and arguments' 'logically', 'English grammar, punctuation and spelling' go together so naturally that it may take an effort to see them as a historic grouping, not immutable. *Write sentences!* is implied by the whole rubric; but to say that would seem so unnecessary as to be unnatural. The spirit of *sentence* is identically present in this remark of Evelyn Waugh's: 'My education, it seems to me, was the preparation for one trade only; that of an English prose writer.'[2] Waugh at Lancing, unlike any medieval boy at Winchester, was drilled in writing sentences. Shakespeare, unwillingly sitting exams at school, must have understood that rubric as the instruction not to write the verse which in his age might have come more naturally. Chaucer simply could not have understood the rubric, because although he wrote a considerable body of prose he could not have known what was intended by 'continuous'. 'In fact Middle English prose is not written in sentences at all.'[3] After publishing this by-academic-standards-sensational statement in a volume in a very popular series I received a grand total of two (private and favourable) comments.

[1] Oxford and Cambridge Schools Examination Board 9620/1 English Literature Paper 1: Shakespeare and the Drama, Monday 5 June 1995, morning.
[2] Evelyn Waugh, *A Little Learning*, New York, 1964, p. 140.
[3] Robinson, 'Prose and the Dissociation of Sensibility', p. 263.

So I try again, and shall begin by establishing the sensational contention and explaining why it matters.

Before asking what the *clerkes* of the Middle Ages thought they meant by *sentence*, it will be prudent, however, to make sure we know what we mean ourselves.

1 Sentence and period

i Sentences now

We shall be considering some obscurities, but also some things so well known that the only difficulty may lie in the need to be explicit, so let us start with one of the latter. In ordinary writing we spell words with letters, we recognize the spelled things as words by separating them with spaces, and we end groups of words with full stops. These practices, none of which is universal, express a particular grammatical attitude towards the written language, centring for us on sentences.

The very ancient practice of word division[1] has already made an essential step towards Western grammar. If words were shown to exist every time something was written down, the study of the behaviour and interaction of words was a natural enough development. Our grammars are principally of different forms of words (accidence) and the rules for the combination of words (syntax).

'Well may men knowe, but if it be a fool, / That every part dirryveth from his hool,' as Chaucer's Duke Theseus declares. It is axiomatic in modern grammar that the wholes from which written words derive are called sentences. Transformational analysis always begins with the big S for sentence as the root of the famous inverted trees. 'The **sentence** is the highest grammatical level in the grammatical hierarchy.'[2] Within

---

[1] 'The division of writing into words . . . appears to have been customary in the writing of various languages in cuneiform characters. The practice may have reached the classical peoples through Crete, for word-division is clear on the Phaistos-disk, which may be as early as 1700 B.C.' (Wingo, *Latin Punctuation*, p. 14).

[2] N. F. Blake and Jean Moorhead, *Introduction to English Language*, 1993, p. 17. The paragraph is a visual representation of a larger unit of discourse, where our conventions of writing are still, as they have been for about three thousand years, some jumps ahead of the grammarians, for we have neither a syntax of the paragraph nor a proof that such syntax is impossible. The anaphoric use of pronouns to refer back to earlier sentences raises the possibility of a syntactic element in the paragraph. Radulphus Brito discussed this question early in the fourteenth century and came to the conclusion that anaphor and antecedent do form a *constructio*, i.e. are syntactically related. (Cf. Covington, *Syntactic Theory*, p. 116.)

transformational-generative grammar *the sentence* is where we start even before *the language*: a sentence can be made out of two different languages.[3]

The grammar of the sentence is autonomous: the question what makes a sentence well-formed can be answered without invoking nonsyntactic categories.[4] *The sentence* is understood within the system of syntax; if we try to define *sentence* we are unlikely to do better than Dr Levinson:

the minimal theoretical entity required to account for the formal syntactic relationships found to exist among the constituent syntactic units of a language. It is the entity which allows coherent statements about the lower-level constituents of the language, identifying a domain within which other units can be specified.[5]

The simpler traditional notion is 'the syntactic domain of a finite verb', which depends on an understanding of *verb* that could only be a reference back to the system: a finite verb is that part of speech whose domain makes a sentence.

Our understanding of the sentence is embodied all the time in writing. Many contemporary linguists think their task is to describe, and never say that one form is better or worse than another, though exceptions are mysteriously made for politically incorrect but well-attested forms. No attempt, however, is made to apply descriptivism to the written language. When complaints are made in the press about standards of literacy, what is usually meant is that spellings are bad and sentences not properly written; and teachers correct spellings and prescribe the grammar of written sentences (if they are able) without any qualms.

Modern punctuation has a variety of rhetorical uses, but one of its tendencies is the clarification of sentence structure. It is sometimes punctuation alone that conveys to a reader the syntactic structure of a sentence, for instance just by the insertion of a question mark or not. M. B. Parkes (the necessity of whose work to mine will appear in frequent citation) discusses copyists' mistakes in punctuation:

[3] E.g.

it provides a
moyen d'habiller, pour ainsi dire, notre pensée, de la rendre sensible . . . (Noam Chomsky, *Cartesian Linguistics*, New York, 1966, p. 47)

An English subject, verb and indefinite article belonging to the object are followed by the complex remainder of the sentence in French.

[4] 'Grammatical definitions of the sentence avoid reference to either semantic factors or to subjective notions and depend on purely formal features,' as Dr Levinson says (*Punctuation*, p. 123).

[5] Levinson, *Punctuation*, p. 123.

Such mistakes become more readily excusable when it is realized that the same grammatical structure can sometimes be pointed in several different ways . . . For example the written statement—George said Paul is an idiot—can be pointed either as—'George', said Paul, 'is an idiot'—or as—George said, 'Paul is an idiot'—.[6]

No, this is not the same grammatical structure pointed two ways, but two quite different syntactic structures, distinguished by punctuation. In the first *Paul* is the subject of *said*, in the second *George*, as is shown by the different placing of inverted commas. There are other possibilities for that string of words: George might be the subject and what George said indirect not direct speech, or it could be ' "George," said Paul, "is————" "An idiot?" '

Sometimes lexical or syntactic differences can be indicated aloud by phrasing, stressing, intonation . . . but not always. The different spellings of homophones specifically differentiate words that sound the same. We can't *say* differences between pairs like pears and pares, which we make and see in writing. Any apostrophe, as a sign of omission, i.e. the written indication of something *not* said, can only be written-grammatical, not a record of sounds. The novelist who 'records' uneducated speech with forms like "E said 'e would 'eave the 'ole 'ouse hup to 'eaven' is simultaneously conducting a grammatical commentary, for the speaker does not use these apostrophes and does not omit anything, except by the standards of the novelist's standard grammar. 'Brackets were useful,' as Percy Simpson says, 'in making a construction clear to the eye.'[7] Some uses of brackets can have no spoken equivalent; for instance there is no way in the spoken language of distinguishing round, square and pointed brackets.

We need to be clear both about the autonomy of the modern grammar of the sentence and about its limitations.

The development of the grammar of the well-formed sentence is one of the great achievements of linguistics. Great intellectual achievements can, however, notoriously become imperialistic, like Darwinian theory. The grammarians, having conceptualized the sentence, are tempted to think of language as made of nothing but sentences. 'I will consider a *language* to be a set (finite or infinite) of sentences' and therefore 'Syntactic investigation of a given language has as its goal the construction of a grammar that can be viewed as a device of some sort for producing the sentences of the language under analysis.'[8] There are,

[6] Parkes, *Pause and Effect*, p. 5 and note.
[7] Simpson, *Shakespearian Punctuation*, p. 91.
[8] Noam Chomsky, *Syntactic Structures*, The Hague, 1957; repr. 1962, pp. 13, 11.

however, other units in language as well as sentences—verses, for instance. It is not unknown even in prose for conspicuously well-written novels to do without sentences, sometimes for a page at a time like the opening of *Bleak House*, sometimes for shorter periods:

Awful years—'16, '17, '18, '19—the years when the damage was done. The years when the world lost its real manhood. Not for lack of courage to face death. Plenty of superb courage to face death. But no courage in any man to face his own isolated soul, and abide by its decision. Easier to sacrifice oneself. So much easier![9]

A paragraph without a well-formed sentence: two 'sentences' with temporal clauses; four with infinitives; and one without any verb at all! After such knowledge what forgiveness? These can no doubt be treated one way or another as derived elliptically from well-formed sentences or underlying strings, but with what explanatory force? Johnson told the story that

I once dined in company with ['Demosthenes' Taylor], and all he said during the whole time was no more than *Richard* . . . Dr Douglas was talking of Dr Zachary Grey, and ascribing to him something that was written by Dr Richard Grey. So, to correct him, Taylor said . . . '*Richard*.'[10]

No doubt ellipsis can also be made to 'explain' this *Richard*, but I repeat my question.

With notes for lectures, the notion of derivation from underlying strings or well-formed sentences is absurd, the point being to use the notes as strings and generate the right sort of well-formed sentence when the occasion requires. Many notes are quite intelligible, though not well-formed sentences, i.e. their syntax, the way of putting words together to make them intelligible, is not that of sentences.

There are in fact many ordinary and grammatical uses of the written language not made of well-formed sentences, for instance timetables, income-tax forms, crosswords (answers usually, clues often) and the game of Scrabble, posters, glossaries, programmes (including most of *The Radio Times*), menus, running titles, title and contents pages and indexes. Dictionary definitions are not written in sentences.

It is common for teachers to object to some nonsyntactic string of words in a student's text with a marginal 'not a sentence!' The objection is not itself made in a well-formed sentence. This, I hope, is not mere class-distinction (*you* must write sentences but *I* in authority needn't): it merely recognizes that though sentences are often required, for instance in the writing of essays, the requirement is not universal for all writing.

[9] D. H. Lawrence, *Kangaroo*, 1923; repr. 1930, pp. 239–40.
[10] Boswell, *Life of Johnson*, 25 April 1778.

As for speech: the radio commentator, as the winning-post, the goal or the knock-out punch is imminent, is unlikely to be using well-formed sentences, though his shouted syntax is quite correct for the occasion:

Adam Bede from Felix Holt now neck and neck Adam Bede Adam Bede Brother Jacob coming up on the outside but still Adam Bede and now Silas Marner putting on a spurt and Felix Holt overtaking Adam Bede on the fence half a furlong to go Brother Jacob fading Felix Holt now clear of Adam Bede Felix Holt as they pass the post Felix Holt then Adam Bede then Silas Marner and what a day for Mrs Cross her third winner of the afternoon!

In view of the common presupposition, which we shall glance at, that the well-formed sentence will convey information, it may be surprising that some styles developed specifically to convey factual information do not use well-formed sentences. For more than fifty years the BBC has been reporting football results without using finite verbs. The listener knows from the intonation whether the result is a home win, an away win or a draw, but there is nothing that could be called sentence structure. That prominent feature of the external world, the weather, is dealt with in broadcasts that make very little use of sentences. The shipping forecast frequently goes on for several minutes without the use of a finite verb. It is likewise to concentrate the conveyance of information that the human race has long since given up addressing envelopes in well-formed sentences, and the idea of a well-formed sentence as an address for e-mail hardly arises.

TG grammar analyses, with some elegance, the syntax of the well-formed sentence, but that is all it does. Some grammarians, however, still demand that for something to be properly called a sentence it must make sense. The quotation above from Blake and Moorhead's *Introduction to English Language* (1993) continues, 'Grammatical completeness on its own is not enough . . . That it should make sense is another essential feature of a sentence.' This needs unpacking. We do, let's hope, make sense in language, often with the well-formed sentences that are central to modern prose, and the aim of the present work is to throw some light on the kinds of sense well-formed prose sentences may make. But an isolated well-formed sentence, 'the highest grammatical level in the grammatical hierarchy', rarely if ever makes sense, even if it is a combination of proposition with reference. To begin a conversation with 'This is a chair,' even if a chair is there, would be to ask for psychiatric attention. It would be as senseless as the nonsense-sentences grammarians amuse themselves by constructing, 'Colourless green ideas sleep furiously,' and the like (Blake and Moorhead's is 'the wisdom drove the table succulently'). That is what they are: sentences that make no sense, but still sentences. 'A nonsense sentence' is not a contradiction in terms. The autonomy of the grammar of the sentence was not easily achieved and we should hang on to it.

In practice, though, our understanding of the sentence may still carry quite a load of metaphysical and ideological and stylistic baggage—most of it refurbished in the late seventeenth century from Aristotelian leftovers—about the kinds of sense we expect sentences to make, and the mental ways in which they do it. So it is worth emphasizing that since the syntax of the sentence is autonomous, 'the sentence' implies no extra-linguistic views about the workings of the human mind nor anything about the relations of language with the physical universe. The dictionary definition of the sentence nevertheless begins: 'A series of words in connected speech or writing, forming the grammatically complete expression of a single thought.'[11] Neither 'expression' nor 'single thought' are within the province of TG grammar; the first is psychology and the second logic.

Whether Aristotle originated the notion of the sentence as the expression of a single thought I do not know, but he was certainly the authority who established it in Western tradition. It is amazing to think how much we still live under the shadow of Aristotle! He set the tone of the next two and a half millennia by treating words as signs representing ideas:

Words spoken are symbols or signs of affections or impressions of the soul; written words are the signs of words spoken. As writing, so also is speech not the same for all races of men. But the mental affections themselves, of which these words are primarily signs [*semeia*], are the same for the whole of mankind, as are also the objects of which those affections are representations or likenesses, images, copies. With these points, however, I dealt in my treatise *peri psyches*.[12]

Words are taken to be signs of conceptions that exist separately from language in the mind.

This is what Locke and Saussure, Aristotelians both, almost identically mean by the arbitrariness of the sign: that words are arbitrarily adopted by languages to signify ideas that precede *any* expression. 'Words, in their primary or immediate signification, stand for nothing but *the ideas in the mind of him that uses them*,' says Locke. Words came so to be used 'not by any natural connection that there is between particular articulate sounds and certain ideas, for then there would be but one language amongst all men; but by a voluntary imposition,

---

[11] *The Oxford English Dictionary*, prepared by J. A. Simpson and E. S. C. Weiner, 2nd edn, Oxford, 1989. All the definitions I quote have been retained unchanged from the great *New English Dictionary*.
[12] Aristotle, *de Interpretatione* 16a; *The Organon*, transl. Harold P. Cooke, Loeb edn, 1938, p. 115.

whereby such a word is made arbitrarily the mark of such an idea.'[13] This confuses the undoubted facts that meanings are not found in nature with sounds attached, and that more or less the same sound will do very different work in different languages, with the belief that meanings are found before any linguistic expression whatever.

But: 'When I think in language,' says Wittgenstein, 'there aren't "meanings" going through my mind in addition to the verbal expressions.' I believe that once this is said it is just about self-evident. Lower down the same page Wittgenstein challenges us to 'Say a sentence and think it; say it with understanding.—And now do not say it, and just do what you accompanied it with when you said it with understanding!'[14] It is all too easy to say a sentence without thinking it, but there is no equivalent thinking a sentence without saying it. See this and the whole Saussurean apparatus of signifier and signified, that goes by way of Locke's 'ideas' and the Modistae all the way back to Aristotle, can be discarded. There is no difference (not to mention *différance*) between signifier and signified.

It is not my contention that all thinking takes place in language. There are images and dreams. As I walk away I see the car lights left on: I go back and turn them off without saying to myself 'I left the lights on' or 'I must turn them off' or anything else. If this can be called thinking, the thought is in seeing from a certain point of view and acting accordingly. What I do contend is that when we think in language that's exactly what we do: not think separately then translate the thought into language.

Linguists, however, still habitually think in terms of Saussure's 'speech circuit' which tries to account for the conveyance of a thought from one brain to another.[15] A thought is supposed to arise, complete, before it is *coded* into language, then into sound, 'the coding process from meaning to expression', as Halliday calls the notion,[16] and at the other end decoded from sound into language and then from language back into thought (*The New Grammarians' Funeral*, pp. 74–8). The thoughts, unluckily, are always and only producible in their 'coded'

---

[13] *An Essay Concerning Human Understanding*, Book 3, ch. 2, ¶2, ¶1 (which harks back to the notion (below) that ideas are dictated in turn by the nature of the world).

[14] Wittgenstein, *Philosophical Investigations*, p. 107e.

[15] Cf. my review of Roy Harris, *Language, Saussure and Wittgenstein*. The only hint I have come across in recent linguistics that the lesson of Wittgenstein has been learned is Frédéric Nef's essay 'The Question of the *Significatum*: a Problem Raised and Solved', transl. Christian Fournier, in Lia Formigiari, (ed.), *Historical Roots of Linguistic Theories*, Amsterdam, 1995, pp. 185–202. There is much to challenge in this essay, but I agree with the very Wittgensteinian conclusion: 'If the significatum can no longer be viewed as a state of affairs or even as a thought, then the very meaning of the problem vanishes' (p. 197).

[16] M. A. K. Halliday, *An Introduction to Functional Grammar*, 2nd edn, 1994, p. xiv.

form, and nothing at all changes if one denies their separate existence. How do we know that a thought (in the mind) is complete? As Levinson says, 'There is no independent way of identifying a "thought", whatever that thought may be, except as it is embodied in language . . . The only clue to an incomplete thought is an incomplete sentence.'[17]

Arthur Koestler, not being a card-carrying linguist, innocently made one thing clear that the professionals should have noticed for themselves. He puts at the top of the syntactic diagram not the Chomskyan S for Sentence but I for Idea (*The New Grammarians' Funeral*, p. 32). If one takes *I* to include the joining of ideas in propositions, this constitutes linguistic orthodoxy from Aristotle to Saussure, but *I* for Idea cannot enter syntactic analysis. The connection between *I* and *S* is a line not a fork: which means that from the point of view of the grammarian there is *no difference* between the sentence and the idea. I believe this is true, but linguists are still unwilling to remove the *I* as an unnecessary postulate already included in *S*.

If all that Locke meant by the *ideas* of words were words heard, seen, said to ourselves or imagined, I would not disagree, but that is not all. 'Words, by long and familiar use, as has been said, come to excite in men certain ideas so constantly and readily, that they are apt to suppose a natural connection between them. But that they signify only men's peculiar ideas, and that *by a perfect arbitrary imposition*.'[18] I am following Wittgenstein in arguing not for natural connection between word and idea but for identity. The word properly understood, heard or said to oneself, *is* the idea; one use of the sentence *is* the proposition.

The assumption about sentences commonly associated with the basic belief that they signify mental propositions, and present in the above quotation from Aristotle ('the objects of which those affections are representations'), is that the ideas of which the propositions are made will refer to objects or categories in the external world. According to the 'traditional interpretation of Aristotelian semantics—to be found, e.g., in Boethius, Avicenna, Albert the Great, and Thomas Aquinas,' Jan Pinborg tells us, 'words signify concepts which in turn represent the objects signified.'[19] I quote William Barnes's neat reformulation of ideas more than two thousand years old:

The formation of language is always a conformation to three things in nature— (1) the beings, actions, and relations of things in the universe; (2) the conceptions of them by the mind of man; and (3) the actions of the organs of speech.[20]

[17] Levinson, *Punctuation*, pp. 121–2.
[18] Locke, *An Essay Concerning Human Understanding*, Book 3, ch. 2, ¶8.
[19] Pinborg in *The Cambridge History of Later Medieval Philosophy*, p. 262.
[20] Quoted in Lucy Baxter, *The Life of William Barnes Poet and Philologist*, 1887, pp. 136–7.

The conceptions of (2) are to be *of* the 'things' of (1); and language has to signify the process. The Wittgensteinian short-cut means that Barnes's item (2), the conception of things by the mind of man, is an entity not found in grammar. (Whether it may be found anywhere else is a question we need not ask.) I think the same about Barnes's item (1), the beings, actions and relations of things in the universe. Grammar has enough on its plate without trying to take in the universe. This is not to deny, as do some deconstructionists,[21] that language can refer. But language does many other things too; and when it does refer the sense made is rarely determined by the referent and only then in the right situation. Some questions like 'Where is the dog?' may be answered more or less simply by references to the external world. If an oddly designed object is in question even 'This is a chair' is possible. But for instance to say 'dog' every time a dog happens to be present would be a pathological symptom rather like the above-mentioned contextless 'This is a chair.'

The reasons why some grammarians still take what Chomsky calls the 'simple declarative sentence' as the norm are not grammatical, but because it (usually the third person indicative) has the prestige of signifying a complete thought by way of *making true statements*. Whether a sentence is making a statement, however, is not decided by its status as a sentence. Some indicative sentences make propositions, some tell stories. The basic subject plus predicate form belongs equally to both; there is no reason grammatical, logical or chronological, to give the propositional uses priority. Outright lies are deplorable but need not be ungrammatical. It may be that, as Milton reports, angels are easily deceived because they expect rational creatures to tell the truth; but this is plainly a moral not a grammatical expectation nor even, as regards humans, realistic.

How to know when something is not meant 'straight'? To parallel the imperative, indicative, subjunctive, optative . . . there is no ironative mood marking tongue-in-cheek. We can 'roguishly accent' an ironical word,[22] but is not the best irony quite deadpan? Earnestness can also be expressed in speech rhythm, but earnestness is commonly meant ironically.

There is no reason *in grammar* for the indicative to have precedence over, for instance, the imperative. Reputable linguists have conjectured that the imperative was the primitive form of the verb in Indo-European. In fact as I shall demonstrate in chapter four, the well-formed sentence

---

21 Robinson, 'Reconstruction', p. 183.
22 Herman Melville, *Bartleby*, repr. 1995, p. 27.

as a central mode of thought came into English by way of the imperative not the indicative.

It can be a moment well spent to remind ourselves, perhaps again with the help of Wittgenstein,[23] that many senses are made in language which can only with some ingenuity be called making statements.[24]

Exclaiming (and the varieties of *that*, as Wittgenstein remarks). *Praying. Commanding*—which even has its well-recognized grammatical mood, the imperative, but which can be done in many ways not using the imperative.[25]

Expressing an attitude or relationship to the subject of the 'proposition'. *Expressing feeling. Expressing doubts, irony, sarcasm.*

Valuing: conferring value upon or seeing value in some object which may or may not be the grammatical subject of a sentence. (Many, perhaps *all*, poems do this one way or another.)

Imagining, by way of enactment and the old Aristotelian *making* and *imitation*.[26]

None of these can be discussed directly by the TG grammarian. Ordinarily, many of them will go on at the same time. Any of them will simultaneously perform a surprising feat I discuss in chapter seven below: suggest a world.

Wittgenstein is the prime philosophical anchor for what I am saying about the identity of language and thought, but as a matter of fact I came to it myself as an ordinary part of a literary education. Pound, Eliot, Richards, Leavis, demonstrated the fallaciousness of the old idea of language as the *dress* of thought, which was merely the aesthetic version of the belief in separable ideas. Poems are notoriously not translatable (as the Venerable Bede says very clearly[27]) not because only the poet's words can express his separable idea but because the poem *is* this ordering of words. The quoted work of Aristotle is commonly

---

[23] Cf. Wittgenstein, *Philosophical Investigations*, para. 27, p. 13, and many other places.

[24] This is a passing glance at one of the central themes of information technology, hermeneutics and also of epistemology. A meaning laugh or an expletive can be said to convey information, but only if we define *information* so as not to make it propositional.

[25] Cf.'Grandcourt put up his telescope and said, "There 's a plantation of sugar-canes at the foot of that rock: should you like to look?"' (George Eliot, *Daniel Deronda*, ch. LIV). In context this is certainly a command, though grammatically a most polite interrogative subjunctive.

[26] The basic notions of creation and imitation make together, I believe, a necessary paradox, but this is not the moment to discuss it.

[27] Bede apologizes in the (Latin) *Eccesiastical History of the English* for translating the English verses of Cædmon (Book IV, ch. 24; Loeb edn of *Opera Historica*, ed. J. E. King, 1930, vol. II, p. 144).

referred to by its Latin title *de Interpretatione*. Leavis consistently denied the basic Aristotelian notion of *interpretation* of language. There is no superlanguage (called ideas or any other name) for language to be interpreted into. We do not interpret poems, we read them.

Behind Leavis was a tradition going back to Coleridge, by way of Newman and Carlyle: 'Language is called the Garment of Thought: however, it should rather be, Language is the Flesh-Garment, the Body, of Thought.'[28] The talk about signs, ideas, decoding, leads away from the living body of thought which is much more accessible than the central philosophical tradition of Europe would allow it to be.

Whether you agree with all this or not, I hope it is uncontroversial to assert that when linguists talk about objects, or nonlinguistic ideas in the mind, or electrical circuits in the brain, whatever they are doing or think they are doing it is not grammar. If we are thinking about language we can only understand any possibly relevant brain activity as language, not *vice versa*.

Well-formed sentences, even indicatives conveying information about the external world, are *of course* very important in language. I even believe that most of the time we do talk in well-formed sentences (*pace* Chomsky, who thinks of actual speech, Saussurean *langage*, as largely composed of degenerate sentences, and *pace* Quirk, who I believe exaggerates the ill-formedness of common speech[29]). One may notice, nevertheless, how much of *style* adheres even to the grammar of the sentence.

There are traditionally three kinds of well-formed sentence, the simple, the compound and the complex. In these, no terminal full point must be used within the sentence boundary. A sentence for instance that begins 'Not only . . . ' arouses the expectation of at least two clauses, as does a 'When' (as against 'then', one of the differences between the syntax of Old and Modern English), and it is going to be incorrect to interrupt this evolution by a sentence-boundary, equally with a compound sentence whose subject is brought into construction with two or more verbs: 'She woke, yawned, turned over and went back to sleep.' But as well as these three, which I shall follow Nunberg in calling 'lexical sentences', there are also what he calls 'text sentences', which happen to be the building-blocks of prose, and to which the basic rule about full points does not apply.

Printed pages include many sentences of the traditional three kinds,

---

[28] Thomas Carlyle, *Sartor Resartus*, 'Prospective'.
[29] Cf. *The Corpus of English Conversation*, ed. Jan Svartvik and Randolph Quirk, Lund, 1980.

but also many sentences declared by their punctuation to be sentences but which can be analysed into more than one simple, complex or compound sentence. It is about these 'text' sentences that Dr Levinson's remark has force: 'The characteristics of the sentence in written English are such that syntactic rules alone (or even mainly) cannot capture them.'[30] Sentences including two main clauses divided by a colon or semi-colon can always be rewritten as two or more simple or complex or compound sentences without any ungrammaticality. It is always, equally, legitimate in grammar to join simple or complex or compound sentences into 'text' sentences. In the age of the word-processor there is nothing, grammatically, to prevent an author either turning every chapter into one 'text' sentence, by replacing all full points by semi-colons and colons or, conversely, turning every long 'text' sentence into shorter sentences by replacing all semi-colons and colons by full points, with appropriate adjustment to capitalization. (C. P. Snow wrote before the word-processor age, or I would have suspected him of adopting the latter method.) Although this certainly has to do with sentence bound-aries it is a stylistic not a grammatical matter. Grammar can give rules for deciding whether the sentences in an extant text are well-formed, but it has to leave to us the possibility of other well-formed sentences made from exactly the same constructions.

When the grammarians are remembering to be conceptually precise they do not use 'generative' literally to mean that as the mud of the Nile used to be thought to generate living creatures, or as dynamos meta-phorically generate electricity, the TG grammar generates the sentences of the language, though in common speech *generative* is bound to make some such suggestion, and the speculations about the internalization of a grammar by a physical language-acquisition device go further than suggestion (*The New Grammarians' Funeral*, ch. four). Transforma-tional-generative grammar is analytic and descriptive and prescriptive, but does not generate anything. We make text sentences as we please, within whatever constraints are imposed by grammatical rule and stylistic decorum.

How actually to shape sentences is a stylistic question. Nunberg tries to give rules for the use of semi-colons as against full points, but they turn out to be pieces of good advice about style or about logic, not anything decreed correct or incorrect by the grammar of the sentence. *Clumsy* pertains to style, *incorrect* to grammar, and some of Nunberg's examples marked with an asterisk as incorrect are only clumsy: one or two are not even that. 'This set, then, will be (if I can use a technical

---

[30] Levinson, *Punctuation*, p. 8. Her term for 'text' sentences is 'orthographic' sentences.

term) subsected by the other one'[31] gets the asterisk to indicate ungrammatical, but seems to me perfectly all right. To call clumsy or inelegant sentences ungrammatical looks like an effort to elevate one's taste into laws.

Classical Latin, extensively imitated in the English of the sixteenth century, had a common practice of starting what Nunberg would call a 'text' sentence with a relative whose antecedent is in the previous sentence. In every case of this construction the decision whether the sentence is indeed new or whether the relative makes it an extension of the previous sentence is purely stylistic.[32]

In modern writing, then, we put into practice a clear sense of syntactic structures, many of which have been elucidated by modern grammar. I have to bring out, however, that 'modern' is not redundant.

Chomsky has always been a conspicuously synchronic linguist, and the question whether the sentence itself might change never arises for him. The history of the well-formed sentence must surely have been attempted; the useful *datum* is that it is not easy to find. I do not even know of any history of the concept of the sentence.[33] But if sentences have much to do with style, the possibility of a change in the sentence does arise.

ii   Sentences then

Medieval grammar, following the classical tradition, was of course highly developed, but there never emerged in the medieval period any conception of the sentence as syntactic unit. Levinson says, 'During the manuscript era . . . the orthographic sentence existed neither in practice nor, apparently, even in concept.'[34] I believe that this understates the matter, for I do not think that even *simple* sentences were clearly recognized either by medieval grammar or by the practices of medieval writing.

Aristotle's attention to language was and is of profound importance, but as far as we know he never wrote a *Grammatike*; the remarks we can

---

[31] Nunberg, *The Linguistics of Punctuation*, p. 41.

[32] St Peter, a writer of prose of surprising syntactic complexity, uses this construction frequently, for instance 1 Peter i. 5, 8, 12, 20, 21, all faithfully rendered in the English Bible of 1611. Modern editors punctuate these as new sentences or not at their discretion.

[33] There is no trace of either in E. F. Konrad Koerner's *Western Histories of Linguistic Thought, an Annotated Chronological Bibliography, 1822–1976*, Amsterdam, 1978, or in Lia Formigiari, (ed.), *Historical Roots of Linguistic Theories*, Amsterdam, 1995.

[34] Levinson, *Punctuation*, p. 117.

call grammatical are found in the *Rhetoric*, the *Poetics* and the *Organon*. None of them either state or imply the modern grammatical unit. Aristotle is interested in what could be reasonably translated as units of thought, and in figures of speech. His (logical) syllogism is the one and (rhetorical) enthymeme is the other, though he says that the enthymeme is a kind of syllogism. The tensions between logic and rhetoric go back at least one generation further than Aristotle, and one might say they have lasted ever since, with grammar caught in the cross-fire. What I can't find in the old grammarians, right down to the fourteenth century, is any specifically syntactic definition of the unit of sense.

The ordinary grammars of antiquity and of the Middle Ages were literary grammars, aimed at elucidating the classics. Prosody was traditionally an essential branch of grammar. In prosody and rhetoric, the unit is likely to be the stanza, the verse or the period, none of which are more than coincidentally the same as sentences.

On the other (logical) hand, an *oratio*, in Priscian's standard definition, is 'ordinatio dictionum congrua, sententiam perfectam demonstrans'[35]—'a correct ordering of words pointing to a complete thought'. We need to see firstly that *oratio* is a little closer than *sententia* to our *sentence* and next that grammar comes into this definition with neither word, but with *congrua*. What makes an *oratio* complete is not the domain of a finite verb but the completeness of meaning by way of the (logical) predication of something or other about a *suppositum* or topic, distinguishable (by us) from our grammatical *subject*.

The *word* 'sentence' is of course common enough in Middle English, following Latin *sententia*. Neither is obscure, and neither ever includes the modern grammatical sense. Much is still to be learned from the great *New English Dictionary*, not least at the points where its definitions are inadequate or inadequately supported. After satisfactorily defining senses of *sentence* like *opinion* ('My sentence is for open war'), *authoritative decision*, and others including the very useful 'An indefinite portion of a discourse or writing', we get to grammar in a definition already partly quoted, which continues:

6. In *Grammar*, the verbal expression of a proposition, question, command or request, containing normally a subject and a predicate (though either of these may be omitted by ellipsis).

This is all right as an account of how the sentence was understood in the late nineteenth century. What I doubt is whether the earlier texts cited in support mean syntactically anything like all that this definition tries to

[35] Keil, *Grammatici Latini*, II, p. 53.

make them. These citations are in any case quite late, the oldest being from Osbert Bokenham on St Agnes (1447): 'Fro sentence to sentence, I dar wel seyn,/ I hym haue folwyde euen by & by', where the poet means no more than 'I have given an exact translation, following him closely from one sense to the next.' The following, from 1526, looks more grammatical, and may be so: 'Euery lettre, syllable, worde & sentence of his prayer & duty from the begynnynge to the end.' This does make *sentence* look like a grammatical term completing the order *letter*, *syllable*, *worde* as it would for us (though *syllable* is, as often, the odd man out); but this *sentence* is still more like the *member* (below), a unit of sense with no exact syntactic requirement. Despite any momentary *heureka* feeling, we are actually further from the modern sentence and more clearly in the older world of rhetoric with the Dictionary's following quotation, still in support of our grammatical *sentence*, from Sir Thomas Elyot, 1538: '*Tetracolon*, a sentence hauyng .iiii. membres'. It may well look to the modern eye as if *members* must be the clauses of a complex sentence; but the word is very well established in the sense of a group of words within a 'period'. We shall meet *tetracolon* again, but not meaning 'complex sentence'.

The most ordinary Middle English sense of *sentence* is NED 7, 'the sense, substance, or gist (of a passage, a book etc.). *Obs.*' Professor Mueller, whose work I shall use gratefully later on, makes a whole chapter-section out of misinterpreting this sense syntactically.[36] She rightly draws attention to the intelligence of Purvey's Preface to his English translation of the Bible but takes his 'open sentence' to mean something like 'sentence structure rendered into English recursive forms using many *ands*' when he just means 'plain meaning'. If Latin is rendered a word at a time, the meaning will not be plain, so the constructions will have to vary. But Purvey never mentions any syntactic unit bigger than preposition plus noun within which the variety is made. 'A translatour hath greet nede to studie wel the sentence bothe bifore & aftir/ & loke that suche equivok wordis acorde with the sentence.'[37] This is not about grammatical concord but about the different senses of words in different contexts.

In Chaucer *sentence* just means *sense* or perhaps *sense particularly worth remembering*. Chantecleer explains to Pertelote:

> *Mulier est hominis confusio*:
> Madame the sentence / of this Latyn is
> Womman is mannes joye / and al his blis.[38]

---

[36] 'Open Sentences', the beginning of ch. 3 of Mueller, *The Native Tongue and the Word*.
[37] Cambridge University Library Kk. I. 8, f. 29 r.
[38] Chaucer, *Canterbury Tales*, B 4354–6.

This *sentence* goes with *authority*: some scribes were in the habit of marking particularly weighty moments with the word *auctor* in the margin. *Auctor* of course means *author* but has a sense more like 'This is worth making a note about.' The passages so marked would be *sentences*. Chaucer, naturally, makes sarcastic use of the practice when he so glosses the most scandalous sentiments in *The Merchant's Tale*, a nice touch retained by the Victorian Skeat but dropped without comment by all modern editions. 'Thou speakest sentences,' says Pantilius Tucca to Ovid Sr in Jonson's *Poetaster*: by which he means not that Ovid is speaking grammatically but that he is speaking sense and, in particular, uttering weighty, authoritative dicta. The Waldensians offended the contemporary orthodox by learning by heart what were called *sententiae*: by which they meant particularly memorable verses of the Bible. This idea of *sentence* as a weighty saying obviously connects with the *sentence* of the law-court. It comes straight from classical Latin. The *Rhetorica ad Herennium*, so far from supposing that all language consists of sentences, treats *sententiae* (pithy dicta) as figures of speech which should not be over-used.

In older tradition, then, sentence is indeed meaning and *a* sentence a unit of meaning, but not necessarily a syntactic one.

If our conception of the well-formed sentence was not found in medieval Latin it will come as no surprise to hear that it was not found in English either.

The Toller-Campbell Supplement to the *Anglo-Saxon Dictionary* (1921) cites in support of *cwide* as 'a (grammatical) sentence, period', 'Bebeád hé thæt him mon lengran cwidas (*sententias*) cwæde', but that just means (most probably, given that the *him* might be singular), 'He ordered that the man should make longer speeches to them.' This is from Bede's narrative[39] of the miraculous cure by Bishop John of Hexham of a dumb man, who showed the beginning of his improvement by speaking monosyllables, then worked up to longer utterances. There is no reason to suppose that the cured man could possibly have understood a command to talk in longer sentences even if it could have been given him.

The contention that medieval grammar had nothing like Chomsky's 'sentence' needs argument, which I give to the necessary extent in the first Appendix. The two decisive matters that must be mentioned at this stage are the attitude of the old grammarians to inflections, and the scribal practices of punctuation.

[39] Bede, *Ecclesiastical History*, Book v, ch. 2.

In Old English, 'The nominative . . . is the case of the subject and
its appositional elements,' says Mitchell.[40] Teaching this inflected
language (with Mitchell's help) at the present day I would not know
how to start unless I could say such things about the structure of the
sentences.[41] How could one begin to explain the differences between
nouns and verbs without pointing to their different roles in the
sentence? Donatus does it. He gives the same definition of a verb in
the *magnum opus*, the *Ars Grammatica*, and the *Ars Minor*, the very
potted accidence (without a word about syntax) which was the
grammar most commonly used for teaching Latin throughout the
Middle Ages, and is still extant in thousands of copies, recensions,
rifacimenti. 'A verb is the part of speech that has tense and person but
not case, signifying either doing or suffering something' (or neither, as
Donatus rather confusingly continues): 'Verbum est pars orationis cum
tempore et persona sine casu aut agere aliquid aut pati aut neutrum
significans.'[42] As clear as mud, many a poor medieval lad must have
thought before these words were beaten into him. Donatus doesn't say
anything whatever about the syntactic domain of the verb. There is no
difficulty in reconciling the modern grammar of sentences with what
Donatus has to say about tense, person and case, but he shows no
interest in sentences himself. In this he is just the same as the Greek
Dionysius Thrax.[43]

Priscian is concerned to establish the proper order of precedence of
the cases, and takes the nominative as, so to speak, the true form of a
word from which the other cases temporarily depart. Much later, in the
days of the schoolmen, this fitted with misleading ease into the philosophy of substance and accident. To this day nouns are called substan-
tives; the forms represented by any other case endings were thought of
as the accidents that befell the substance. Priscian concludes that the
nominative is correctly so called because 'Per ipsum enim nominatio fit,
ut "nominetur iste Homerus, ille Virgilius."'[44] ('For in itself it does the
naming, as "*He* is named Homer, *he* Virgil."') I don't know whether
anyone made the obvious retort that the vocative seems to exist just to
address by name and that the accusative could equally well have been
used in naming, as the object of a verb. In the same paragraph Priscian
himself says that 'Quarto loco est accusativus sive causativus: "accuso

---

[40] Mitchell, *Old English Syntax*, I, p. 530.
[41] It does not follow that I, any more than Mitchell, believe that Old English writing was
composed in sentences. See below, ch. 3.
[42] Keil, *Grammatici Latini*, IV, p. 381; cf. *ibid.*, p. 359
[43] Cf. below, p. 170.
[44] Keil, *Grammatici Latini*, II, p. 185.

hominem" et "in causa hominem facio." ' ('Coming in fourth is the accusative or defendant [in a court of law], as in "I accuse a man" and "I name a man in the case" ') which seems a pretty direct way of naming the man. But he leaves it there, without any hint that the two or three kinds of naming are explained by different relations to the verb. *Declensions* are so called because the other cases are thought to be a *falling away* from the nominative, so called because it is the pure name. This, which proceeds from the view that names are the really essential part of language, is not syntactically enlightening. Much later, the accounts of case given by Petrus Helias or Radulphus Brito are much more logically sophisticated, but still don't mention the sentence.[45] Sergius's *Explanation* of Donatus is one of many grammars that offers the folk-etymology that *verbum* is so called because 'aerem verberat vox' (sound makes the air reverberate).[46] This is obviously not about syntax.

The Difficult Apollonius[47] did devote himself to syntax. Closely followed by Priscian, he was in the grip of a bright but untrue idea about analogy. He thought that at different levels language must behave in the same way. Letters can occasionally be missed out of words and so words out of *logoi* (complete units of sense, but whether our *sentences* is the point at issue); there is occasional metathesis of letters and so sometimes words may be transposed; but generally the order of letters to spell a word is essential, and therefore so must be the order of words in a *logos*. This would be plausible about modern analytic languages, but in the case of the inflected language Apollonius Dyscolus was actually discussing clearly leads in a wrong direction, in particular away from the overarching Chomskyan S. If one's first language is English one has the great advantage of noticing that in Greek and Latin word order doesn't affect syntax, because the grammatical relations within the sentence can be indicated by case endings. English *man bites journalist* is not the same as *journalist bites man*, but in Latin the word order would not alter the sense.

It was possible for Apollonius Dyscolus to get into this muddle because for him grammar was not autonomous. 'The noun necessarily precedes the verb, since influencing and being influenced are properties of physical things, and things are what nouns apply to.'[48] This is an argument from the Aristotelian picture we met above, and is about logic and the external world, not about grammar. Priscian followed: 'ante

---

[45] Radulphus Brito, *Quaestiones super Priscianum Minorem*, pp. 349, 350–1.
[46] Keil, *Grammatici Latini*, IV, p. 488.
[47] The surname Dyscolus seems to mean 'difficult' both as to thought and as to temper.
[48] Apollonius Dyscolus, *The Syntax of Apollonius Dyscolus*, I. 16, p. 25.

verbum quoque necessario ponitur nomen, quia agere et pati substan-
tiae est proprium, in qua est positio nominum, ex quibus proprietas
verbi, id est actio et passio, nascitur.' ('The noun is necessarily placed
before the verb, because to act and to suffer is the property of a
substance, from which the position of nouns follows; from which the
property of the verb, that is action and suffering, is born.'[49]) Even the
later medieval grammarians thought that the *suppositum* should come
first, though they allow that in actuality it does not always. According to
Roger Bacon,

Et recte sequitur verbum post pronomen et nomen: quia ista naturaliter priora
sunt verbo et ab eis actus verbalis egreditur . . . et ideo preponi habent ordine
naturali.

And the verb rightly follows after [in order of precedence] the pronoun and
noun, because they naturally are prior to the verb and the verbal action proceeds
from them . . . and therefore they have to be put first in natural order.[50]

He does say on the next page that 'Per accidens autem potest ante
verbum poni' (the verb can *accidentally* be placed first): but this way of
thinking is dominated by philosophical considerations: in the substance,
the non-verbal idea, what the noun signifies must come first.

It is so natural to think something like 'But they *must* have known about
sentences: even if they didn't talk about it the understanding must have
been there in the background, and they *wrote* sentences.' To any student
of language, however, unconscious 'knowledge' is one of the commonest
if most startling of phenomena. It is *quite* possible that the classical
orators and the medieval scholars practised the grammar of complex
sentences unawares. To us it is crashingly obvious that Cicero's style is
just about the same as the eloquent management of long complex
sentences, often culminating in a main verb. Cicero, the most influential
practitioner of oratory as well as one of the most important writers on
style and rhetoric from the great age of Latin prose, seems to have been
himself quite unaware of this.

What is not available is the possibility of unconscious knowledge *in
grammarians*. It is precisely the aim of the grammarian to make
conscious what a speaker or writer may not explicitly know. If the
classical grammarians did not elucidate the syntax of the sentence it was
because they had as little conception of the sentence as the writers on
whom they commented.

[49] Keil, *Grammatici Latini*, III, p. 116.
[50] *The Greek Grammar of Roger Bacon*, ed. E. Nolan and S. A. Hirsch, Cambridge, 1902,
p. 164.

iii   Medieval punctuation

If the boundaries in medieval texts are practically the same as our syntactic ones even though there was no grammar of the well-formed sentence, we can say that the difference is at most one of explicitness. But if medieval scribes marked different divisions . . .? I think it would follow that they were putting into practice a conception of language and the units of language different from ours. This is why the generally despised topic of punctuation is well worth pursuing as one of the strongest sets of hints we can get from those ages themselves about how the construction of prose and verse was perceived.

I have never come across a medieval manuscript punctuated in anything like the modern syntactic way. Allowing for the great and obvious overlap between syntactic and rhetorical units, one can say that in all the medieval traditions, both in theory and practice, punctuation (if any) is metrical, or rhetorical, or periodic, never except coincidentally syntactic. Many manuscripts have hardly any punctuation at all. Many others are punctuated: lightly, sparsely or (like the Hengwrt Chaucer) obsessively. The punctuation, if any, is always aimed at helping the voice to phrase and shape.

Advice to the medieval writer to remember the speaking voice would have been otiose, for what else would he have in mind? Parkes argues not quite convincingly[51] that silent reading became the norm during the early middle ages, but even if one ignores the important exceptions of liturgy and psalm-chanting, the reading aloud in the refectories, university lectures and the declamation of poetry, it remains true that texts thought by Parkes to be intended for silent reading are punctuated by phrase-markers and pause-directions to the voice, whether internal or aloud.

The last phrase needs a gloss. Parkes asserts that 'From the sixth century onwards . . . writing came to be regarded as conveying information directly to the mind through the eye.'[52] This suggests to me the modern practice of 'speed reading' whereby the eye glides through a text without any accompanying internal vocalization which, I frankly confess, I am personally unable to do. Everything I read I hear, with the exception of items on a list I am flicking through, but even then, when I get to the one I want I hear that. Comparing notes with friends and

---

[51] For a view different from Parkes's and strongly supported by evidence, cf. Paul Saenger, 'Silent Reading: Its Impact on Late Medieval Script and Society', *Viator*, Berkeley, 13 (1982), pp. 367–414. Saenger argues that reading aloud was normal until about the fourteenth century.

[52] Parkes, *Pause and Effect*, p. 1.

pupils I find this disability is still not uncommon.[53] Anyway, I think it brings us closer to the middle ages. The great divide is not between reading aloud and reading silently, but between reading with a voice real or imagined and reading without a voice at all. It is possible that a text meant for the inner voice will take less account of the need to pause for breath than a text meant for public performance, and I think this is reflected in the longer periods of some later medieval writings, but I have never come across any hint from the Middle Ages that the possibility of reading without an inner voice was ever imagined, and *pace* Parkes I shall assume that all medieval texts need a voice.

Wingo reports that the primitive Latin practice, perhaps taken from the Etruscans, was to separate words, and it is established that some quite elaborate form of punctuation was practised by the Romans in the first century BC.[54] But the fashion of Greek writing at the time was what the Romans called, imitating it, *scriptura* or *scriptio continua* and similar phrases; in this words were unseparated. The Roman adoption of this inconvenient practice, during the first century AD, must have followed from cultural awe, in this case misplaced.

In *scriptura continua* texts consisted of strings of letters unseparated into words or any other units shorter than the paragraph or, in verse, the line. Even for a scholar working in one of the great libraries, reading must have been quite different from reading at the present day. The papyri could be thought of more as we think of musical scores; complete notations but calling for considerable skill and art in the oral performance at which they were aimed. It is easy to understand why punctuation was reintroduced.

The earliest punctuated books were called 'distinguished', *codices distincti*, i.e. writing in which divisions were marked. There is some suggestion that these were rather looked down upon by late Roman literati who prided themselves on the capacity to do without punctuation, rather as some contemporary pianists scorn editorial fingering suggestions. Punctuation could be added to an already written manuscript as aid to performance. Medieval punctuation was sometimes in a different coloured ink from the original text.

Word-division by spaces has to be the work of the original scribe,

---

[53] I did a little research: I asked the well-read members of a corresponding society I belong to. David Holbrook and Brian Lee both answered that they don't know what it is to read without some sort of inner voice, and Duke Maskell thought nothing else is theoretically possible.

[54] Wingo gives a lucid account of the punctuation inscribed on stone monuments, but the possibility that it may not have been meant syntactically just did not occur to him, which makes him judge a number of marks anomalous that can be easily explained as indicating non-syntactic units or pauses.

though revisers sometimes separated words by vertical lines. Word-division as the norm seems to have been reintroduced by the Irish monks of the Dark Ages, and in particular when they were copying Latin. When they wrote Irish, 'In the earliest surviving records of Old Irish prose those words which are grouped round a single chief stress, and which have a close syntactical connexion with each other, have been copied as a single unit.'[55] Writing Irish they produced not words but phrases. The implication is that Latin was being treated more grammatically than Irish, but not necessarily that the grammar was that of the well-formed sentence.

The distinguishing of words (sometimes even in the high middle ages by spaces so thin that the reader has to look quite hard), must be grammatical, the recognition of 'lexical items'. No further *grammatical* development in punctuation took place before the Renascence, nor is there any hint in the discussions of punctuation by the grammarians that punctuation was thought to have anything like the syntactic function of the modern full point or semi-colon (see Appendix 2).

Reading an 'undistinguished' manuscript one might easily identify the words wrongly. Should we read 'exilio' or 'ex Ilio'? Servius twitted Donatus for reading *collectam ex Ilio pubem* instead of *collectam exilio pubem*.[56] Comparable questions arise about what we would think of as sentence breaks, the units divided by punctuation. For Augustine the possibility of ambiguity raises questions of orthodoxy. It would be heretical to end a sentence thus at the beginning of the Fourth Gospel: 'In principio erat Verbum et Verbum erat apud Deum et Deus erat.' ('In the beginning was the Word and the Word was with God and God existed.') It has to go 'et Deus erat Verbum. Hoc erat in principio apud Deum.' ('and God was the Word. This was in the beginning with God.' As against: 'and God existed. This word was in the beginning with God.') The erroneous 'distinction' is heretical because it implies a denial of the equality of the Persons of the Trinity.

So here, we may naturally suppose, we have the demand for punctuation of a grammatical/syntactic kind. Take the words one way and the disputable *verbum* is in one sentence in apposition with *deus*; take them another way and it is the subject of the next sentence. The question would be settled in a modern text by a full point, as in all modern editions of the Vulgate. Augustine, however, doesn't put it like this. He

---

[55] Parkes, *Pause and Effect*, pp. 23–4. The close connections are those of the age-old understanding of separate syntaxes of classes of words, such as preposition-with-noun. As a matter of fact, there is also plenty of running together of words in the (Latin) Book of Kells.

[56] Parkes, *Pause and Effect*, p. 10.

rightly says that each reading gives *alius sensus*; but he doesn't go into the syntactic reasons, any more than Dositheus (cited in Appendix 2).

It is not controversial to say that substantially different punctuations of the same passage are commonplace in medieval texts, as I illustrate in Appendix 3. Curiously enough, though all the medieval bibles I have seen (Greek, Latin and English) avoid the trap Augustine imagines, they ordinarily punctuate at verses 3–4 to give a sense rejected in 1611 but adopted by modern authorities including the New English Bible and the Jerusalem Bible: 'All things were made by him and without him was nothing made. That which was made was alive'—as against the 1611 'All things were made by him; and without him was not anything made that was made. In him was life.'

There are in fact *many* places in the New Testament where syntactic boundaries are unclear and consequently the sense varies with the editor; the cited Greek edition's apparatus 'includes some six hundred passages in which difference of punctuation seems to be particularly significant for interpretation of the text.'[57] Six hundred! I have lost count of the number of well-formed sentences in 1 Corinthians which some scholars take as questions, others as statements, e.g. 1. Corinthians vii. 18, 21, 27.

Rebuking the Church at Corinth for its factions Paul wrote, according to the 1611 Bible,

12 Now this I say, that every one of you saith, I am of Paul; and I of Apollos; and I of Cephas; and I of Christ.
13 Is Christ divided? was Paul crucified for you? or were ye baptized in the name of Paul?[58]

This traditional period/verse division has been accepted by all the modern versions I can easily find. Authorities differ as to the status of some members of verse 13 as question or exclamation or statement, but the cited Greek text records nobody offering a different syntactic boundary. I don't suppose, however, that I am the first person in the history of biblical commentary to suggest what seems the obvious sense, which can be brought out by rendering *de* as *but* instead of *and* and by modern punctuation:

12 Now this I say, that every one of you saith, 'I am of Paul,' 'But I of Apollos,' 'But I of Cephas.'
13 But *I* of Christ! Is Christ divided? was Paul crucified for you? or were ye baptized in the name of Paul?

My point is not to establish my reading, but that it is certainly

---

[57] *The Greek New Testament*, p. xxxv.   [58] 1 Corinthians i. 12–13.

disputable. There is no way of proving from the manuscripts that one reading is possible but not the other.

The choice between readings here makes a significant difference. But need it always?

The possibility I wish to raise is that not all syntactic imprecision need be seen as unwelcome ambiguity. The Authorized Version of 1611 gives 1 Corinthians xiv.33 as: 'For God is not *the author* of confusion, but of peace, as in all churches of the saints.' The cited Greek text, however, makes a paragraph in the middle of the verse and takes the phrase rendered 'as in all churches of the saints' to go with the next one, given in 1611 as 'Let your women keep silence in the churches.' To the modern reader these clearly give different senses: but must it follow that we have to differentiate them? May it not be possible that the 'as in all the churches of the saints' goes with all the other phrases in the passage, with, from our point of view, syntactic vagueness, but perfect intelligibility? Some examples of medieval treatments of this passage are given in Appendix 3.

The same Greek edition begins the chapter of Luke xxiv in the middle of a 1611 sentence, by taking the clause about the women followers resting on the sabbath to go with what they did on the first day of the week rather than what they did after preparing spices and ointments. But must we choose? To insist on one rather than the other is quite unnecessary! Matthew Arnold thought that the famous verse from Isaiah used by John the Baptist should go: 'The voice of one crying, In the wilderness prepare ye the way of the Lord.' Others including the Greek text I am using follow the traditional phrasing: 'The voice of one crying in the wilderness, Prepare . . .' This only matters if one thinks it important to know whether only the preparation or the voice also is in the wilderness. In places like these it may be a mistake to opt firmly for *either* syntax. The phrasal habit of antiquity makes it probable that *both* are intended. These are examples of what I call 'syntactic drift', which quite often means there is *no* way of accurately representing medieval texts in well-formed sentences. This will not be surprising to any reader who accepts my argument that they were not written in sentences. Some more examples are given below.

The least disputable use of medieval punctuation was *metrical*. 'Scribes and readers [of verse] throughout the Middle Ages usually introduced punctuation only when they thought it was necessary to avoid possible confusion,' says Parkes.[59] This is not quite true if we bear in mind that

59 Parkes, *Pause and Effect*, p. 106.

verse was almost always either lineated as we still do, or punctuated to indicate lines and, frequently in English, half-lines. Some earlier English manuscripts of verse were written out as we write prose. This practice may have been introduced 'for reasons of oeconomy' in the days before paper. But these manuscripts usually do indicate metre in their punctuation. For instance the Junius manuscript of Old English verse follows Bentham's definition of prose (written as far as the right-hand margin), but Krapp reports punctuation including 'dots marking the hemistich divisions of the lines of verse. This latter is obviously a metrical punctuation, and is used with remarkable regularity and correctness throughout the whole manuscript.' As Krapp remarks, 'This metrical punctuation must obviously have been of the very greatest assistance to anyone who undertook to read the poems of the manuscript aloud, and it is still helpful.'[60] From the early Middle English period that metrical oddity *The Ormulum* is written out continuously and therefore looks nothing like the modern editions, but is meticulously punctuated to indicate metrical units. Similarly the very stanzaic Old Norse poem the *Thrymskvitha* is written out continuously in the Codex Regius of the *Elder Edda*, but stanza breaks are clearly indicated as we indicate sentence divisions, by a point followed by initial capital. As late as *Piers Plowman* at least one manuscript still does not lineate, but relies on punctuation marks to indicate line- *and half-line* division.[61]

The purely metrical use of punctuation marks survives into the sixteenth century. Parkes quotes Gascoigne:

> Nor frame one warbling note to passe, out of hir mournfull voyce.

> And there to marke the jests, of every joyfull wight[62]

The mid-line comma is just the descendant of the medial punctus found in so many manuscripts of Chaucer and Langland, and in the sixteenth-century editions of the latter.

In many medieval verse manuscripts there are some points inserted at places where it would spoil the sense not to pause, or at places where the scribe wants us to go particularly slowly and weightily. The Cotton Caligula A. ix text of *The Owl and the Nightingale*, for instance, of the mid thirteenth century, puts a stop at the end of almost every line whether they are end-stopped or not—which must be taken as part of the metrical marking like lineation and starting a line with a capital letter—and then just a very occasional attention-calling stop within the

---

[60] *The Junius Manuscript*, ed. George Philip Krapp, 1931, pp. xxii, xxiii.
[61] Skeat reports of the Bodleian MS Digby 102, that 'The poem is written as prose, to save space; but the divisions into lines and half-lines are marked' (*Piers the Plowman* in *Three Parallel Texts*, ed. Walter W. Skeat, Oxford, 1886; repr. 1954, vol. II, p. lxxi).
[62] Parkes, *Pause and Effect*, p. 111.

line to slow us down. So in these texts punctuation performs two functions: it indicates the verse form, and it sometimes tells us when to pause. One surprising thing is how easy these manuscripts are to read. A text by our standards unpunctuated might be expected to trip the reader up constantly. Not at all. There are occasional awkward moments but I doubt whether in a careful manuscript of competently written verse they are any more frequent than in the modern printed book. Rhythmic/ metrical suggestions to the voice look after the syntax.

With verse, the primacy of the voice is comparatively easy to grasp. But something very similar, allowing for the basic fact that it is not metrical, has to be true of medieval prose.

Punctuation in the middle ages varied very much with place and context as well as time; liturgical writing developed its own system; the later Schoolmen naturally drew attention by theirs to logical connec- tions.[63] The art of writing letters called for rather different practices from the art of writing sermons, and verse always had its own conven- tions. It is not necessary here to go into detail beyond the assertion that very much medieval prose was divided into *periods*, divided into *members*.

The theory of punctuation used to mark periods and their members goes back to the Greeks. Wingo says, 'So far as I know, there is no Latin manuscript which embodies this [classical] system of punctuation.'[64] He means, I take it, no Latin manuscript from before the Barbarian invasions. There are *thousands* of medieval Latin prose manuscripts to the punctuation of which the accounts of the grammarians (Appendix 2) make a very good introduction.

The text of medieval Latin bibles is a vast subject, but I would hazard from the experience of taking every opportunity of looking at them that there was a central tradition of Bible phrasing, and that it went back to St Jerome. He introduced into his translation this classical system of division into members, by way of oratorical punctuation *per cola et commata*.[65]

It will be convenient to postpone our look at how periods are constructed, not *sine die* but to the next section. At present it is enough to assert that they are made rhythmically out of phrases, and are only coincidentally syntactic.

In medieval perception not even the classical Latin orators were seen syntactically. The medieval scribes habitually divide Cicero up into

---

[63] Cf. Parkes's citation of Roger Bacon (*Pause and Effect*, p. 89) as an example of logical, rather than rhetorical punctuation. This is still not modern-grammatical.
[64] Wingo, *Latin Punctuation*, p. 25.   [65] Parkes, *Pause and Effect*, pp. 15–16.

different periodic structures which may or may not be modern well-formed sentences (see Appendix 3). In the first thousand years or so of English prose there are likewise countless examples, a few quoted below, of periods that do not overlap with well-formed sentences.[66]

Correctness belongs to our sentence not the period. Medieval punctuation is always a matter of taste. As Levinson says, 'it all depended on how one chose to "orate" the passage';[67] which does not imply that punctuation cannot be reliable. There may, however, be several good punctuations of the same passage.[68] Take this bit of the prose life of Seinte Katerine of about 1225, as it appears in the Royal ms: 'beoth blithe ic bi seche ow. Yef ye me blisse unnen. for ich iseo iesu crist the copneth ant cleopeth me.' But the Titus manuscript here punctuates: 'Beoth blithe ich biseche ow yif ye me blisse unneth. For ich seo [. . .]'—and any grammatical difference doesn't matter much, though one may certainly prefer one version to the other.[69] I know best the Chaucer manuscripts, and there one does learn to appreciate the scribes who punctuate best— notably, in the case of *The Canterbury Tales*, those of the Ellesmere, Hengwrt and Cambridge Dd.iv.24 manuscripts.

Quite often an editor punctuates to make one particular syntactic structure when the manuscript punctuation does nothing so precise. The 1961 reprint of *The Book of Margery Kempe* has photographs of two pages of the unique manuscript. The one used as a frontispiece appears in the printed text like this:

As this creatur lay in contemplacyon, sor wepyng in hir spiryt, sche seyde to owyr Lord Ihesu Cryst, 'A, Lord, maydenys dawnsyn now meryly in Heuyn. Xal not I don so? For be-cawse I am no mayden, lak of maydenhed is to me now gret sorwe; me thynkyth I wolde I had ben slayn whan I was takyn fro the funtston

---

[66] At the excellent British Museum exhibition *The Making of England: Anglo-Saxon Art and Culture AD 600–900* (1992) I noticed that the following Latin and English manuscripts use varieties of periodic punctuation: Bodley Hatton 20 (*The Pastoral Care*); British Library Harley 7653 (eighth-century Latin); Durham Cathedral B.II.30 (Cassiodorus on the Psalms, Northumbrian eighth century); British Library Addn 47967 (Old English Orosius); British Library Harley 208, (Letters of Alcuin, ninth-century Latin). The Corpus Glossary (Corpus Christi College Cambridge 144) sets out words in columns, the Latin word followed by a comma, then the English equivalent and a comma. The Ceolfrid Bibles present the text in *cola et commata* making verses, though (see Appendix 3) the habit of the later Middle Ages was to indicate periods without displaying them as verses. The charters on display were all unpunctuated, no doubt because not designed for public performance. Levinson reports that as in modern ones there was 'virtually no pointing' in Anglo-Saxon legal documents (Levinson, *Punctuation*, p. 44).

[67] Levinson, *Punctuation*, p. 26.

[68] Cf. Parkes, *Pause and Effect*, pp. 14 and 85, where he quotes two fifteenth-century punctuations of the same passage.

[69] *Seinte Katerine*, re-ed. S. R. T. O. d'Ardenne and E. J. Dobson, EETS, SS7, 1981, p. 123.

that I xuld neuyr a dysplesyd the, and than xuldyst thu, blyssed Lorde, an had my maydenhed wyth-owtyn ende.'

As photographed, the mansucript actually reads:

A S this creature lay in contemplacyon sore wepyng in hire spiryt sche seyde
to owyr lord Ihesu cryst . A lord Maydenys dawnsyn now meryly in
heuyn ꝓ xal not I don so . for be cawse I am no mayden . lak of
maydenhed is to me now gret sorwe . me thynkyth I wolde I had ben slayn whan
I was takyn fro the funt ston. that I xuld neuer a dysplesyd the . & than xuldyst
thu blyssed lorde an had my maydenhed with owtyn ende .[70]

Whether the creature was weeping only in spirit is decided by the punctuation of the edition but not that of the manuscript; given her experiences of a quarter of a century it seems equally possible that as she lay sore weeping (lying flat was her habitual posture for both weeping and roaring) she spoke to our Lord in spirit. Whether Margery should be taken as linking her being deprived of the celestial dance to her lack of maidenhood is another question settled by the editor, this time in the negative, though surely at least part of our understanding is that she shall not dance in heaven because she is no maiden. The point, however, is not so much to argue against particular editorial interpretations as to observe that they are unnecessary. It is against the spirit of her book to insist on one syntactic structure here rather than another. Margery, who dictated her book to a German, from whose semi-legible text it was copied by an initially reluctant priest, was quite unlike Henry James dictating his novels, and was not talking with syntactic precision. She certainly did not put in that semi-colon after *sorwe*. I think the spirit of many medieval texts is to leave several syntactic possibilities open.

I have done next to no work on languages other than English, Old Norse, Greek and Latin, but I would be very surprised if what I have reported of medieval punctuation in Latin and English did not hold more or less throughout Christendom, with consequent implications about sentence-structure. Even German, the modern prose of which seems to the non-German reader congenitally clotted, with its long sentences looking forward to perhaps as many as three finite verbs one after another that will finally clinch them and absolutely demand a syntactic full point, was not so written in the middle ages. Medieval German was much more paratactic, and its prose manuscripts are punctuated like those of other languages *per cola et commata* to indicate periods, not syntactic structures.[71] Another obvious line of investigation is Italian. It would not be

---

[70] *The Book of Margery Kempe*, ed. Sanford Brown Meech, EETS, 1940, p. 50; MS f. 25 r.
[71] Cf. examples in Heinz Mettke, (ed.), *Älteste Deutsche Dichtung und Prosa*, Leipzig, 1976 and Charles Clyde Barber, (ed.), *An Old High German Reader*, Oxford, 1951. Cf. also

surprising if the change from phrasal to syntactic prose occurred earlier in Italy than elsewhere—Italy the first home of the Renascence and modern punctuation, Italian with its peculiarly close relation to Latin. Machiavelli's style reminds me of the English empiricist philosophers of the eighteenth century. On the other hand, though the narrative of the *Decameron* is neat and elegant, the prose is phrasal not syntactically complex. I leave this investigation to others.

Just one French example, from the witty but syntactically drifting opening of Gaston Phoebus' well-known treatise on hunting, in an unidentified ms reproduction:

Je gaston par la grace de dieu surnomme phebus. Conte de foys Seignieur de bear[n]. qui tout mon temps me suis delite par especial en .iii. choses. Lune est en armes. Lautre est an amours. Et lautre si est en chasce. Et car des deux offices il y a eu de meilleurs maistres trop que ie ne suy. Car trop de meilleurs cheualiers [folio ends before grammatical sentence.][72]

I Gaston by the grace of God surnamed Phoebus, Count of Foix Lord of Béarn, who have delighted all my days especially in three things, The one is arms, The next is love, And the other is hunting, And because there have been far better masters of the two former than I am, For many better knights'

Punctuation to indicate pauses or more ambitiously periods went on being normal in England more than half a century into the era of the printed book. I differ here from Dr Levinson, who attributes modern punctuation to the introduction of printing. By Caxton's day punctuation in the book trade had settled down into the use of a few apparently all-purpose marks, but the pauses and periods in Caxton's vernacular printing are if anything further from syntactic boundaries than those in the manuscripts of Ælfric:

/ ¶ The auncyent fonde awaye for to vse of certeyn tokens by whyche they gaffe hastly knowlege thurghe al the oost what they shuld doo/ ¶ Other by the sowne of trompettys / or by dyfferent sowne / as of hornes that men called bnyssynes / as of other manere of thyngys/ ¶ But to thende that by often herynge of suche manere of sowne/ the ennemyes shulde not be wyse nor knowe what hyt ment / made som tyme a dyfference in hyt / but fyrst was thys wel notyfyed emonge them / ¶ And from theyre chyldhede that men taughte hem the vse of armes/ thees maneres where [*sic*] shewed vnto them / by cause they shulde bettre Remembre hem self at a nede /[73]

Eric A. Blackall, *The Emergence of German as a Literary Language 1700–1775*, Cambridge, 1959.

[72] Probably Français 616, Bibliothèque Nationale, Paris; reproduced at the beginning of *Medieval Hunting Scenes*, text by Gabriel Bise after Gaston Phoebus, transl. J. Peter Tallon, Fribourg and Geneva, 1978.

[73] [Translation from Christine de Pisan], *The Fayt of Armes & of Chyualrye*, Westminster, 1489, f. E iii r.; facsimile repr. Amsterdam, 1968.

We are looking at so many dubious matters that it comes as a relief to find something that can rightly be called obvious. The compositor/ editor of this passage obviously still thought of the units of prose not as we do, syntactically, but as phrases, constructed by the voice. The subject of 'made' has to be 'the auncyent' two periods/paragraphs earlier. These paragraph marks seem to be meant to separate periods as breath lengths which may also be understood as 'complete thoughts', as with the grouping of the three advantages the general should take. But the thoughts are not *syntactically* complete. We are still being offered periods not sentences. The tension between the two is becoming more noticeable as prose becomes rather more syntactically complex at the end of the Middle Ages.

Many a medieval prose-work can only be saved from being seen as the dreaded million-word sentence by the realization that it is not written in a sentence or sentences at all. With the long unsyntactic phrase-successions of many a medieval prose work, the question whether to analyse into sentences is settled arbitrarily by the modern editor. This is why modern punctuation of a medieval text quite often looks peculiar: it can even be thought of as an unrecognized form of translation (Levinson uses the word). Is every *and* a new sentence or is the whole book one long sentence? We are asking the wrong question, brought on by modern grammatical instinct and the effort to fit a text to modern typographical practice.

The authentic reading of medieval texts is seriously impaired by modern punctuation, but editors learned enough to know better still sometimes suppose punctuation to be either a matter of no importance or one in which they have complete freedom or both. The printing of *Piers Plowman* without medieval punctuation but with modern punctuation means that the recent Schmidt four-text edition is much less reader-friendly than the old Skeat three-text, which did give us the mid-line punctuation. In his useful Everyman edition of the B-text Schmidt shows himself to be aware of the importance of half-line punctuation, but doesn't reproduce it there either. He ought to restore the half-lines to the next edition.[74]

Even when the importance of punctuation is realised, a scholar's results may be invalidated by dependence on edited texts. 'I have

[74] William Langland, *Piers Plowman: a Parallel-Text Edition of the A, B, C and Z Versions*, ed. A. V. C. Schmidt, vol. I, Text, 1995. 'All punctuation, capitalisation, word-division and paragraphing are editorial' (p. xv). We shall have to wait for volume two for Schmidt's reasons for preferring fussy syntactic punctuation to best manuscript tradition.
    Cf. my (forthcoming) discussion of the Kane-Donaldson-Russell edition, 'Doing a Bentley on Langland', *The Cambridge Quarterly*, 1998.

proceeded by taking my cues from punctuation (or its lack) in the prose under discussion,' says Professor Mueller when discussing the question how we know when a sentence/sentences made of many *and* . . . clauses begins and ends. Praise given to the sentences of a fifteenth-century cookery book which 'perspicuously groups into separate sentences the respective steps of mixing the batter, coating and frying the apple slices, dishing out the fritters, and bringing them to the table' is really due to the nineteenth-century editors not the fifteenth-century author or scribe. Conversely, when she says that the earlier sections of Capgrave's *Chronicle of England* are written in 'a high concentration of short, simplex sentences',[75] the true state of affairs is that this is what the nineteenth-century editors did with a text out of which, if so inclined, they could equally well have made longer sentences.

What would 'English' medievalists do without the Early English Text Society? But I seriously believe that the well-formed-sentencing of more than three quarters of the texts the EETS has published makes their re-editing an urgent necessity; for which at least there should be gratitude from graduate students looking for dissertation-subjects.

As Professor Mitchell says, raising the question how modern editions should punctuate Old English texts, 'Modern punctuation is syntactical, produces modern sentences, and so forces unnecessary and irrelevant decisions on editors.' Mitchell hopes for a new punctuation which 'will involve at least a partial retention of the OE system', and in *An Invitation to Old English and Anglo-Saxon England* (Oxford, 1995), has made a useful start towards providing one. He asserts that

The unit of both prose and poetry in Old English . . . is certainly not the sentence of today's formal English . . . I believe that the heavy use of modern punctuation, especially the division of the Old English paragraph into sentences, destroys the flow of both prose and verse.[76]

But as Mitchell is well aware, there are problems. If the manuscripts vary from each other and if no punctuation is 'correct' what is to be done? I hope the answer is not going to be *nothing*. In fact there is a mountain of work waiting to be done, once the principles of medieval punctuation have been grasped. And this is not just an academic-specialist matter: the present discussion is aimed at reading.

Modern syntactic punctuation is a Renascence development, and it anticipates the grammar that explains it by up to three hundred years.

---

[75] Mueller, *The Native Tongue and the Word*, pp. 18, 120, 116.
[76] Mitchell, *Old English Syntax*, I, pp. 770, 771, 21. Mitchell's belief is that the unit in Old English texts is 'not the phrase or the sentence but the paragraph'. I hope he will go into more detail about this.

Something very like our own system of punctuation developed in Italy in the late fifteenth century, not coincidentally contemporary with the roman and italic hands and their imitations in early printing fonts. The modern reader will be quite at home with the Aldine editions, though the older virgule-dominated punctuation survived in vernacular texts for more than a century. The use of the semi-colon in the modern way seems to have originated at that time in Venice.[77] Parkes quotes a page from P. Bembo, *De Ætna*, Venice, Aldus Manutius, 1494, that looks to me fully modern in its punctuation as well as its type face.[78]

Not all grammatical punctuation of the Renascence survived. We no longer bother with the *percontativus*, which was used to mark indirect questions. There is no rhetorical need for it; to point indirect questions is unmistakably to write in the grammatical way I began by noticing.

The Italian printers and scholars, however, who introduced the semi-colon and standardized parentheses, seem to have had no grammatical theory of what they were doing. The semi-colon was explained as yet another refinement of pause.[79] This is not very plausible, though efforts on these lines were still found in the eighteenth century and later (see below). The new contribution of the humanists was to *practise* modern syntactic punctuation. But this development does not give a *terminus post quem* for the modern editorial repunctuation of old texts. From the sixteenth century there are thousands of pages of unmistakable well-formed sentences of a size too much for modern editors, who repunctuate into more fashionable lengths and so rewrite the text as decisively as the repunctuating editors of medieval prose. Parkes gives examples from Nashe and Bacon, both of whom surely knew the effects they intended. We shall see that editorial re-sentencing did not even stop at Dryden.

The punctuation poem, a late medieval joke that survived into *A Midsummer Night's Dream*, in which verses read with one punctuation give a sense opposite to the one indicated by another punctuation, might seem to prove a modern syntactic understanding. But even this could if necessary be explained as different groups of sense made by different pauses. Shakespeare's Duke Theseus, leading up to Peter Quince's version of the punctuation poem, remembers that he has heard great clerks 'make periods in the midst of sentences', which most probably is not syntactically precise, *periods* and *sentences* both being taken in their old senses.

Shakespeare and Jonson both come where we might expect as regards rhetorical and syntactic punctuation: they both have elements of both. It

---

[77] Parkes, *Pause and Effect*, p. 49.   [78] *Ibid.*, plate 31, p. 214.
[79] *Ibid.*, p. 49.

should not be surprising if acting texts are conservatively rhetorical in their punctuation: obviously actors would welcome help with phrasing and need not be expected to bother too much about grammar. So it is worth remarking that both Jonson and the Shakespeare first folio also have a good deal of syntactic punctuation.[80] Brackets are, as usual, a reliable indicator; the exhibition of grammatical construction need not always worry a speaker. Simpson acutely notices that the bracketing in Sonnet xxix gives a sense different from that of the modern editors.[81] But even commas need not always be rhetorical. There are for instance commas 'marking the logical subject'.

The relation of the punctuation of the Shakespeare quartos and first folio to what he wrote remains controversial, but Jonson supervised the printing of a number of his own plays and his own first folio, and is known to have been an obsessive tinkerer. Some of Jonson's punctuation, however, is plainly rhetorical not syntactic. To the modern reader the most noticeable use of rhetorical punctuation is the 'full stop in an incomplete sentence'.[82] These are not infrequent and are quite comprehensible if taken as marking the end of a period, to which grammatical punctuation is here subordinate—a winding-down at the end of a series of members, not the conclusion of a syntactic unit.

The great *theoretical* change in the attitude to sentences comes with the enlightenment of the mid seventeenth century. By about 1700, our modern assumptions about grammatical punctuation have triumphed and the appropriate grammar for explaining modern punctuation has been developed. Contrast the late-eighteenth-century David Steel with any of the Humanists. Steel 'complained that many treatises on punctuation advocated that punctuation should represent pauses in speech, and so offered "too much accommodation to the reader, and too little attention to grammatical construction".'[83] By Steel's time, in fact, there was already a backlash against the tyranny of syntax. After the revolution in grammar and punctuation, Johnson's friend Thomas Sheridan in his interestingly named *Rhetorical Grammar of the English Language* advocated *declamatory* or *elocutionary* units and made it a complaint that 'certain parts of speech are kept together, and others, divided, according

---

[80] Sir Thomas Wyatt, the best part of a hundred years earlier, was already using both rhetorical and syntactic punctuation, virgules and parentheses: Parkes, *Pause and Effect*, p. 107, and below, ch. five.

[81] Simpson, *Shakespearian Punctuation*, p. 93.

[82] *Ibid.*, p. 79; his examples are from Jonson as well as Shakespeare and include one from Jonson's prose on p. 81. Cf. examples in Graham-White, *Punctuation*, p. 113, including one said to be in Shakespeare's hand, in the fragment of *Sir Thomas More*.

[83] 1786; cited Parkes, *Pause and Effect*, p. 4.

to their grammatical construction, often without reference to the pauses used in discourse'.[84] By then it was far too late to recur to a rhetoric-based punctuation. Bishop Lowth's attempt to make punctuation virtually like musical rests (two commas one semi-colon, two semi-colons one colon) is clearly hopeless, although the excellent Fowlers were still attempting it in the twentieth century. We don't count pauses like rests in music. Lowth's idea was a minor eccentricity in a grammarian for whom syntax was unassailable. As Parkes says, 'His rules are expressed not in terms of elocution but in terms of rhetorical structure and grammar':

Simple Members of Sentences closely connected together in one Compounded member, or Sentence, are distinguished and separated by a Comma . . . So likewise, the Case Absolute; Nouns in apposition, when consisting of many terms; the Participle with something depending on it; are to be distinguished by the comma; for they may be resolved into Simple Members.[85]

There the evolution of rhetoric into modern syntax is about as complete as it is ever likely to get.

In the eighteenth century there was a certain come-back of rhetorical punctuation in imaginative works. The dash, called by printers em rule, was used in the printing of plays around the turn of the seventeenth and eighteenth centuries, but came into its own in the novel of the later eighteenth century. This was true not only of the deadly serious joker Sterne, who uses the dash in just the old way to indicate the succession of phrases that are anything but clauses in a complex sentence, but was something taken for granted in the novels of the turn of the nineteenth century:

While the ladies remained in the same room with Dorriforth, Miss Milner thought of little, except of him—as soon as they withdrew into another apartment, she remembered Miss Woodley, and turning her head suddenly, saw Miss Woodley's face imprinted with suspicion and displeasure—this at first was painful to her—but recollecting that in a couple of hours time she was to meet her guardian alone—speak to him and hear him speak to her only—every other thought was absorbed in that one, and she considered with indifference, the uneasiness, or the anger of her friend.[86]

That, complete with frequent *cursus* forms, is a good old period rather than a sentence.

So: what do we understand by *period*?

---

[84] Cited Graham-White, *Punctuation*, p. 24.
[85] ?1763; cited Parkes, *Pause and Effect*, p. 92.
[86] Elizabeth Inchbald, *A Simple Story*, introd. Jeanette Winterson, 1987, p. 69.

iv   Period

I spent rather a long time searching for the medieval sentence, and what place more natural than grammar? If I had been more alert I would have started with the *period*, and for that would have gone to the rhetoricians not the grammarians. Naturally, however, the first place to look for the period as for the sentence seems to be the dictionary—which blithely conflates the two: 'Period 10 (a): A complete sentence . . . Usually applied to a sentence consisting of several clauses, grammatically connected, and rhetorically constructed. Hence, in *pl.*, rhetorical or grammatical language.' *Rhetorical*, unfortunately, does not go so easily with *grammatical*; nor need what is rhetorically constructed be grammatically connected. The NED's first citation in a clearly syntactic sense is from 1875. George Puttenham, in the sixteenth century, is not grammatical at all: 'a complement or full pause, and as a resting place and perfection of so much former speech as had bene vttered . . . your three pauses, comma, colon and periode'. The only move towards syntax there is to think of *period* as the separation rather than that which is separated.

The Latin dictionary is not much more distinctive. After defining *periodus* as *A complete sentence, a period*, which begs the question we are asking, Lewis and Short quote from Cicero 'in toto circuitu illo orationis, quem Graeci *periodon*, nos tum ambitum, tum circuitum, tum comprehensionem, aut continuationem, aut circumscriptionem dicimus'. ('In that whole cycle of discourse which the Greeks call *period*, we sometimes the orbit, sometimes the circuit, sometimes the apprehension,[87] or the continuation, or the encircling.') This gives us the alternatives of seeing a thrashing about in the general direction of the sentence without getting there, or of recognizing that periods were not thought of as much like modern sentences.

The basic terminology of the period as the unit of oratorical discourse punctuated *per cola et commata* seems to have originated with the Sophists; Thrasymachus is said to have been the inventor of the period and the colon; Gorgias himself is credited with originating the *schemata verborum*, the categories of verbal figures; which may explain the perhaps surprising absence of the topic from Plato, notoriously suspicious of rhetoric because it is supposed to put persuasiveness before truthfulness. Aristotle seems to have set himself the task of finding a place for rhetoric

---

[87] The dictionary explains *comprehensio* firstly literally, as *seizing with the hands* and also cites from Cicero the phrase *verba comprehensione devincire*: to conquer words by laying hands on them!

and verse without denying the pursuit of truth. I am not sure the task is yet completed.

All the later definitions of *period*, anyway, as of *rhythm*, are unpackings of Aristotle, though the discussion by Demetrius is probably the most usefully accessible to the modern reader.[88]

Aristotle introduces the word *periodon* in a passage of the *Rhetoric* that distinguishes two styles within what we call prose.[89] This witty treatment of the period is short enough to quote. I will give a very literal translation:

The speech [*lexis*] [is] to be joined: either strung together[90] and fastened just by the conjunctions[91] as in the dithyrambic preludes, or turned-back,[92] and so like the antistrophes of the ancient poets. But the strung-together speech/prose is the ancient one, [e.g.]: 'Of Herodotus of Thurii here is the story of the investigation.' This was used formerly by everybody, but now not by many. I say of the strung-together style that it has no end in itself should not the matter bring the saying to an end. It is annoying through its boundlessness/ having no way out; for everybody wants an end in sight. That is why at the turning-points [in a running-course] they run out of breath and faint, but seeing the end they are not worn out before. Such is the strung-together speech/prose; but the turned is in periods. I say that a period-diction has a beginning and an end in itself and a size easy to see at once. This is pleasing and easily intelligible: pleasing through having qualities opposite from the boundless and because all the time the hearer [*sic*] has good hope of getting something [and] that something has bounded itself; but it is unpleasing neither to know what is coming nor to come to an end. [The periodic] is good for learning because good for memorizing. This is because in periodic discourse there are numbers, of all things the best memorable. That is why all verse is memorized more easily than a flood [of words]; for it has number by which it is measured/put in metre.

Whatever may be unclear here, some important matters about the period are clear enough. The period is one particular style of constructing meaningful units out of sounds and pauses. Aristotle is discussing one style of the written language intended for performance,

[88] *Demetrius on Style*, transl. T. A. Moxon, *Essays in Classical Criticism*, 1953; but beware of Moxon's gloss '"Members", i.e. "limbs"; here "clauses"' (p. 199): no, locutions perceived to be units of sense, not syntactically well-formed.

[89] Aristotle, *Rhetoric*, 1409a–b (III. ix in the Loeb division, transl. John Henry Freese, 1926; repr. 1939). Quite possibly Aristotle was pressing a nonscientific term into service with *periodon*. The more common senses are for instance 'a way round', 'a book of travels' and 'a course at dinner' (Liddell and Scott).

[90] *Eiromene* is glossed by Liddell and Scott as 'a continuous, running style' with this passage cited, but the word comes from *eiro* which they say means 'to fasten together in rows, string, plait'.

[91] *Syndesmos*: cf. Aristotle, *Poetics*, 1456b.

[92] This represents an untranslatable participial adjective from *katastrepho*, the range of which includes: to bring a speech suddenly to an end, to turn or bring back, to twist strongly; glossed here as 'a close periodic style'.

not trying to say anything generally true of all non-verse written language. As his descendant Demetrius puts it, 'One kind of style is described as "connected", as, for example, the style which is expressed by periods.'[93] His examples are the speeches of Isocrates, Gorgias and Alcidamas, which 'are expressed as completely by the medium of periods as Homer's poetry is by the medium of hexameters.' Period itself, as well as *commata* and *cola*, is treated as a *figure* by the *Rhetorica ad Herennium*. Aquinas still distinguishes Demosthenes in Greek and Cicero in Latin as orators 'qui prosa scripserunt per cola . . . et commata'[94]; that is, not all prose writers did.

Aristotle is distinguishing nicely rounded speech-units from ones that just seem to be strings of phrases linked by conjunctions, and he thinks the difference is that the periods have *number* though they are not metrical. I don't think it is pushing anything far to apply what he says of Herodotus to the barer entries in the Anglo-Saxon Chronicle, and what he says of periods to Ælfric's Homilies.

The modern English descendants of the word *periodus* include, as well as the American *full point* (end of a (grammatical) sentence): a division of the school day, an age in history, and a woman's monthlies. You may well ask what the English examples have to do with government by a finite verb or syntactic perfection. They have, though, everything to do with the sense of *a coherent unit* or *one of a series complete in itself* or *something coming round*.

Aristotle goes on to use one of the basic terms for the units of the period which survived until they turned into the names for modern punctuation-marks, the *colon*. The period, he says, can either be simple or in *cola*, the simplest form being the *monocolon*. He gives the good advice that neither *cola* nor periods should be too short or too long.

The word *rhythm* comes into the same passage of Aristotle as necessary for the understanding of the *period*. Punctuation, he says, should not be imposed to signal the end of a period: the rhythm itself should do that.[95] The importance of this notion of rhythm should not be neglected. 'The "harmony", "number" or "rhythm" of a period depends chiefly upon the relations between the members,' says Croll.[96] If our present interest leads us to *rhythm* before sentence-syntax it is much in the spirit of Aristotle.

Neither Quintilian nor Cicero thinks of *commata* as lesser units making the greater *cola*. The *Rhetorica ad Herennium* treats *commata* as a separate style of short staccato phrases.[97] Quintilian agrees and gives the

---

[93] *Demetrius on Style*, p. 203.   [94] Hubert, *Corpus Stigmatologicum Minus*, p. 147.
[95] Aristotle, *Rhetoric*, 1409a.   [96] Croll, *Style, Rhetoric and Rhythm*, p. 325.
[97] *Rhetorica ad Herennium*, IV. 19. 'Veni, vidi, vici' would be an example.

single word *diximus* as an example of a *comma*, but reports it as the opinion of most that a comma is a part of a member (or *colon*).[98] The latter became the ordinary medieval notion.

One style of rhetoric became, under the patronage of the Church, universal and therefore the ancestor of our *prose*. The *commata* came to be taken as elements of *cola* in much the way that *cola* were elements of periods. I shall keep these in italics, to minimize the likelihood of confusion between them and the modern names of punctuation marks that are their descendants. Our modern commas often do mark the boundaries of *commata* but the coincidence can be misleading.

The parts of a period were not subordinate clauses but *limbs* or *members*, to which the organic terminology is necessary. The *commata* and *cola* approximate more closely to stress- or tone-groups than to grammatical clauses, though they were also thought of as groups of sense within the *sententia*. Naturally, the marks tell the reader where to pause, and how important the pause is.

This is one rhythmic style, not nature. There is no such thing as *natural* pausing, unless we think of going on until the breath runs out then fetching breath and recommencing. All pauses in speech are conventional. Some are syntactic, some are periodic, some neither. Many sentences in speech and especially the odd speech of the 'real world' of interviews on 'the media' have no pause at the end. I frequently hear public readings in which there is no pause between 'She said' and the direct speech of what she said. On the other hand, one style of contemporary public speaking even puts pauses between articles and nouns. Periodic prose is one stylization of phrase-lengths and pauses.

Cicero and Diomedes both say that a period should be the same as a breath-length.[99] There must be breaths; Cicero's argument is that periods are a way of making the units harmonious and not just dictated by the breath's expiry. Quintilian (who seems to my inexpert judgement to be a very intelligent writer) notices, however, that 'it is at times necessary to take breath without any perceptible pause'.[100] Here, of course, the connection between periodicity and medieval punctuation comes clear, and continues clear as late as the fifteenth century:

Item nota, si distinctio sit nimis prolixa, lector poterit pausare per unum paruum punctum, quotiens uoluerit, sustentans equaliter in tono tube. Sed caute caueat quod hoc faciat congruenter, quoniam si taliter pausaret inter

---

[98] Quintilian, *Institutio Oratoria*, IX. iv. 122.
[99] Cf. Cicero, *De Oratore*, III. xlvi. 181; Loeb transl. H. Rackham, repr. 1960, p. 145.
[100] Quintilian, *Institutio Oratoria*, XI. iii. 39; Loeb transl. H. E. Butler, IV, 1921; repr. 1959, p. 263.

substantiuum et adiectiuum, uel inter suppositum et appositum sibi inuicem
contigua, insipienter ageret et reprehensibiliter haberetur et confusione dignus.

N.B.: If the [distance between] punctuation is rather long, the reader will be
enabled to pause by a little punctuation mark as often as he need, sustaining the
monotone without variation. But let him be careful that this should be done
grammatically, since if he should pause in this way between the noun and
adjective or between the topic and predicate in turn next to each other, he will
do foolishly and will be held reprehensible and worthy of being called
confused.[101]

Grammatical categories still make their appearance by way of rhetoric,
and there is no instruction to pause at the end of a syntactic structure.

Croll reports Landry's opinion that the number of members or *cola*
that make a period is undefined but rarely more than eight. Numbers of
rhetoricians follow Quintilian in recommending four as the norm, the
tetracolon, though Cicero preferred three, and Demetrius says four is the
maximum. Even the simplest period, mentioned by Aristotle, the
monocolon, need not be the same as a simple sentence: Cassiodorius
gives *arma virumque cano* as an example, which turns out to be the
beginning of a complex sentence. Croll also says that the number of
emphatic accents in a *colon* varies between one and four and that a *colon*
rarely exceeds twenty syllables in length (the length, of course, of a
heroic couplet) because of the breaths required in oral delivery. Here is
one versifier's informative definition:

> KOMMA. Particulae membra efficiunt, haec circuitum omnem.
> Particula est comma, ut versu tria commata in illo:
> 'Arcadiam petis, inmensum petis, haud tribuam istud.'
> KOLON. Membra ea sunt quae cola vocant; ea circuitum explent:
> 'Nam qui eadem vult ac non vult', colon facit unum;
> Huic adiunge sequens: 'is demum est firmus amicus'.
> PERIODOS. Circuitus, peri quam dicunt odos, orta duobus
> Membris, ut praedicta, venit tetracolon adusque:
> Nam si plura itidem iungas, oratio fiet.

Comma: The little parts make the members, they the whole period. A little part
is a *comma*, as the three *commata* in this line of verse: 'Arcadiam petis, inmensum
petis, haud tribuam istud.' *Colon*: These members are what are called *cola*; they
fill out the period. 'Nam qui eadem vult ac non vult', makes one *colon*, to which
this next one is joined: 'is demum est firmus amicus'. *Period*: The circuit, which
they call the way around (parts as aforesaid from two members) becomes
completely the *tetracolon*: for if you join a number in the same way, the *oratio* will
be made.[102]

---

[101] *Unification Carthusienne*, in Hubert, p. 165. *Tuba*, originally the (trumpet)-tone of epic
poetry, is used for the monotone sometimes varied at the ends of clauses or periods by
melodic phrases quoted in this document.

[102] *Carmen de Figuribus vel Schematibus*, 4–12; *Rhetores Latini Minores*, pp. 63–4.

The ways of characterizing the members may look impressionistic, as when Fortunatianus says, 'Structurae qualitas est tripertita: aut enim rotunda est, id est volubilis, aut plana, id est procurrens, aut gravis, id est stabilis ac resistens.' ('The quality of the structure is one of three kinds; for it is either rotund, that is, voluble, or plain, that is, running on, or grave, that is, stable and unyielding.')[103] The *raison d'être* of the schemes and members is, as Bede says, 'per hoc quodam modo vestitur et ornatur oratio'.[104] This is evidently about style not grammar as we understand grammar.

Quintilian says that we have to watch the beginnings and endings most: hence the emphasis on *cadence*, which is emphatically a rhetorical not a grammatical concern, for instance in the extensive formal and informal practice of the *cursus* (see Appendix 4). If the period was, in Cicero's quoted definition, the complete circuit of rhythmically connected members, the *cursus* was the set of recommended ways of rounding off a period or a *colon*. Like all rhetoric this could degenerate into mannerism, but need not.

The classically-derived medieval arts of rhetoric and dictamen (manuals for writing letters) define numbers of comparisons between the members of a period, as well as numbers of ways of constructing members. The *tropes* sometimes equated with *figurae sententiae*, figures of meaning like metaphor and antithesis, apply to only one phrase at a time. *Schemata verborum*, the figures of sound, are more inherently rhythmic.

Prose rhythm consists of linking the units appropriately. Croll gives a useful summary of the *schemata verborum* as found in the English Euphuists:

first, isocolon, or equality of members (successive phrases or clauses of about the same *length*); secondly, parison, or equality of sound (successive or corresponding members of the same *form*, so that word corresponds to word, adjective to adjective, noun to noun, verb to verb, etc.); thirdly, paromoion, similarity of sound between words or syllables, usually occurring between words in the same positions in parisonic members, and having the form either of *alliteration*, similarity at the beginning, or *homoioteleuton* (*similiter cadentes* or *desinentes*), similarity at the end.[105]

Some of these can be repetitions of syntactic shape, but the rhetoricians' interest is in *sound*.

Within the period everything relates to everything else. The likenesses such as isocolon and parison are thus bounded, though of course the

---

[103] *Rhetores Latini Minores*, p. 127.   [104] *Ibid.*, p. 607.
[105] Croll, *Style, Rhetoric and Rhythm*, p. 242; cf. a useful discussion in Brian Vickers, *Francis Bacon and Renaissance Prose*, Cambridge, 1968, p. 97.

linking of periods into larger rhythmic units is also important and the beginning of the next period will be affected by and refer back to what has gone before. As Michael wittily puts it, 'The period refers to an expression as if it were a journey in which it is important only to arrive, provided one has travelled stylishly, visiting the best places en route, even if a detour is needed.'[106] This appeals to the etymology *peri odon*, a way round, of which Aquinas was aware.[107] The well-formed sentence is not a way round.

Nobody seems to have thought there was any contradiction between treating the periods in terms of breaths and pauses and treating them as groupings of sense. *Sententia* or *oratio* is a unit seen in the aspect of propositional content, *period* in the aspect of rhythmic shape. There was no term for the same unit defined syntactically.

Period of course very often covers exactly the same words as our *sentence*, but they are still different. It is extraordinarily difficult, though so simple, to avoid confusing the two.[108]

In the Middle Ages, periodic prose was the ordinary good style of Latin. R. W. Southern's edition of Eadmer's *Life of Anselm* is a handily available text that gives useful examples. Southern is able to reproduce the punctuation of the author, and gives a close English translation *en regard*. The periods that differ from well-formed sentences can be readily seen by glancing at the places where the English sentence divisions have to depart from the Latin periodic structure, for instance the first two English sentences on p. 79.

Periodic structure survives in Coverdale's psalms, classically pure because they are designed to be spoken or sung as, thank God! they are still in most English cathedrals. In these verses from the hundredth Psalm, the alternative to the Benedictus in Morning Prayer, punctuation

---

[106] Michael, *Grammatical Categories*, pp. 42–3.

[107] Hubert, *Corpus Stigmatologicum Minus*, p. 147.

[108] Even Michael talks of sentences in Plato when he should say periods; and Croll, though he agrees that the period is rhetorical, wavers. Croll did not himself revise his essays for collection and had he done so would, I expect, have resolved a contradiction:

The things named by these terms are identical. *Period* names the rhetorical, or oral, aspect of the same thing that is called in grammar a *sentence* (Croll, *Style, Rhetoric and Rhythm*, p. 231).

That this is not always true is later conceded:

Though the period ordinarily coincides with the sentence, theoretically it is not the same, and in practice it may (in certain kinds of style) consist of elements not syntactically connected (*Ibid.*, p. 324).

I of course agree with the latter statement.

by verses, commas and colons, here purely medieval in function, marks each verse as a period made out of two *cola* each made out of *commata*:

O go your way into his gates with thanksgiving, and into his courts with praise : be thankful unto him, and speak good of his Name.
For the Lord is gracious, his mercy is everlasting : and his truth endureth from generation to generation.

'In Psalmody the period is the verse,' says Clemoes.[109] All that needs for complete periodic pointing is commas after *gates* and *endureth*.

The English Bible of 1611 is traditionally printed in verses which are the most important descendant of the periodic tradition into our world. The verses are by no means always the same as sentences. Often a sentence takes up more than one verse:

8 Then Peter, filled with the Holy Ghost, said unto them, Ye rulers of the people, and elders of Israel,
9 If we this day be examined of the good deed done to the impotent man, by what means he is made whole;
10 Be it known unto you all, and to all the people of Israel, that by the name of Jesus Christ of Nazareth, whom ye crucified, whom God raised from the dead, *even* by him doth this man stand here before you whole.[110]

On the other hand verses are often made of more than one sentence: 'And the earth was without form, and void; and darkness *was* upon the face of the deep. And the Spirit of God moved upon the face of the waters.'[111]

Periodization can in some circumstances appear artificial. In the Book of Common Prayer some verses of the Te Deum appear like this:

> The Father : of an infinite Majesty;
> Thine honourable, true : and only Son;
> Also the Holy Ghost : the Comforter.

These are not the boundaries we would notice if the passage were written out as ordinary prose, where syntax would have more influence on phrasing. This phrasing has been reorganized presumably for the sake of singing. I asserted above that no pauses are natural. In unusual circumstances prose periodization can alter, too. The *commata* get very short in *Through the Looking Glass* when Alice pants.

Text sentences that correctly separate main clauses by commas, rather than major punctuation, are curious. There is some survival of logic into the demand that their topic must be unified. 'Napoleon lost the battle of Waterloo, when ice melts it forms water, and there are fifty-two weeks in

[109] Clemoes, *Liturgical Influence on Punctuation*, p. 10.
[110] Acts iv; cf. Appendix 3.   [111] Genesis i. 2.

the year' would be unacceptable as an opening, though imaginable as an answer in a quiz programme. But why can commas be used in such sentences? I think the most likely reason is the survival of the period. Here are three or more syntactic structures not connected syntactically but rounded off into a structure of sense whose overriding unity is recognized by the minor punctuation. 'They were ready and waiting on the starting grid, the engines were revving, the flag was raised and lowered, and they went roaring off into the first bend.' That is a *tetracolon*. The use of commas, semi-colons, colons or full points between the lexical sentences will depend on our sense of rhythm, not on syntax. The same period punctuated with semi-colons would go rather slower, and repunctuated to make four sentences would go ponderously.

We make units of sense not governed by the syntax of the well-formed sentence, and our sense of these units tells us when to use commas or semi-colons rather than full points:

It was as big a fish as was ever catched in the Mississippi, I reckon. Jim said he hadn't ever seen a bigger one. He would 'a' been worth a good deal over at the village. They peddle out such a fish as that by the pound in the market-house there; everybody buys some of him; his meat's as white as snow and makes a good fry.[112]

Whether this punctuation is the author's I don't know, but the last sentence with the two semi-colons is right, though Huck Finn would never write semi-colons. It would have been quite possible for these to have been separate sentences like the short ones at the beginning of the quotation. As it is they make a *tricolon*, and are all the better for it.

---

[112] Mark Twain, *Huckleberry Finn*, ch. x; introd. Walter Allen, 1948, p. 72.

2   Prose rhythm

Numerosa fiat oratio   Cicero

So far I have been taking for granted that we know what *prose* means.
What could we know better? But the word is suprisingly hard to define
formally as a kind of language. Samuel Johnson, master both of English
prose and of the art of defining, does what can be done: 'Language not
restrained to harmonick sounds, or set number of syllables, discourse
not metrical'. We shall return to the sense there may be in the old joke
that prose is not verse. The great *New English Dictionary* is less formal
than Johnson. It begins: 'the ordinary form of written or spoken
language', before going on to 'without metrical structure' and the
commonest of common speech: 'Opposed to *poetry, verse, rime*, or
metre'. I think *spoken* should be omitted: otherwise this is all fair enough
as long as we realize that except for the negative phrase 'without metrical
structure' we are not being offered any formal linguistic definition. I also
notice that even this omits the other part of Aristotle's remark. As well
as being without metrical structure this form of language must also have
number and *rhythm*.[1]

It is an objection to a value judgement, not to a formal definition, to
ask how 'dull or commonplace expression, quality, spirit'—a sense of
prose that goes back to the sixteenth century—fits such leading examples
of prose as the traditional Latin Collects or their English equivalents, or
Jane Austen's[2] or Charles Dickens's novels.

'The ordinary form of written or spoken language' is still historic not
formally linguistic: 'ordinary' to whom? Not to the Greeks of the age of
Homer, who would not have known what to make of the definition. The
ordinary order is for prose to succeed heroic poetry; prose is well known
to appear *late* in the history of many civilizations. The *Shorter Oxford*
tells us that prose is 'straightforward discourse'. But, again, what is

---

[1] '*Dio rhythmon dei echein ton logon, metron de me*' (Aristotle, *Rhetoric*, 1408b; III. viii. 3).
[2] Cf. George Whalley's essay 'Jane Austen: Poet' in *Studies in Literature and the Humanities*, 1985.

45

46   The establishment of modern English prose

straightforward for us is not so as a fact of nature and need not be so in all ages.[3] 'Opposed to . . . *verse, rime* or *metre*', with which the definition continues, returns us to Johnson and the joke.

Saintsbury declines, on his first page, to quote that classic dialogue between M. Jourdain and his Maître de Philosophie because, he says, it is too well known. In case, however, that there might be any substance in Saintsbury's immediately consequent prediction ('and which, in the near future of what is now called education, nobody at all will know'), I will do so. 'Il n'y a, pour s'exprimer, que la prose ou les vers . . . Tout ce qui n'est point prose est vers et tout ce qui n'est point vers est prose.'[4] To the following question what it is that we speak, the answer is firmly *prose*. In the act of appearing to generate its comicality from a mere tautology this in fact extends the falseness, for we don't speak prose. To say so is not to deny a necessary connection between speech, prose and character. But, as T. S. Eliot puts it:

An *identical* spoken and written language would be practically intolerable. If we spoke as we write we should find no one to listen; and if we wrote as we speak we should find no one to read. The spoken and the written language must not be too near together, as they must not be too far apart.[5]

We expect prose to be analytic and succinct, also ordinarily *less* syntactically complicated than speech. But this is still a stylistic expectation, not one that defines the non-verse forms of written language.

It becomes much more difficult to state the difference between prose and verse if we take prose as a sort of natural base on which verse is built. *Both* sides in the classic controversy in English about the difference between verse and prose, between Wordsworth in the *Lyrical Ballads* Preface and Coleridge in *Biographia Literaria*, take it for granted that there is no great difficulty in defining the difference, and that verse is so to speak a specialized prose, made different by the addition of metre. As well as being almost instinctive, the position is still sometimes held by academics. 'Prose follows only the rules of the English language,' says Attridge, 'but verse introduces some additional principle or principles that heighten our attention to its rhythms.'[6] But if the best we can do for a formal linguistic definition of prose is to say that it has no metrical structure we must have a sense of metrical structure prior to prose.

What is useful in these non-definitions is the recognition that prose is

---

[3] The Latin original of the phrase *straightforward discourse, prosa oratio*, is probably mistranslated by 'ordinary prose'. How ordinary was Cicero?

[4] Molière, *Le Bourgeois Gentilhomme*, II. vii.

[5] T. S. Eliot, 'Charles Whibley', *Selected Essays*, 3rd edn, 1951, p. 497; cf. Abercrombie, *Studies in Phonetics and Linguistics*, ch. I, 'Conversation and Spoken Prose'.

[6] Derek Attridge, *Poetic Rhythm, an Introduction*, Cambridge, 1995, p. 5.

not a syntactic category, though for us prose certainly has strong syntactic implications. If prose is not verse the discussion is within the province of rhythm.

Rhythm is another word that needs attention, though, surprisingly enough, it seems to me much easier to define than *prose*. Shortage of space here compels me to present, unsupported, some results of a work in progress for which I shall propose the title *Shakespeare's Rhythmic Descent from Chaucer*. Rhythm is not a regular alternation of different elements like *tick-tock*, nor is it as some think a *flowing*; rhythm is whatever forms a whole out of parts. This is variously applicable in language, including to syntax, the rhythm of the well-formed sentence; but as commonly used, the *rhythm* of language has to do with sound in speech, verse or prose.

In English, the rhythms of sound are made out of patterns of stress. *Stress* may be absolute but is always comparative. Accentual-syllabic verse, the ordinary verse of modern English, makes lines by the repetition and variation of certain patterns of comparative stress, called the *metre*. Iambic, for instance, is not unstress followed by stress but lesser followed by greater stress, the domain of the greater stress being the *foot*. The words *foot*, *syllable* and *stress* are interdependent. Within the foot there is one syllable more stressed than the rest, and the relation of the stress to the unstress(es) defines the kind of foot it is. The metrical line consists of a given number of feet. Provided this works in practice, as I believe it has often been shown to do, this is enough to establish the existence of feet, challenged though it is by some contemporary theorists.[7]

Even in this summary, however, it must be emphasized that formal is not critical: everything depends on how the patterns are made. The rhythm of verse is metrical, certain patterns put together in a certain order; the rhythm of a poem is not the metre but what a poet does with metre.

All a syllable needs to count as stressed within a foot is to have more stress than the other syllable(s), so the stressed syllable may or may not be what David Abercrombie calls a 'stress-pulse'.[8] Stress-pulses do seem to exist; as we talk or read we are conscious of occasional surges of energy separable from the binary or trinary comparisons of stress that make feet. This may seem less opaque if I drop Abercrombie's term. What Abercrombie calls *stress pulse* I shall just call *beat*.

---

[7] E.g. Cureton, *Rhythmic Phrasing in English Verse*, p. 88.

[8] 'Less frequent, more powerful contractions of the breathing muscles which every now and then coincide with, and reinforce, a chest-pulse' (Abercrombie, *Studies in Phonetics and Linguistics*, p. 17): the 'chest-pulse' is the stress that defines a syllable.

By *stress* I always mean a prominence dependent on a relation to a (comparatively) unstressed syllable or syllables; *beat* fits into the comparative pattern but also demands an absolute expenditure of energy. Much bad reading of verse follows from treating metrical stress as beat.

If the metrical stress governs the foot, the main beat probably governs the *phrase* or in some styles the *breath-length*. But there need not be only one beat to the phrase. In the leading formalization of beat in English, the alliterative half-line, there are by definition ordinarily two beats per phrase. I report as ordinary experience that though these beats vary considerably in sensitive reading, they have a tendency towards equality which we just do not find in the foot-stresses of the blank verse line.

D. W. Harding asks whether Saintsbury's scansions of prose are more than an arbitrary notation.[9] If it is granted that there need be no pause between one foot and the next, that there is no relation between word boundaries and foot boundaries, and that any syllable is either more or less stressed than its neighbours, it must be possible to score any passage in feet whether or not the feet are actually part of the rhythmic construction. If prose is defined as being without the repeated stress-patterns that demonstrate the feet in verse, do we really form syllables into feet as we read prose?

I think there is some reason to suppose that we do. The range of possible stress-patterns in a prose phrase is often wider than the range in verse; but there are many prose phrases which are naturally rhythmized (D. W. Harding's very useful word) one way rather than another, and where the terminology of feet seems to give the most convincing explanation why. The *cursus* forms on which I offer a short Appendix are most simply defined metrically as successions of prescribed feet.

Words of alternative accentuation will often receive the one that makes a more convincing foot-pattern. This cannot be conclusively demonstrated, because the other accentuation will always make another foot pattern, but some instances seem fairly clear.

That there are disyllabic words of alternative accentuation in English is beyond dispute.

The trouble was a damned trades union demarcation dispute.

The *tendency* (not a rule) is to put the accent on the second syllable in my first example, and on the first in my second. If so, the simple explanation is the run of feet of the same metre (iambic, rising rhythm in the first, trochaic, falling in the second) which, I agree with Quintilian in

---

[9] Harding, *Words into Rhythm*, pp. 116 ff.

thinking, the prose-writer (and reader) will make where it is easy to do so up to about the number of three (Cicero's number[10]), beyond which the prose lapses into verse.

To slip into verse is notoriously a blemish in a prose writer, though as Quintilian observed, we do it all the time in *oratio*. In English it is most commonly blank verse, as all over the place in *A Christmas Carol*, or this from a contributor to *The London Review of Books* waxing plangent about the efforts of a warder to prevent the suicide of Frederick West: 'To no avail he tried the kiss of life'[11]; I have a list of about twenty examples from Martin Amis's well-paid work *The Information* (1995). Other verse forms lie in wait. Every Sunday some hapless pilgrims recite lines purporting to be the Gloria in Excelsis which I would guess to be intended as prose but which begin

> Glory to God in the highest,
> and peace to his people on earth.[12]

—the same metre as ''T was Christmas day in the workhouse'. *Lorna Doone* is ruined by compulsive trochaic tetrameters; George Gissing, whose novelist hero Reardon in *New Grub Street* found himself exhaustedly writing metrical phrases, himself produced the far too dactyllic 'Though Miss Barfoot had something léss thăn ă wómăn's ávĕrăge státŭre, thĕ nóte ŏf hĕr présĕnce wăs pérsŏnăl dígnĭtў.'[13] There is even at least one ballad quatrain, complete with rhyme, in the prose of *Middlemarch*:

> 'No, really, Mrs Farebrother,
>   I am glad of both, I fear,'
> Said Mary, cleverly getting rid
>   Of one rebellious tear.[14]

If we just follow Cicero and say that repetition of the same foot-pattern more than about three times establishes metre, we notice these passages becoming verse because we are reading in feet. There are other possible descriptions, but this does have the merits of simplicity and comprehensibility.

The classical rhetoricians take it for granted that prose is made of feet, and I think we would be rash to ignore them, this being their home ground. Quintilian goes straight on from discussing the members of the period to the feet that may compose them, which he discusses at much

---

[10] Cicero, *De Oratore*, III. xlvii. 182.
[11] *The London Review of Books*, 29 January 1995, p. 8.
[12] *The Alternative Service Book 1980*, 1980; repr. 1993, p. 121.
[13] George Gissing, *The Odd Women*, New York, 1893, p. 65.
[14] George Eliot, *Middlemarch*, ch. LVII.

greater length. He doesn't regard the existence of feet as doubtful. This, for him, was how verse *and* oratorical prose are composed and read. It is possible, of course, that Quintilian may have been mistaken, but when Cicero and Quintilian both recommend some feet but not others as suitable for prose it seems at least to follow that they did consciously compose *oratio* in feet. Here they agree with modern linguists. 'The foot . . . is the basic unit of rhythm in English,' says Halliday; Catford discusses 'stress-group' or 'foot'.[15]

Saintsbury was therefore right to employ terms from (verse) metrics for discussing prose, but did not see clearly enough what follows. From the point of view of stress-patterns, which seems to be our only signpost towards a linguistic definition, prose and verse use the same building blocks. But feet are easier to discern in verse, which may explain why it seems easier to come to prose from verse than *vice versa*. It is certainly untrue that verse is prose with something added.

This is not to say that we read *vers libre* exactly as we read prose. We take separate lines more deliberately, and put in more of a pause at the line end, than we would with the *cola* written out as ordinary prose. Members of the Church of England are often invited to declare that

> Though we are many, we are one body,
> because we all share in one bread.[16]

This biological *non sequitur* is made heavier by the disposition of the words on the page as if they were verse.

The rhythmic shaping of the sound of prose, however, does not depend only on feet. At this point I believe Abercrombie's stress-pulses, which I wish to rename *beats*, come into their own. To take a still well-known example of prose:

> I N. take thee N. to my wedded wife to have and to hold from this day forward for better for worse, for richer for poorer, in sickness and in health, to be bonere and buxum in bed and at the board till death us departe, if holy Church it will ordain; and thereto I plight thee my troth.[17]

Whether these two-beat phrases were in some proto-Germanic language before alliterative verse, or whether they came from verse, or whether the present situation arose from a reinforcement of the custom of the

---

[15] M. A. K. Halliday, *An Introduction to Functional Grammar*, 2nd edn, 1994, p. 9; J. C. Catford, *A Practical Introduction to Phonetics*, Oxford, 1988, who says that 'each [foot] contains one major stressed syllable' (p. 181).

[16] *The Alternative Service Book 1980*, p. 142.

[17] The Sarum rite marriage vows, as reported in modern spelling in Procter and Frere, *A New History of the Book of Common Prayer*, p. 614. The now disused clause about being *bonere and buxum* is a regular enriched alliterative line, though unusually ending with a beat.

language by its verse tradition, can hardly now be established. Howbeit, it is just a basic fact that modern English prose (for instance in a passage of Norman Lamont quoted below) is made out of rhythmic phrases of about the same length as the alliterative half-line, very often constructed like them out of the relations within the phrase of at least two beats and the balance between phrases. Classical Latin, of course, went differently, but *mutatis mutandis* I think Quintilian is saying something rather similar when he points out that *oratio* is made out of members *as well as* out of feet.[18]

It is much truer of much prose—the prose of speeches, sermons, news bulletins—than of blank verse that the main stress of successive units tends to be similar. Prose certainly makes its rhythmic units from contrast between levels of stress, and can call on the infinite differences used by verse, but often doesn't. In long stretches of ordinary prose, as of alliterative verse, there *are* only two levels of stress, the beats, and the unstressed syllables. This sometimes makes for unclarity of notation because it raises the possibility that the scansion of prose can use the same marks for stresses and beats. As in verse the two may or may not coincide.

Beats in parliamentary speeches are quite often as frequent as foot-stresses, and in some more frequent. Any day while Parliament is sitting you can see MPs beating with a hand as they talk, but not quite beating time, because the beats are not anything like equidistant in time. All they beat is beats. This morning (13 March 1996) I saw one emphatically beat every single syllable. There was some comparative foot-stress too, but the beat was what counted. Syllables are still necessary: I have never seen anyone beat *two* per syllable.

The last system of stress in prose rhythm I shall mention (there may well be others) defines the prose-rhythm unit. I think that as well as feet, and phrases made out of beats, we discern a stress-contour usually extending over several phrases. This is best shown by an example, for which I take the section of the Prayer for the Church Militant added to the Book of Common Prayer in 1662:

And we also bless thy holy Name for all thy servants departed this life in thy faith and fear; beseeching thee to give us grace so to follow their good examples, that with them we may be partakers of thy heavenly kingdom: Grant this, O Father, for Jesus Christ's sake, our only Mediator and Advocate. *Amen.*

The quoted sentence can be taken as beginning with an acephalic blank verse line, though on the whole I think it is better to diminish the iambic

---

[18] Quintilian, *Institutio Oratoria*, IX. iv. 121 ff.

element and take the first four syllables as a run of unstresses leading to the first beat *bless* balanced by the second *Name*. 'Beseeching thee to give us grace' is not quite verse, a succession of four iambs. The two-beat alliterative phrases are prominent and sometimes overlapping with the feet ('faith and fear', 'give us grace'). I offer this, however, as a beautifully clear stress contour. There are opportunities for breath before the full point, at the semi-colon and colon, and at the comma after 'examples', but it is clear that the whole is one rhythmic structure (actually a *tetracolon*). Here the 'relative prominence' that is the best I can do for a definition of stress makes its sense in a way that may seem self-evident: if so we are relying on an implicit grammar of stress-relations. The quite daring juxtaposition of the two pronouns *them* and *we*, each a beat, emphasizes the closeness of ourselves and the departed with perfect grammaticality but also with a putting-together that is not in the ordinary sense syntactic. This is a small example of the expressiveness of stress-rhythms.

Compare Edmund's 'I should haue bin that I am, had the maidenlest Starre in the Firmament twinkled on my bastardizing.'[19] I doubt whether there is a pause at the comma. The sentence goes as one rhythmic unit with a stress-peak on the first syllable of *firmament*, the third of three dactyls followed by two paeons. *Stress peak* implies that within the unit all the stresses are related to all the others. It matters for the body of this sentence that the stress-peak comes where it does and that the main verb of the conditional clause, *twinkled*, is the beginning of a *diminuendo*, with the little-stressed *bastardizing* a kind of bitter Parthian shot.

We are not just now aspiring to anything like a complete grammar of rhythm. Intonation must sometimes be structural: whether we raise the voice at the end of a *colon* will often decide whether or not it is the end of a period, as well as sometimes having a syntactic function like indicating a question, and many medieval manuscripts will indicate some or all of these with an appropriate punctuation mark. A document quoted by Hubert gives a catalogue of proper intonations for ending periods.[20] It is nevertheless my opinion that the rhythm of English prose has, systemically, grammatically, to do with stress not intonation.

Intoning, the reading aloud of prose all on one note (better called monotoning to avoid the suggestion of changing tone), was a practice customary in medieval low masses and the reading of the saints' lives during monastic meals, and permitted in the rubrics of the 1549 Book of Common Prayer:

---

[19] *The Tragedie of King Lear*, I. ii; Folio, p. 286.
[20] Cf. above, pp. 38–9; Hubert, *Corpus Stigmatologicum Minus*, p. 164.

And (to thende the people may the better heare) in such places where they doe syng, there shall the lessons be songe in a playne tune after the maner of distincte readyng: and lykewise the Epistle and Gospell.[21]

You can still hear monotoning any week in any highish church. It turns out to be important to our discussion, for in monotoning, the extreme opposite of melodic music, all the other elements of rhythm are excised and periods constructed only (in English) by stress-relations, with some possible contribution from *lengths* of syllables.

In the common understanding coming from the classical rhetors, the smallest prose unit is the foot, then the short phrase or *comma* often in English of two beats; the phrase made out of two or more *commata* is the *colon*, and the complete rhythmic unit in prose, made out of the balancing *cola*, is the *period*. It will be seen that these units resemble, if inexactly, the three rhythmic systems I think are discernible in prose. The manner of the modern world is for rhythmic units to coincide with sentences. All we have to do to get into older prose is to see that this need not be so; do this and one begins to understand the *period*. In English the period is the stress-contour, the domain of stress-relations in prose. Medieval punctuation marks the relevant divisions.

The period, as a structure of sense not governed by the syntax of the well-formed sentence, is simultaneously a structure of *sound*. This does not mean that it is unintellectual or unimportant. To look at the periodicity of prose is to get at its body. It need not follow that we are ignoring the mind. In fact the body/mind dichotomy more than accidentally resembles the misleading language/idea dichotomy.[22] If there is no need to separate ideas from words I think it follows that there is no need to separate words and sounds. The sound can be taken without the sense if for instance we don't know the language, and sound is frequently treated as a separate level without sense if we are drilling ourselves in the sounds of a foreign language. (The written equivalent is the formation of letter-shapes.) But *in* language, when we are not deliberately separating the sound, there is no corresponding taking the sense without the sound. The 'verbal expressions going through my mind' are sounds, heard or imagined. Provided that the sounds are taken as the sounds of language or, in medieval terminology, provided

---

[21] Rubric in both the 1549 and 1552 Prayer Books, Mattyns. It is possible that the 'playne tune' means a plainsong melody, but 'after the maner of distincte readyng' makes it more likely that intoning was intended, the 'reciting in a singing voice . . . usually in a monotone' of the NED's definition *intonation* 2. Cf. above, ch. 1 n. 101.

[22] Cf. R. G. Collingwood, *The New Leviathan*, Oxford, 1942, 1. iii, pp. 14–17, 'The Body as Mind'.

that *vox* is taken as *dictio* and *sermo*, there is no separation between language and sound.

Appeals to music are not unfashionable in the contemporary linguistics of metrical phonology: here is one that I think settles this matter. If the sound is not really the word but only a sign of the word, must we also say that we don't really *hear* a tune, but understand a musical idea into which it is decoded? Locke does say so. 'A musician used to any tune will find that, let it but once begin in his head, the ideas of the several notes of it will follow one another orderly in his understanding'[23]—the ideas, not the notes themselves or the imagination of them. There is no need to believe anything so dispiriting about music or about words either. We do really hear the tune, by connecting its sounds. Bach's *Art of Fugue* can be realized on different instruments; what is not available is the idea of music without any realization (actual or imagined) at all. The musicologist, perhaps the musical equivalent of the literary speed-reader, who points to the score and says '*There* is the idea' may be combining marks in some other way, but can be supported or refuted only by sounds. And as Wittgenstein said, 'Understanding a sentence is much more akin to understanding a theme in music than one may think.'[24]

The sense of a word is its sound understood as language, just as music is the sound understood as music not noise. The move to the understanding, where both language and music really exist, need not be thought of as a move away from what we hear towards what it signifies, only towards the reality of what we hear. If we hear music *as* music, not for instance with the ear of the piano-tuner listening for sound, we are hearing what music really is, not adding anything to it: but it is still the sound we hear. To understand the sounds of language from the point of view of language is to take the sounds as what they really are.

'For Leavis,' Dr MacKillop acutely observes, 'it was *sound* that was at the heart of Cambridge.'[25] He is certainly not saying that Leavis was uninterested in thought, or demanded only beautiful noises. 'In plain expository prose, such as this book is written in,' says another scholar, 'both writer and reader are consciously concerned not mainly with rhythm but with sense.'[26] This is a false dichotomy. The sounds of a poem connected by rhythm are indeed the 'living body of thought'. Take the sound as poetry and there is no further stage of interpretation into

---

[23] Locke, *An Essay Concerning Human Understanding* Book 2. ch. 23, ¶6.
[24] Wittgenstein, *Philosophical Investigations*, p. 143e.
[25] Ian MacKillop, *F. R. Leavis: a Life in Criticism*, 1995, p. 78.
[26] G. S. Fraser, *Metre, Rhyme and Free Verse*, 1970, p. 1.

poetry. Just the same is true of periodic prose: the rhythm of the period organizes sound into a unit of sense.[27]

My criticism of the logical tradition in grammar is just that stress, pitch, attitude, emotion are not *suprasegmental* matters added to the basic logic or syntax but other glimpses of a linguistic whole which includes grammar as usually understood. Grammar as a whole is the study of what is done in language, and a grammar that restricts itself to logic or to syntax is in a self-imposed prison. I accept the now unfashionable view of all the old grammarians that prosody is a necessary part of grammar. *Of course* the meaning of any locution whatever will depend on how it is stressed as well as its syntactic structure.

The rhythm of the period (patterns of relative prominence) is often more important, just with respect to a reader's making sense of a passage, than the syntax of the sentence; and as we saw with a bit of the Prayer Book this can apply even with genuine sentences that certainly do depend on tightly controlled syntax. Cf.:

Still, however, though he by change of place had lost sight of the negro for a few minutes, it was not long ere he again discovered him at a distance too far for a companion, but near enough to serve all the purposes of a spy.[28]

This of course is another perfectly competent complex sentence, the opening three words and the later 'too far . . .' both indicating complicated subordinations much in the mould of Dryden whom Scott edited. Syntactically the main verb is *was*. There is some sense in remarking that the relative importance of the parts of speech has more to do here with rhythmical prominence than syntactic role. In an older sense of *sentence* this works by the antithesis of *companion* and *spy*. The rhythm makes this contrast, the period ending with a word of distinct 'relative prominence'. The periodicity tells the reader more than the syntax, unless one understands syntax as *any* joining of words.

I suppose it is too much to hope that anyone else will follow Dionysius Thrax into accepting that the 'noblest part' of grammar is literary

---

[27] The matter is not affected by the traditional distinction in rhetoric between figures of sound, figures of sense and figures of thought. Alliteration is a relation of sounds that links syllables in a kind of syntax unrecognizable by contemporary linguistics; it simultaneously links the ideas expressed in the words, though here it is natural to talk about the sounds. Conversely Quintilian's definition of a trope as 'an artistic change of word or phrase from its proper signification to another' (cited Murphy, *Rhetoric in the Middle Ages*, p. 369) need not mean that both significations are somewhere other than the words, only that sounds usually used one way are used another. Figures of thought like understatement or emphasis are no more and no less expressed in sound than anything else.

[28] Sir Walter Scott, *Count Robert of Paris*, London and Glasgow, Collins Pocket Classics, n.d., pp. 151–2.

criticism,[29] but it seems to me that what I have just observed of a bit of Scott is grammar used in literary criticism. Why not?

In the ancient world they presupposed periods and had a sort of aspect-blindness to our well-formed sentence. We reverse the situation and ignore periodicity. If modern prose is periodically bad we notice that the style is jerky or undistinguished, but it never occurs to us to use the traditional rhetorical terms to explain why.

Modern prose, however, can no more do without something like periodic structure than it can do without syntax. Let us glance at a modern document, a report of a budget speech delivered by Mr Norman Lamont, not a notably rhetorical speaker, on 10 March 1992. I happened to notice as the speech was being broadcast how unsyntactic it was in its phrasing, and in this I believe it to be typical of many public performances. The *Financial Times* thus reported part of the speech:

The challenge before us is not to provide some artificial short-term stimulus to the economy. It is to continue the supply-side reforms of the 1980s. Low tax and light government have produced an economic environment which spurs competition and rewards enterprise. Our job now is to build on them to help people and businesses make the most of recovery. And that will be the theme of my Budget today.

I have no recording of the speech, and do not know for instance whether Mr Lamont emphasized the beats with hand gestures; my own med-ieval-style punctuation of it is probably not quite the same as Mr Lamont's. Some scribes, bear in mind, would punctuate much more lightly and others not at all. Howbeit, here is another version, punctu-ated *per cola et commata* with commas to divide *commata*, colons *cola* and paragraph-marks periods:

The challenge before us , is not to provide , some artificial short-term stimu-lus , to the economy : it is to continue , the supply-side reforms , of the 1980s. ¶Low tax and light government , have produced an economic environment : which spurs competition , and rewards enterprise. ¶Our job now , is to build on them : to help people and businesses , make the most of recovery : and that will be the theme , of my Budget today. ¶

Mr Lamont certainly delivered the speech in phrases more like those of the second punctuation than the first, rather monotonously (I use the technical term without pejorative intent), with equal beats, similar breath lengths and plenty of cursus endings (the first, 'reforms of the 1980s', the scarcest of the three, *velox*). I would suggest that in a speech

[29] 'The Tekhne Grammatike of Dionysius Thrax', p. 172.

for public delivery this second kind of punctuation is in fact more useful to the reader and listener.

In my modern examples ordinary syntactic sentences usually coincide with periods. One of the processes between the delivery of a speech in Parliament and its recording in the prose of *Hansard* not infrequently makes the sentences better formed but less periodic.[30]

I asked a sort of riddle: When is a sentence a text sentence? *Answer*: When it's a period, i.e. when it is a rhythmic unit. The formal definition of prose has to be prosodic: that form of the written language in which the feet do not form metrical patterns. That prose be written in well-formed sentences and that it convey information are stylistic demands. The question whether any sequence of nonmetrical well-formed sentences may be denied the name of prose must be a question about rhythm and style: paraphrase it as: Is any writing unrhythmic?—to which the answer has to be *no*, though some prose seems to be aspiring after that condition.

The writer of prose is at the opposite extreme from the composer of a symphony who, allowing for different interpretations, controls loudness, intonation, rhythmic phrasing . . . The writer of prose has only words and punctuation and the rhythmic habits of the language. This does not mean that the prose writer has no rhythmic control, only that the writing of prose is an art.

---

[30] Cf. Stef Slembrouck, 'The Parliamentary Hansard "Verbatim" Report: the Written Construction of Spoken Discourse', *Language and Literature* I. 2, 1992, pp. 101–19.

3   Syntax and period in Middle English

In Middle English we often find even in carefully written, lucid verse and prose, a syntactic drift (as I habitually call it) which modern editors cannot tolerate. Cædmon's hymn, copied over a period of about six hundred years before and well after the Norman Conquest, would be blue-pencilled by any modern editor.

> Nu we sculan herian   heofonrices Weard
> Metodes mihte   and his modgethonc
> weorc Wuldorfæder   swa he wundra gehwæs
> ece Dryhten   ord onstealde
> He ærest gesceop   eorthan bearnum
> heofon to hrofe   halig Scyppend
> tha middangeard   moncynnes Weard
> ece Dryhten   æfter teode
> firum foldan   Frea ælmihtig[1]

A very literal translation, with half-line division indicated by em dash, may show what I mean:

Now we shall praise—heaven-kingdom's Guardian / Creator's might—and his heart-thought / works of the Gloryfather—as he of each wonder / eternal Lord—established the beginning / He first shaped—earth for men / heaven for a roof—holy Shaper / then middle-earth—mankind's Guardian / eternal Lord—afterwards made / for men earth—Lord almighty

This is syntactically unlike prose, even Old English prose, and about as far as you can get in language from the modern ideal of the brisk conveyance of information. The active verbs of creating are necessary, but not as part of a text sentence; the relation of these phrases to a main verb (which probably is there if anyone wants it) is a minor matter. I hope this need not mean that the poem is not a work of mind. One half-line phrase about the wonder of creation, which may or may not have a finite verb, suggests or varies another, constantly interspersed with

---

[1] Tanner MS version as in Sweet's *Anglo Saxon Reader*, ed. C. T. Onions, Oxford, 14th edn, 1959, p. 43, with modern punctuation removed.

exclamatory turns to the Creator; the rhythm of this movement is the real thought of the piece.

Or take this passage from *The Phoenix*:

> Nis thær on tham lande   lathgenithla
> ne wop ne wracu   wea tacen nan
> yldu ne yrmthu   ne se enga death
> ne lifes lyre   ne lathes cyme
> ne synn ne sacu   ne sarwracu
> ne wædle gewin   ne welan onsyn
> ne sorg ne slæp   ne swar leger
> ne winter geweorp   ne wedra gebregd
> hreoh under heofenum   ne se hearda forst
> caldum cyle gycelum   cnyseth ænigne

There in that land is no foe, nor weeping nor misery, no sign of sorrow, old age or grief, nor the narrow death, nor loss of life nor visitation of misfortune, nor sin nor conflict nor sad grief, nor the strife of poverty, nor want of wealth, sorrow nor sleep nor grievous sickness, nor winter-storm nor rough change of weathers 'neath the heavens, nor shall the fierce frost, with icicles chill, harm anyone.[2]

The modern reader probably takes these lines as all governed by the opening *nis* until at *cnyseth* a clause is retrospectively constructed for that verb to govern, having for subject only *se hearda forst*. But there is no way of being grammatically sure that the other singulars are not meant to go with *forst* as subjects of *cnyseth*. Perhaps more intriguingly there is also no way of being sure that it is wrong, as modern syntactic habit would suggest, to take the hard frost as the last in the succession of tribulations not found in that land, *as well as* (in modern terminology) the subject of *cnyseth*. To the small extent that verbs are necessary at all, this is more like a train with an engine at both ends than a well-formed sentence. It doesn't make much sense to ask which engine is pulling which coaches.[3]

This is an extreme example of a poetic mode that survived into Shakespeare's soliloquies. Hamlet's 'To be or not to be' soliloquy moves away from modern well-formed sentences as it proceeds. The passage about sleeping and dreaming in the middle is much more like Cædmon than the syntactic structures at the beginning. The infinitive halfline 'to die to sleep' (quite ambiguous as it appears in the Folio) suggests the thought 'To sleep perchance to dream', but not within the shape of a well-formed sentence.

---

[2] *The Phoenix*, 50–9; text from Parry, *Excerpts*, p. 68, Parry's translation.

[3] Cf. Blake's discussion of 'a kind of hanging syntax in which certain phrases are left hanging by themselves so that their exact grammatical relationship to the rest of the sentence is uncertain' (N. F. Blake, *The English Language in Medieval Literature*, repr. 1979, p. 143).

It is also true, however, that in Old and Middle English, competent syntactic complication is the province of verse, not prose,[4] appearing when it is expressive: for instance in these words of Satan in the *Later Genesis* where the elegant politeness needs syntactic complexity:

> Gif ic ænegum thegne   theodenmadmas
> geara for-geafe,   thenden we than godan rice
> ge sælige sæton   and hæfdon ure setla ge-weald,
> thonne he me na on leofran tid   leanum ne meahte
> mine gife gyldan,   gif his gien wolde
> minra thegna hwilc   ge-thafa wurthan,
> thæt he up heonon   ute mihte
> cuman thurh thas clustro,   and hæfde cræft mid him
> thæt he mid fether-homan   fleogan meahte,
> windan on wolcne,   thær ge-wohrt stondath
> Adam and Eve   on eorth-rice
> mid welan be-wunden,   and we synd aworpene hider
> on thas deopan dalo.

'If I ever gave princely treasures to any thane in former times, while we lived in delight in that good kingdom and had command of our seats, he could find no better time for repaying my gift, if yet each of my thanes would consent to this, than that he might get up out of here, move through this darkness, if he had such skill about him that he might fly with a feather-coat, turn up to the clouds, where stand created Adam and Eve in earth-kingdom, wound round with good, while we are thrown out here, into this deep dale.'

Cf. the dramatic interruption of his syntax by Satan in the same poem; Parry's modern punctuation is actually helpful at this point:

> Wala! ahte ic minra handa geweald,
> and moste ane tid   ute weorthan,
> wesan ane winter-stunde,   thonne ic mid thys werode——
> ac licgath me ymbe   irenbenda,
> rideth racentan sal;   ic eom rices-leas.

'Oh! if I had power over my own hands, and could get out for one moment, be one winter-hour, then I with this army—but iron bands lie about me, the rope of chains swings, I am kingdomless.'[5]

I note, though, the necessary feebleness of a modern prose version compared with the rhythmic *making* of the original. Line 369 goes more literally 'and might *one* time, *out* become', with the stress on *ute*, rather like modern American 'I want out'. This is the 'syntax' of putting

---

[4] Syntactic complication in verse is far from an exclusively English phenomenon. The merest dip into Greek shows that Homer and the Greek dramatists are often very syntactically complex, e.g. Achilles' climax to the first great row, *Iliad*, I. 233–44; Aeschylus, *Agamemnon*, 12–19, or the first Chorus which calls for no major modern punctuation between lines 40 and 55.

[5] 409–21, 368–72; Parry, *Excerpts*, p. 106; my translation.

sounds, words as sounds, next to each other rather than the syntax of the well-formed sentence. But the interruption is naturally for us of syntactic structure, though even this can be accounted for rhetorically.[6]

Two or three centuries later, *The Owl and the Nightingale* can be surprising in its *syntactic* command:

> Oft than hundes foxes driveth
> The kat ful wel him sulve liveth
> Thegh he ne kunne wrench bute anne
> The fox so godne ne can nanne
> Thegh he kunne so vele wrenche
> That he wenth eche hunde atprenche
> Vor he can pathes righte & wowe
> An he kan hongi bithe bowe
> An so forlost the hund his fore
> An turnth ayen eft to than more
> The vox kan crope bithe heie
> An turne ut from his forme weie
> An eft sone kume tharto
> Thonne is the hundes smel fordo
> He not thurh the imeinde smak
> Wether he shal avorth the abak
> Yif the vox mist of al this dwole
> At than ende he cropth to hole
> Ac natheles mid alle his wrenche
> Ne kan he hine so bi thenche
> Thegh he bo yep an suthe snel
> That he ne lost his rede vel

Often when hounds chase the foxes, the cat gets on with his own affairs very nicely: though the cat knows only one trick, the fox doesn't know one so effective, for though he knows so many tricks that he expects to outwit every hound, for he knows paths both straight and crooked and how to hang from a bough, so that the hound loses his scent and turns back again to the moor, and the fox knows how to creep along the thicket and turn out of his earlier path and afterwards soon come back to it (then the hound's scent is all done up—he doesn't know, through the mixed up scent, whether he should go forward or back) and if the fox fails despite all this cunning, in the end he can still creep to his hole, yet nevertheless, with all his tricks, he doesn't know how to arrange matters for himself, though he is alert and very bold, in such a way as not to lose his red skin.[7]

There is no grammatical need to take this as one sentence, and

---

[6] 'Aposiopesis (*praecisio*) occurs when something is said and then the rest of what the speaker had begun to say is left unfinished. (Also: *interruptio*.)' (Murphy's analysis of the *figures* from the *Rhetorica ad Herennium*, *Rhetoric in the Middle Ages*, p. 369).

[7] *The Owl and the Nightingale* 809 ff.; my text edited from MS Cotton Caligula A.ix; *u* and *v* regularized. My opinion, argued in the edition I am working on, is that this poem was composed in or about 1193.

J. W. H. Atkins punctuates it as five, but I think the sustaining of sense through a long sentence is preferable, and that the rhythm carries this syntax: you hold the voice up. The enactment of the fox's deviousness is by way of the interwoven syntactic clauses. Parentheses are not all that easy to handle in reading modern prose aloud, but there is no trouble here.

The Canterbury Tales begins with an enormously long sentence (the word is again called for in its modern sense), the repeated 'when' being necessarily syntactic in pointing forward to a main clause to which these temporal clauses are subordinate. The function of the syntax is to hold several periods together and unify the senses of the natural world in the new life of Spring and the impulse, at least partly spiritual, to go on pilgrimage.

Chaucer's contemporary the *Gawain* poet gives a set-piece contrast between the styles of Sir Gawain and the Green Knight, and quite fittingly part of the contrast here is syntactic. In his effort to taunt King Arthur into accepting a challenge the whole court knows to be foolish, the Green Knight utters a really archetypal epic insult, Anglo-Saxonate, paratactic, constructed out of simple forceful half-lines, and appearing in that sophisticated court positively archaic:

> What is this Arthures hous   quod the hathel thenne
> That al the rous rennes of   thurgh ryalmes so mony
> Where is now your sourquydrye   & your conquestes
> Your gryndellayk & your greme   & your grete wordes
> Now is the reuel and the renoun   of the Rounde Table
> Ouerwalt wyth a worde   of on wyghes speche
> For al dares for drede   withoute dynt schewed.

'What! is this Arthur's house?' said the knight then, 'that all the fuss is made about through so many kingdoms? Where is now your pride and your conquests, your fierce games and your anger and your big words? Now the revelry and the fame of the Round Table is overturned with one speech from one man's talk, for you are all cowering for dread, without any blow offered you!'[8]

When Sir Gawain intervenes, the contrast in style is more of a lesson in manners even than what he says, and that contrast is amongst other things syntactic; what is more, the connection between syntax and rhythm, in the most practical form of social movement, is here particularly clear:

> Wolde ye worthilych lorde   quoth Wawan to the kyng
> Bid me bowe fro this benche   and stonde by yow there

[8] *Sir Gawain and the Green Knight*, 309 ff, ed. Sir Israel Gollancz, EETS 1940; modern punctuation removed but half-line spaces added. The scribe of the unique Cotton Nero a.x manuscript did not mark the half-line.

That I wythoute vylanye   myght voyde this table
& that my legge lady   lyked not ille
I wolde com to your counseyl   bifore your cort ryche
For me think it not semly   as it is soth knawen
Ther such an askyng is heuened   so hyghe in your sale
Thagh ye yourself be talenttyf   to take hit to yourseluen
While mony so bolde yow aboute   vpon bench sytten
That vnder heuen I hope   non hagherer of wylle
Ne better bodyes on bent   ther baret is rered
I am the wakkest I wot   and of wyt feblest
& lest lur of my lyf   quo laytes the sothe
Bot for as much as ye are myn em   I am only to prayse
No bounte bot your blod   I in my bode knowe
& sythen this note is so nys   that noght hit yow falles
& I haue frayned hit at yow fyrst   foldez hit to me
& if I carp not comlyly   let alle this cort rych
       bout blame.

'If you would, noble lord,' said Gawain to the King, 'bid me move from this bench and stand by you there, so that without ill-manners I might leave this table, and provided that it did not displease my liege lady, I would come to advise you in front of your noble court; for it seems to me not proper, as all would agree, when *such* a request is raised so noisily in your hall, though you are fully capable, to take it upon yourself while so many bold companions are sitting on benches—than whom I believe there are no more undaunted, nor more valiant in the field when battle is pitched. I know I am the weakest, and feeblest in mind, and my life would be the smallest loss, to tell the truth: I am only praiseworthy in that you are my uncle; I know no distinction in my body except your blood; and since this business is so silly that it does not fall to you, and I have requested it from you first, turn it over to me: and if I am not speaking fittingly, let all the whole court correct me without blaming me.'[9]

Sir Gawain is even more polite than the Satan of the *Later Genesis*. Seated on the Queen's left and addressing in the first place the King who is standing in the hall in front of the high table, he begins with a conditional clause in the subjunctive necessarily suspending the main verb of the lexical sentence, with a vocative to the king interpolated, then (obviously with a turn to the Queen: this poem *does* ask to be staged, at least in the theatre of the imagination!) a parenthetical continuation of the subjunctive conditional with 'And that my liege lady liked not ille'; but any expectation that the 'if' clause will be completed in the usual way by a 'then' or the like is much delayed by a 'so that'. I will not follow the speech through its continuing complications, but will only observe, firstly, that in the poem it sounds not only easy, but a demonstration of Gawain's masterliness of courtly ease; secondly that it

[9] *Ibid.*, 343 ff.

would have been just about unimaginable in prose. At the same time as making a most complex sentence Sir Gawain is naturally uttering a beautifully rounded period.[10]

In the long passages of courtly conversation in this poem, so much more like a novel than anything in Chaucer, the modern editors are often at their wits' end with punctuation, using dashes, parentheses, semi-colons, devices quite foreign to the movement of the original, to try to keep pace with its syntactic complication. What *this* complicated syntax needs is the alliterative verse, not modern punctuation.

One of the ways in which Milton is stubbornly archaic is that in *Paradise Lost* as much as the *Later Genesis*[11] the syntax is somehow carried by the verse movement. If necessary, a teacher of English might have to explain that imperatives always come either right at the beginning of a sentence or close to it. (*By the right, quick march!* does put an adverbial phrase before the imperative, but that is unusual.) Milton begins *Paradise Lost* by defying this rule: he suspends the imperative right to the beginning of line six, inserting a relative clause dependent on the indirect object and another clause subordinated to this relative before getting to the imperative *Sing*.

> Of Mans First Disobedience, and the Fruit
> Of that Forbidden Tree, whose mortal tast
> Brought Death into the World, and all our woe,
> With loss of *Eden*, till one greater Man
> Restore us, and regain the blissful Seat,
> Sing Heav'nly Muse,[12]

I leave the sentence midway at this imperative. In ordinary grammatical or syntactic terms this is just impossible[13] and would be rewritten by any modern sub-editor. I would also say that if one committed the experimental barbarity of trying to read the passage as prose it would at once dissolve into impossible syntactic wandering, which is the state in which (below) I do find much of Milton's prose. As verse, there is no trouble

---

[10] Not all the syntax is so controlled. The Lady, anxious to learn all kinds of latest fashions from Sir Gawain, sometimes wanders—possibly thereby showing us something of her character, for instance at lines 1508–27. Editors wrestle with her syntax, unnecessarily.

[11] It has long been recognized that the link may be direct. Milton was acquainted with Junius, the seventeenth-century Dutchman who edited the poem, and Milton read everything. It is even possible that he may have picked up a stylistic hint or two.

[12] John Milton, *Paradise Lost*, 1–6; *The Poetical Works of John Milton*, ed. H. C. Beeching, Oxford, 1900—a much better text than its successor in the same series.

[13] This objection was already copiously made in the eighteenth century, together with the saving clause I wish to reaffirm, that Milton's poetry justifies the ungrammaticality. Cf. Michael, *English Grammatical Categories*, pp. 471–2. Cf. also A. D. Nuttall, *Openings*, Oxford, 1992, pp. 74–5 and Christopher Ricks, *Milton's Grand Style*, Oxford, 1963.

with the passage. The rhythmic mastery tells the voice what to do, and that in turn conveys the syntax.

It is true that structures we cannot but recognize as long complex sentences were occasionally written in vernacular prose in the Middle Ages. For instance there is a rather startling long sentence at the beginning of Ari's account of the settlement of Iceland in which he inserts his authorities into a parenthesis.[14] This is nevertheless quite unusual in vernacular prose. 'As far as I know,' says Auerbach, 'there is virtually no example of intricate sentence structure in French prose before Alain Chartier.'[15] Much the same can be said of English.

Of all the subjects I touch on, medieval English prose is the hugest, and all I can say is: it more or less falls into two classes. The simpler bits of the Anglo-Saxon Chronicle are not periodic; Ælfric and Wulfstan are in different ways at the other extreme, expertly rhetorical. The two traditions, a simply paratactic prose at one end and a periodic or oratorical one at the other, run through the English Middle Ages.

The common word for the Chronicle prose is this *paratactic*: characteristically it works not like the modern complex sentence with its relations of subordinate clauses, but by successions of main clauses linked by *And* or *Ac*. Syntactic complication rarely goes further than the frequent *Tha . . . tha . . .* construction (When . . . [then] . . .).

Many of the Chronicle entries are bare and sparse enough to put one in mind of what Aristotle said of Herodotus.[16] At random:

985. Her Ælfric ealdorman was ut adræfed.
986. Her se cyning fordyde thet biscop rice æt Hrofeceastre. And her com ærest se myccla yrf cwalm on Angel cyn.
987 Her Wecedport wes ge hergod.

985. In this year the Ealdorman Ælfric was exiled. 986. In this year the king suppressed the bishopric of Rochester, and in this year the great beast pest came for the first time amongst the English. 987. In this year Watchet was ravaged.[17]

Paratactic prose, however, need not be unperiodic. At other times the Chronicle can be rhetorical. The quoted entries are within a page or so of the *verse* epitaph for Edgar (975) and the rising to rhetoric for the death of Edward (979) ('He wæs on life eorthlic cing. he is nu æfter deathe heofonlic sanct' etc.).

By contrast with the barer Chronicle prose Ælfric is periodic in a much more rhetorical way:

---

[14] Gordon, *An Introduction to Old Norse*, p. 34.
[15] Auerbach, *Literary Language*, p. 205.   [16] Above, p. 36.
[17] Laud MS as recorded in *Two of the Saxon Chronicles Parallel*, p. 125.

Drihten sothlice. sæde on his bodunge. ge beoth mine frynd. gif ge wyrcende beoth. tha thincg the ic bebeode. eow to gehealdenne; Micel mildheortnys. thæs metodan drihtnes. thæt we beon gecigede. swa gesæliglice. ures scyppendes frynd. gif we his hæse gefyllath. we the næron wurthe. beon his wealas gecigde. and we habbath swilce gethincthe. thurgh tha gehyrsumnysse;

Rather literally translated, with comma for . and full point for ;

The lord truly, said in his commanding, you are my friends, if you are doers, of those things that I command, you to hold. Great mildheartedness, of this lord god, that we are professed, so marvellously, friends of our creator, if we fulfil his behests, we who were not worthy, to be called his slaves, and we have such honour, through that obedience.[18]

Ælfric's periods have much in common with the movement of Old English verse,[19] but they are a true if ornate prose.

Periods sometimes continue when we expect a sentence end. This is Ælfric's version of a famous passage from Isaiah:

Isaias eft witegode be cristes acennednysse; Us is cild acenned. and us is sunu forgifen. and his ealdordom is on his exlum. and he bith gehaten wundorlic. rædbora. stráng god. and fæder thære toweardan worulde. and sibbe ealdor. his rice. and his anweald bith gemenigfyld. and ne bith nán ende his sibbe;

Isaiah afterwards prophesied about Christ's birth. To us is a child born, and to us is a son given, and his authority is on his shoulders, and he shall be called wonderful, counsellor, strong god, and father to the world, and peace-age, his kingdom, and his monarchy shall be manifold, and there shall be no end to his peace.[20]

In modern English this would be a sprawl and a wander: not in Ælfric, because of the periodic rhythm.

Chambers's basic contention, that Old English prose survived the Norman Conquest unbroken, is borne out by the rhythmic confidence both of the post-Conquest Chronicle entries and of the *Ancrene Wisse*. In the following extract I take the *punctus elevatus* to mark the period:

Grith beo bimong ow · ye beoth the ancren of englond swa feole togederes · twenti nuthe other ma · godd i god ow mutli ⸴ that meast grith is among · Meast annesse & anrednesse · & sometreadness of anred lif efter a riwle · Swa that alle teoth an · alle iturnt anesweis ⸴ & nan frommard other · efter that word is · for thi ye gath wel forth & spedeth in ower wei ⸴ for euch is withward other in an manere of liflade · as thah ye weren an cuuent of lundene & of oxnefort [. . .]

With · represented by , and *punctus elevatus* by . this translates as:

---

[18] *Ælfric's Catholic Homilies*, the 2nd series ed. Malcolm Godden, EETS, 1979, p. 181.
[19] Cf. 'Ælfric's Rhythmical Prose', John C. Pope, (ed.), *Homilies of Ælfric: a Supplementary Collection*, EETS 1967, pp. 105–36.
[20] *Ælfric's Catholic Homilies*, 2nd series, p. 8.

Peace be among you, you are the anchorites of England so many together, twenty now or more, god increase you in good. who have greatest peace among you, Greatest unity and singlemindedness, and agreement of singleminded life following a rule, So that all pull as one, all turn one way. and none away from other, according as that saying is, therefore you walk forward well and prosper well in your path. for everyone is together with the others in one manner of living, as though you were a convent of London or Oxford . . .[21]

The survival of these manuscripts proves the existence of a linguistic community whose medium in this case was an excellent nonprosaic English prose.

Naturally, one danger of the paratactic mode is monotony, from which the Chronicle is certainly not free. But this prose can be very telling, for instance in the last Chronicle entry covering the anarchy under King Stephen.

The very simple paratactic prose of the barer Chronicle entries gave rise to the common late-medieval prose of the romances, and of the over-praised jailbird Sir Thomas Malory.[22]

We had a glance at a Caxton edition as evidence of the survival of medieval punctuation into the age of printing: not surprisingly, periodic prose survived along with virgules.

When prose was more complicated in Chaucer's day, the complexity went not so much into syntactic subordination as towards rhetorical elaboration, in the odd form sometimes called *cadence*, a precious prose made out of bits of verse, rhetorical flourishes, assonance and alliteration, and exemplified in the first few pages (he must have tired of it) of Chaucer's Tale of *Melibee*.

With the beginnings of the Renascence we do, however, see a movement towards modern syntactic complexity in English prose, especially in works that might have been expected to have been written in Latin. I don't think it is coincidence that my example is from a laborious anti-Lollard, Bishop Pecock:

---

[21] *The English Text of the Ancrene Riwle: Ancrene Wisse*, ed. from MS Corpus Christi College, Cambridge 402 by J. R. R. Tolkien, EETS, 1962, p. 130. I have transcribed the passage from a frontispiece illustration of this folio, and I venture to differ from Tolkien about one capital letter.

[22] Cf. 'Hence . . . the endeavour to avoid a punctuation that strings sentences together by innumerable *ands* and so obscures Malory's preference for the short period falling into not more than three parts' (*The Works of Sir Thomas Malory*, ed. Eugène Vinaver, Oxford, 1954, one-vol. edn, p. xi). Vinaver's difficulty arises from the fact that to the modern eye Malory does string sentences together with innumerable *ands*, and Vinaver gives no apparatus by which the reader can know which of the *tricola* go back to Malory himself.

T he . iije . principal poynt may be sped thus / It is open ynough to oure natural resoun that the first man which lyued in this world and hise successouris and progenye fro hise daies hidirto [line breaks *hidir to*] into this present day knowen or myghte if thei wolden haue knowen bi strengthe and light of her natural resoun without eny affermyng or teching maad to hem from thee god ʃ al what is taught fro the bigynnyng of this present book hidir to . and al what schal be taught into the eend of the . ije . party except fewe placis markid for feith / and that vndir notabili greet liklihode . and therwith vndir so greet likelihode that to noon of her contraries is had or can be had so greet a likelihode / and that is right feir and sufficient to reste amannys vundirstonding and resoun therynne / And that this be trewe it may appere sum what bi assay whiche men mowe take in examynyng the skilis which ben sett thorugh al this book bifore hidir to and aftir to be sett / and also her by that we seen openli ynough hardir and derkir treuthis than the now seid treuthis vn exceptid ben : haue be founden of men bothe in sciencis and in craftis soone aftir the bigynnyng of the world ʃ and alwey contynuely sithen / as al the world may herto bere witnes namelich leerned men if thei wolen attende how sutil highe derke privey treuthis men han founden of geometrie [. . . .][23]

Pecock's editor makes well-founded complaints about his prose style:

A new sentence almost always means a new paragraph, for Pecock's sentence is a segmented thing that crawls over the page and often may be divided into self-sustaining units. It is annoying to find a whole section which is too loose to be transcribed as one sentence and too involved to be separated.[24]

Pecock is nevertheless much closer to the modern complex sentence even than Chaucer in the *Astrolabe*. In the quoted passage 'And that this be trewe' has got to be syntactically the subject of a new sentence. But it is putting it mildly to say that Pecock has not much idea of how to manage this syntax in English. This scholarly bishop only a generation before Cranmer can still be read more easily by the help of the old rhetorical marks, in rather rambling periods, than in sentences with the syntactic punctuation that the modern editor thinks called for.[25] Neither, I am afraid, can make the perusal of Pecock either easy or pleasurable.

We shall pick up this thread again with King Richard III and King Henry VIII, below.

---

[23] Pierpont Morgan 519 f. 163 v., used as an illustration to Reginald Pecock, *The Reule of Crysten Religioun*, ed. William Cabell Greet, Oxford, 1927, whose modern-punctuated text is on p. 430. The photograph gives out before next punctuation.
[24] Pecock, *The Reule of Crysten Religioun*, p. xi.
[25] *Ibid.*

4   Cranmer's commonwealth

i   Tyndale and the Bible

Scripture easy of translation! Then why have there been so few good translators? why is it that there has been such great difficulty in combining the two necessary qualities, fidelity to the original and purity in the adopted vernacular?   Newman

The replacement, during the last thirty years or so, of Tyndale-based versions of the English Bible, has been facilitated by much self-congratulation by the new translators on their greater accuracy. All the new translations in various ways, on the contrary, fail on both the criteria enunciated by Newman. As well as being varieties of no-man's-language, a long way from idiom of any kind, they are all very inaccurate.[1] Anyone with enough Greek to find their way through a text with the aid of an accompanying translation—the readers, shall we say, of the Loeb series—can use Tyndale's New Testament as a crib and marvel how close he keeps to the Greek while writing in what is plainly an English style, not Greek imitated in English.

The late Mrs Edith Ehrhardt, who was very far from being super-stitious, thought that one sign of the miraculous inspiration of the Bible is that it will go into many languages almost word for word. Less perceptive New Testament scholars talk of *koine* Greek (misleadingly, as it seems to me, because they tend to overlook the very Hebraic colouring of many passages, and the evident poetry of some) with a more mundane version of the same perception: that the *lingua franca* of the Eastern half of the Roman empire was necessarily cosmopolitan and

---

[1] Cf. A. C. Capey, *Translation* vs *Paraphrase*, in progress; my 'Religious English' in *The Survival of English*; my *Prayers for the New Babel*, and Geoffrey Strickland, 'To understand St Paul, Don't Read the NEB', *The Spectator*, 19/26 December 1992. 'Despite the superior scholarship from which we are continually reminded they were able to benefit, the modern translators [of the New English Bible] offer a less accurate guide to the original than their predecessors, almost whenever I check,' says Strickland, who substantiates the judgement with a number of examples.

71

may be expected to be translatable into ordinary proses. This, however, does not contradict Newman or explain Tyndale. It turned out that when nearly literal versions of the New Testament are made into the idiomatic German or English of the Renascence, and fully satisfying Newman's two conditions, the result is a common prose, but not a prosaic or commonplace one. It is relevant that Tyndale's work on language, however scholarly, was at the behest of something more effective than academic ambition, of which the Wycliffite translators were already well aware. The manuscript of the Wycliffite Bible cited above p. 15 goes straight on from the linguistic discussion of the problem of ambiguities to: 'A translatour . . . hath nede to lyue a clene lyf/ & be ful deuout in preieris & haue not his wit ocupied about worldly thingis.'[2] I think this is true, though the demand for spiritual devotion does not fall within the province of linguistics.

William Tyndale single-handed achieved the backbone of the English Bible. His individual felicities are rightly well-known, and though the Authorized Version often gives a finishing touch, some of Tyndale's phrasing is more direct than that of 1611. 'Care not then for the morrow, but let the morrow care for itself: for the day present hath ever enough of his own trouble.' This is better, though less resonant, than 'Take therefore no thought for the morrow: for the morrow shall take thought for the things of itself. Sufficient unto the day is the evil thereof' (Matthew vi).

Tyndale's greater achievement is a suitable and dependable prose. His well-known remark seems truest applied to prose rhythm:

For the Greek tongue agreeth more with the English than with the Latin. And the properties of the Hebrew tongue agreeth a thousand times more with the English than with the Latin. The manner of speaking is both one, so that in a thousand places thou needest not but to translate it to the English word for word when thou must seek a compass in the Latin & yet shall have much work to translate it well-favouredly.[3]

As Daniell says, 'Again and again, it is Tyndale's arrangement of stresses that helps to grip the reader.'[4] I know by long experience that anyone who talks about the rhythm of Bible prose will be taken to mean only orotundity, sounding brass and tinkling cymbals (a phrase Tyndale remembered from Wycliffe). My argument is that success with rhythm is a necessary condition for accuracy of translation. If prose rhythm has to

---

[2] Cambridge University Library Kk. 1. 8, f. 29 r.
[3] Daniell, *Tyndale's New Testament* p. xxii. Tyndale's translations are quoted from Daniell's editions except where otherwise stated.
[4] Daniell, *Tyndale's Old Testament*, p. xviii.

do with the body of thought, one of the differences between Tyndale and the Good News Bible is that the latter is a dead body.

By praising Tyndale's rhythms I mean that he was able to adapt the basic succession of (usually two-beat) phrases out of which medieval prose and verse were both constructed to make a versatile style, capable of rising to high moments, but pithy and not churchy.[5] His Old Testament begins (of course the grandfather of the 1611 version):

In the beginning God created heaven and earth. The earth was void and empty, and darkness was upon the deep, and the spirit of God moved upon the water.

Then God said: let there be light and there was light. And God saw the light that it was good: and divided the light from the darkness, and called the light day, and the darkness night: and so of the evening and morning was made the first day.

This could be re-lined as phrasal verse, lacking only the alliteration, but it is still true prose. (When Langland paraphrases the Bible into alliteratives he is comparatively diffuse.) The simple, effective accumulation of stress on *light* is brought about both by the repetition of the word in the stressed position at the end of a *comma* and, in terms of the feet, by in the first place trochee plus iamb, in the second weak plus strong iamb. The sense-progression from the emphasis on *light* to *good* and the contrast with *darkness*, metamorphosing into *day* is just what the followers of Aristotle meant by *rhythm* and an example of how the body of sense may not be fully accounted for by syntax. This prose is poetic, in the most literal way *making* a particular sense of common day.

I can only base my agreement with Tyndale on Greek, having no Hebrew; but what I am told of the phrasal organization of Hebrew poetry seems to fit his case. This is anyway plainly to be seen in the Greek quotations of the Old Testament in the New. The balancing varied phrases in the Greek of the Septuagint, the version ordinarily quoted by New Testament writers,[6] go well into a language whose own poetry originates as varied phrases. (The Psalms have always gone beautifully into English since the Anglo-Saxon metrical versions.) Given that the new movement of the Reformation coincided with the Renascence, with its emphasis on going back to the originals, of which in this case it can be said that 'Simple factual progression is characteristic of most biblical narrative',[7] and that both Renascence and Reformation happened in England before the age of phrasal metre and voice-directed

---

[5] For a rhythmic analysis of passages of the 1611 Bible into two-beat phrases, see A. C. Partridge, *English Biblical Translation*, 1973, pp. 144–5.
[6] Cf. G. R. Selby, *Jesus, Aramaic and Greek*, Gringley-on-the-Hill, 1989, especially p. 92.
[7] Partridge, *English Biblical Translation*, p. 28.

prose was over, it may even sound reasonable to say that something like the English Bible was inevitable.

Tyndale did not live to finish the Old Testament, and the first complete printed English bible was the responsibility of Coverdale, who didn't work from the Hebrew. But Coverdale's Psalms do not strike one as of a different stylistic tradition from Tyndale. Even if Coverdale was consciously imitating Tyndale, the point remains true that very rapidly in the 1520s and 1530s a style for the English Bible developed that was available to numbers of translators and revisers until 1885, if not later. Professor David Daniell has recently been campaigning to renew proper recognition of Tyndale's Bible translations. More power to his elbow! He will commonly quote a telling phrase of Tyndale and compare it with the 1611 version or, with hardly a risk, one of the modern *midrashim*. But when the then Archbishop of York picked Daniell's brains he offered as characteristic of Tyndale's successes 'The Lord is my shepherd therefore can I lack nothing.'[8] Alas! this is not Tyndale, but Coverdale, and in phrasing which 1611 improves. Tyndale did supply the language with many proverbs—but so do the parts of the Bible which Tyndale did not live to translate. Nobody quoting the English Bible is aware of the origin of a phrase in Tyndale, Coverdale, Geneva, or Rheims.

The English Bible grew out of a prose tradition stretching back the best part of a thousand years. Tyndale is the heir of the Anglo-Saxon Chronicle. The similarities between Tyndale and the Wycliffite version of about 1389 are too marked to be explained by coincidence, though Tyndale could not be said to be dependent on any earlier English version, and stated that he had not used them.[9] When Tyndale differs from earlier versions it is within the same tradition of phrasal prose. 'Blessid be mylde men, for thei shuln welde the eerthe' (Wycliffite)[10] evidently differs from 'Blessed are the meke, for they shall inheret the erth' (Tyndale), but within very similar assumptions about 'purity in the adopted vernacular' and 'fidelity to the original' Greek (or Latin). Both versions are recognizably in a stylistic line from 'Eadige synd tha lithan, fortham the hi eorthan agun' (995 version). This is not a one-off similarity. 'Tha cwæth se dema to heom, Witdolice hwæt yfeles dyde

---

[8] John Habgood, 'Tyndale: An Extraordinary and Largely Forgotten Englishman', *Faith and Heritage* 38, Spring, 1995, p. 17.

[9] Lewis, *English Literature in the Sixteenth Century*, p. 204, presumably relying on a passage quoted by Pollard (in Tyndale, *The Beginning of the New Testament*, pp. xiii–xiv) which, however, need mean no more than that Tyndale had no copy of a Wycliffite bible with him in Cologne.

[10] Quotations in this paragraph are from *The Gothic and Anglo-Saxon Gospels in Parallel Columns with the Versions of Wycliffe and Tyndale*, ed. Joseph Bosworth and George Waring, 2nd edn, 1874, pp. 16–17, 152–3.

thes? Hi tha swithor clypodon, thus cwethende, Sy he ahangen.'
Wycliffite: 'The presedent seith to hem, Sothely what of yuel hath he
don? And thei crieden more, seyinge, Be he crucified.' Tyndale: 'Then
sayde the debite, What evyll hath he done? And they cryed the more,
saynge, Lett him be crucified' (Matthew xxvii. 23). There, with the
word *debite* that he later altered (a form of *deputy* always rare in English),
Tyndale does not even seem the least archaic.

Similarly, Coverdale often more or less coincides with earlier versions
of the Psalms. A not very inspired version from the Latin, probably
fourteenth-century, even on occasion hits off a more informative
version, as 'The vnwys seid in his hert, God is nought.' 'Unwise' is
arguably a shade better than 'fool', which may to us suggest something
only silly; and 'nought' in the fourteenth century carries an appropriate
suggestion of *not worth bothering about*. (This medieval version follows
the custom of division into verses which, though certainly prose, quite
often resemble the long lines of alliterative verse.) Even when there is
nothing like Coverdale's rhythmic inevitability, it suggests how Coverdale was possible:

1 The heuens tellen the glorie of God, and the firmament telleth the werkes of
his hondes.
2 The daye putteth forthe the worde to the day, and the nyght sheweth conyng
to the nyght.
3 Hij ben nought speches, ne wordes of wiche the voices of hem ben nought
herd.[11]

Phrases from the Primers[12] occasionally go into Coverdale's version
without alteration.

Nevertheless, 'Good must needs come, but blessed is he through
whom it comes.' Much praise is still individually due to Tyndale for his
establishment of what can really be called the natural style of the English
Bible. 'Natural' does not imply 'easy'. Great achievements sometimes
do look inevitable to their beneficiaries; it took the confidence of genius
to see what was natural. We might easily have had a determinedly
Latinate Bible, or English might have taken a leap from the two-beat
phrasal movement of Germanic antiquity straight into the style of
Dryden. Tyndale's great achievement was to see that the original
documents could be accommodated to English provided that the
English was developed from that of the ploughboy (and the poets and

---

11 *The Earliest Complete English Prose Psalter*, ed. Karl D. Bülbring, Early English Text
Society, 1891, Psalm liii. 1, Psalm xix.
12 These books, vernacular aids to devotion when church services were in Latin, included
translations of parts of the mass and the offices, together with private devotions and
exhortations.

Wycliffe) and not that of the Latinising establishment. It is hardly less important that Cranmer, whose own prose is very different, allowed Tyndale to get it right in his own way.

The emphasis on Tyndale's descent from English tradition should not be taken to imply that he wanted to preserve English undefiled by Latin; as a bold neologizer he went indifferently to Greek, Latin and native roots—unlike Cranmer's ally the distinguished Latinist Sir John Cheke, who set his face against words like *resurrection, proselyte, crucified,* and coined Anglo-Saxonate alternatives (*gainrising, freshman, crossed*), none of which has survived in his senses.[13]

Tyndale printed his translations in continuous paragraphed prose not verses, but the sure sign that Tyndale's prose of translation is nevertheless a development from the medieval tradition is that he uses the old unsyntactic punctuation by virgules, at a time when the texts he was translating from, notably Erasmus's Greek New Testament, were already syntactically punctuated. The medieval habit of punctuation began to be replaced in English by something more syntactic in the decade of Tyndale's publishing career, but he kept to the old practices. The bibliography of Tyndale's issues of his translations is complicated, but all the versions I have been able to inspect are printed in black-letter and punctuated by virgules, question-marks and full-points, basically the medieval manner, though with some use of parentheses.

¶Ye are the salt of the erthe. but ann yf the salte be once unsavery / what can be salted there with? it is thence forthe good for nothynge / but to be cast out at the dores / and that men treade it vnder fete [. . .]
¶For Isay vnto you except youre rightewesnes excede / the rightwesnes of the scrybes and pharyses / ye cannot entre in to the kyngdom of heven.[14]

In 1534 Tyndale explained why he needed to revise his text:

Here thou hast (moost deare reader) the new Testament or covenaunt made wyth vs of God in Christes bloude. Whiche I have looked ouer agayne (now at the last) with all dylygence / and compared it vnto the Greke / and have weded

---

[13] Cf. George Philip Krapp, *The Rise of English Literary Prose,* Oxford, 1915, p. 248. Cheke's fragmentary version, unpublished until the nineteenth century, was made as part of the abortive movement towards a new English version of the Bible during Cranmer's brief years of predominance. According to R. F. Jones, Cheke was not one of the most determined opposers of Latinate neologism: cf. *The Triumph of the English Language,* Oxford, 1953, pp. 102–3. Butterworth suggests that Cheke (amongst whose other achievements was the translation of several of Cranmer's English works into Latin) was trying to make the Bible available to an unlearned audience (Charles C. Butterworth, *The Literary Lineage of the King James Bible 1340–1611,* Philadelphia, 1941, p. 152); but his Anglo-Saxonate coinings are sometimes a kind of word-game challenging the reader to guess the meaning. Cranmer could surely not have approved his friend's version.

[14] Tyndale, *The Beginning of the New Testament,* 1525 facsimile repr., f. v v.

oute of it many fautes / which lacke of helpe at the begynninge and ouersyght / dyd sowe therin.

He made extensive revisions to the quoted passage, but only one change in punctuation:

Ye are the salt of the erthe. but and yf the salt haue lost his saltnes/ what can be salted there with? it is thence forthe good for nothynge/ but to be cast oute/ and to be troaden vnder fote of men. [. . .]

For I saye vnto you / except youre rightewesnes excede/ the rightewesnes of the Scribes and Pharises / ye cannot entre into the kyngdome of heuen.[15]

The effect of the ungrammatical virgule after *excede* is to throw an effective rhetorical stress on to that word. That punctuation goes in the three Antwerp and one London editions of 1536 that I have been able to see, but they all retain punctuation by virgules. All credit to Daniell for retaining this one as a comma! though he warns us that not all his punctuation is from the original.[16] None of the Prayer Books of 1549 and 1552 so punctuate.

Tyndale's 1526 version of the second chapter of the Gospel according to St Matthew begins:

When Jesus was borne in Bethleem a toune of Jury / in the tyme of Kynge Herode. Beholde / there cam wysemen from the est to Jerusalem saynge: where is he that is borne kynge of the Jues? we have sene his starre in the est / and are come to worship hym.

Herode the kynge / after he hadd herde thys / was troubled / and all Jenrusalem [*sic*] with hym / and he sent for all the chefe prestes and scribes off the people / and demaunded off them where Christ shulde be borne.[17]

In 1534 he again made a number of verbal alterations but left the punctuation alone:

When Jesus was borne at Bethleem in Jury / in the tyme of Herode the kynge. Beholde / there came wyse men from the eest to Jerusalem saynge: Where is he that is borne kynge of the Jues? We have sene his starre in the eest / & are come to worship him.

When Herode the kynge had herde thys / he was troubled / and all Jerusalem

[15] Anwerp [*sic*], Martin Emperowr, 1534, Cambridge University Library shelfmark Young 152; reverse of title and f. vi v.

[16] 'Basic stops like full points have occasionally to be supplied. . . . Not to supply commas, on quite a number of occasions, would produce a sentence that simply is not English as we know it.' (Daniell, Tyndale's *Old Testament*, p. xxviii.) The (from our point of view) eccentric punctuation of the original editions may indicate that in one important way Tyndale was still *not* writing English as we know it, in particular that he was not writing 'text' sentences.

[17] I have not been able to consult the original edition and used *The First New Testament Printed in the English Language*, reproduced in facsimile by Francis Fry FSA, Bristol, 1862 (made 'by tracing on transfer paper, placing this on lithographic stones, and then printing', p. 16: how's that for devotion?). S. Matthew fo. ii. r.

with hym / and he gathered all the chefe Prestes and Scribes of the people / and axed of them where Christ shulde be borne.[18]

'Beholde' is plainly meant to start a new *sententia* or period, and the rhetorical point is not hard to understand. But syntactically it just has to introduce the main clause of the same sentence beginning with the temporal *When*. Conversely, the modern editor will probably begin a sentence with 'And he sent'.

An exception to Tyndale's normal continuous prose printing is that he sets out the ancient hymns in lines of alliterative-looking verse, in the 1526 version like this:

> Blessed be the lorde god of israhel / for he hath
> visited and redemed his people.
> And hath reysed vppe the horne off health vnto
> vs / in the housse of his servaunt David.
> Even as he promised by the mougth of his holy
> prophetes which were sens the worlde began.
> That we shulde besaved from oureenimys / And
> from the hondis of all that hate vs:
> To shewe mercy towardes oure fathers / And to
> remember hys holy promes.[19]

Later in the sixteenth century there was a reaction against ordinary prose printing. The printing of the Bible in numbered verses, each starting with a new line, makes for ease of reference, and is sometimes defended for that reason, though as in some modern texts verse numbers can easily be inserted into prose. The best reason for verses is the one behind early medieval tradition. English Bible prose does go better if divided into verses, the distant descendants of Jerome's pointing *per cola et commata*. They were reintroduced for instance in the Geneva Bible of 1560 (*not* allowed to be read in churches) and in the Elizabethan Bishops' Bible, and retained in 1611 and most subsequent editions until the twentieth century. By 1611, however, there could be no question of reverting to rhetorical punctuation.

Tyndale stuck to virgules to the last. The innovator who modernized the punctuation of the English Bible was Miles Coverdale. Coverdale's first Bible[20] came out in the same year, 1535, as Tyndale's latest revision of his New Testament, but does not use virgules at all. Coverdale does print, for instance, the Benedictus in prose verses with commas for

---

[18] 1534, cited copy, f. iii r.
[19] Fry, *The First New Testament Printed in the English Language*, f. lxxiiii r.
[20] *The Coverdale Bible 1535* introd. S. L. Greenslade, facsimile repr., Folkestone, 1975. Coverdale also published in 1538 a Loeb-style *Diglott*, parallel Vulgate and English.

medial pause, but most of the book, though still in black-letter, looks far more like continuous modern prose than Tyndale. Coverdale's Bible was followed in its use of modern punctuation by Hollybushe's parallel-text Latin and English version of 1538. Matthew's Bible,[21] of 1537, which used Tyndale, is still, two years after Coverdale, punctuated rhetorically like the manuscripts of medieval English prose. Coverdale's practice was confirmed when the establishment took over the Bible in the late 1530s. 'Cranmer's' Bible of 1540,[22] though it still uses black-letter except for roman notes incorporated in the text, and though it does have the occasional virgule instead of a comma, uses a much more syntactic punctuation than 'Matthew'. The triumph of modern punctuation and of roman type took another century to complete, but the punctuation of 1540 is certainly of the new age and Tyndale's of the old. The words of the Elizabethan bibles, whether Geneva or Bishops', are for the most part the words of Tyndale, but the punctuation is the punctuation of Coverdale. By now it will not appear odd to say that this is important.

I issued a warning that there are numbers of doctorates to be excavated from this field. One is a detailed study of the relations between syntax and periodicity in the English Bible translations of the 1530s. I will set the ball rolling with a suggestion. Tyndale is steadily phrasal and occasionally periodic, as indicated by his use of virgules; Coverdale, a less learned but very intelligent disciple of Tyndale, is nevertheless more syntactic, as indicated by *his* punctuation: Tyndale therefore is matchless in the Gospels, Coverdale's wonderful psalms may well hold the field only because Tyndale never got there, but Coverdale is better in the epistles. Although many of Tyndale's New Testaments have that scandalous Prologue to the Romans declaring that epistle to be 'the princypall and most exellent parte of the Newe testament',[23] Tyndale's style is not at its best in rendering the syntactic complexities so frequent in that epistle. Coverdale's first New Testament made extensive use of Tyndale, but even when the words of the two texts are exactly the same, the syntactic punctuation is enough in itself to make a great difference. Here 1611 is best of all, giving the syntactic complexities more or less as they come in the Greek, but (unlike both

---

21 'Matthew' was one of the devices for getting Tyndale's version past the English censorship. Hollybush is said to be another front-name.

22 Robert Redman and Thomas Petyt for Thomas Berthelet, London, April 1540. Later in the sixteenth century there was still some association of black-letter with the colloquial and even the phrasal as against the sentence-syntactic: see below on Martin Marprelate. A pamphlet so evidently meant to be zippy as Dekker's *Guls Horne-book* of 1609 was printed in black-letter. On the other hand, the 1611 Bible reverted to black-letter. Perhaps by then black-letter was beginning to acquire its aura of the olde worlde, a penchant for which is the main objection to the 1611 Bible.

23 Berthelet, 1536, f. cvi r.

Tyndale and Coverdale) also emphasizing periodic sound-rhythm by way of the *verses*.

Throughout the sixteenth century Tyndale's great work was infiltrated into England by a series of semi-clandestine moves. Tyndale's martyrdom was not, for once, at the instigation of the English; Thomas Cromwell seems to have done what he could to save him. The attitude of the English authorities to Tyndale's translations was nevertheless, to begin with, hostile. Bishop Tunstall expended great energy, that one cannot help thinking would have been better employed, on getting the new books burnt. The state-approved Bibles beginning with the Great Bible of 1539 have to offer themselves as unsubversive, but nevertheless incorporate a great deal of Tyndale. The lessons in the Edwardian and Elizabethan Prayer Books are said to be taken from the 1540 Bible and are often Tyndale minimally modified.[24] As Hilaire Belloc (not a friend to the Reformation) observed, 'The rhythms of [Tyndale's] work run through all successive recensions and adaptations of it.'[25] King James was wise enough to allow the derivation of the 1611 Bible (whether directly or by way of the Geneva Bible) from a source he must have regarded as undesirably Protestant. In 1662 the King James version was used for the lessons in the Book of Common Prayer. Tyndale's phrases as modified in 1611 went into the mainstream English Bible.

The old-style punctuation of Tyndale's translations is important, but not as remarkable as the old-style punctuation of his own polemical and exegetical English works. He frequently writes what have to be taken as long sentences, sometimes using parentheses, but the punctuation is still predominantly rhetorical:

¶Nowe Christ stondeth vs in doble stede/and serveth vs two maner wise. First he is oure redemer/delyverer/reconciler/mediator/intercessor/advocat/atturney/soliciter/cure hoope/comforte/shelde/proteccion/defender/strength/helth/satisfaction/ and salvacion. His bloud/his death/all that he ever dyd/is oures.And Christ him silffe/with all that he is or can doo/is oures. His bloud shedynge and all that he dyd/doeth me as good service/as though y my silffe had done it. And god (as greate as he is) is myne with all that he hath/throw Christ and his purchasynge.[26]

With all the evident feeling and sincerity of this passage, nothing can save the titles in the second 'sentence' from degenerating into a list. The difference between the Bible translations and the English prose Tyndale

---

[24] I do not know whether anyone has checked in detail the sources of lessons in the various Edwardian prayer books.
[25] Hilaire Belloc, *Cranmer*, 1931, p. 180.
[26] Tyndale, *The Beginning of the New Testament*, Prolegge, f. B iii r.

wrote for himself can be quite startling. The *Exposition upon the Sermon on the Mount*, even with the help of modern punctuation, sometimes seems to be doing little more than paraphrase the Biblical text into the expanded Latinate prose that lesser men than Tyndale were then writing all the time:

Whosoever studies to destroy one of the commandments following, which are yet the least, and but childish things in respect of the perfect doctrine that shall hereafter be showed, and of the mysteries yet hid in Christ; and shall teach other men even so, in word or example, whether openly, or under a colour, and through false glosses of hypocrisy; that same teacher shall all they of the kingdom of heaven abhor and despise, and cast him out of their company, as a seething pot casts up her foam and scum and purges itself.[27]

Tyndale seems to follow the general rule (cf. for instance More and Wyatt next chapter) that when he writes down what he hears himself saying, the writing is forceful and pointed, but when he is, so to speak, writing writing, it becomes fatally ponderous. This is meant to be the prose of controversy:

And this same is it that Paule sayeth in the seconde chaptre of the first epistle to the Corinthians / how that the naturall man that is not borne agayne and created anew with the spirite of god / be he never so greate a philosopher / never so well sene in the lawe / never so sore studyed in the scripture / as we haue ensamples in the pharises / yet he can not vnder stonde the thinges of the spirite of god: but sayeth he / the spirituall iudgeth all thinges and his spirite sercheth the depe secretes of god / so that what so ever god commaundeth him to do / he neverleueth [*sic*] serchinge till he come at the botome / the pith / the quycke / the liffe / the spirite / the marye and very cause why / and iudgeth all thinge. Take an ensaumple [. . .][28]

'So that' should really have started a sentence, but the engagement between the *cola* and the well-formed sentences never looks like ripening into marriage. Typographically the passage cries out for the use of parentheses. The tendency towards indiscipline, the lapse into the list, is also apparent at the end. This is much better than Henry VIII's prose, and at least as good as More's (see next chapter), but it has not gone all the way into a true modern prose. The lessons learned in translating the Bible were not applied.

I don't think that in the last decade of his life Cranmer ever wrote like that. Tyndale achieved wonderfully the way of translating the Bible into the real movement of the English language, but it took the other genius of Cranmer to 'change expression' in ordinary prose.

[27] *Writings of the Rev. William Tindal,* Focus Christian Ministries Trust repr., Lewes, 1986, p. 162.

[28] *An answere vnto Sir Thomas Mores dialoge made by VVillyam Tindale,* 1530, f. i v. 'Marye' is marrow.

ii   Cranmer's sentences

We are unlikely ever to have firm external evidence about all the detail of who wrote what in the English Prayer Books of 1549 and 1552. Archbishop Thomas Cranmer had a devoted group of secretaries, of whom Ralph Morice deserves more than a bare mention, though his own prose is just the ordinary mid-century wander. MacCulloch makes something of Cranmer's indebtedness to Richard Taverner.[29] Cranmer did his best not to be original but to use best tradition; he was, moreover, a genuine discusser and often leaned over backwards to allow for the opinions of scholars and ecclesiastics opposed to him. *Cranmer* may be taken as shorthand for the authors/editors of the Edwardian Prayer Books. I nevertheless share the opinion of most observers. Cranmer was the best-read liturgical scholar in the England of his day (we are assured by a trustworthy witness that even after he became archbishop, 'Yf he hadd not busynes of the prince's, or speciall urgent causes before hym, he spent iij partes of the daie in studie as effectuallie as he hadd byn at Cambridge'[30]); his library was the best available for the purpose, an unusual personal extravagance.[31] With marvellous luck, though he himself had doubts about whether good or bad, he was in the central position of power. He shows elsewhere an excellence as a prose writer I do not find in the other possible contributors. And he had a lot of practice. I think the probability is that before and after due consultations, Cranmer wrote the 1549 Prayer Book himself.

When, after the long uneasy years of Reformation headed by a monarch sometimes *plus romain que le pape*, Cranmer at length had the opportunity to negotiate an English liturgy, he showed an originality as a prose writer even more remarkable than Tyndale's, for the creation of an English liturgy was without precedent. The Church of England might even have opted for a book largely in verse, if Cranmer had not been justly dissatisfied with his efforts at verses.[32]

Yet in one way Cranmer's continuity from the Middle Ages is more obvious than Tyndale's. Cranmer is more directly than Tyndale concerned with constructions of sound. Tyndale's pocket volumes were

---

[29] E.g. MacCulloch, *Thomas Cranmer*, p. 336.
[30] Morice's Anecdotes of Archbishop Cranmer, *Narratives of the Days of the Reformation*, ed. John Gough Nichols FSA, Camden Society, 1859, p. 250.
[31] Cf. David G. Selwyn's essay on Cranmer's library in Ayris and Selwyn, *Thomas Cranmer, Churchman and Scholar* and his book *The Library of Thomas Cranmer*, Oxford Bibliographical Society Publications, 3rd series, vol. I, 1996.
[32] Marshall's Primer of 1535 contains a number of unhappy efforts in riding rhyme. King Henry's Primer of 1545 has equally unimpressive trochaic tetrameter verses, but they are quite likely the King's own.

intended primarily for the developing class of private readers, but the Prayer Books were, in a frequent 1549 rubric, to be read 'with a loud voyce'. The Prayer Books' prose rhythm is so reliable that its extraordinary distinction can still be overlooked.

The Gloria in Excelsis could easily have been a disaster, as this kind of rhythmic prose writing must be if not closely governed by a sense of what needs saying, by a confident sense of English prose, and by a fine ear. For in one way of looking at it the piece consists of nothing but repetitions of very similar units. Just to quote the opening, in the 1552 version:

Then shalbe sayd or song.

GLORYE bee to God on hyghe. And in yearth peace, good wyll towardes men. We prayse thee, we blesse thee, we worshippe thee, we glorifye thee, we geue thanks to thee for thy greate glorye, O Lorde God heauenly kyng, God the father almightie.

This begins with what only needs a *g* word in place of *earth* to be a regular alliterative line: the two-beat phrase 'earth peace' is poetic just in putting the beats together, much like the above-quoted (post-Cranmer) 'with them, we'. 'We praise thee, we bless thee,' makes as exact a repetition of foot (amphibrach) as you will find in English prose, varied only by the substitution of one monosyllabic verb for another. The Latin original has a quite different rhythm and internal rhyme, though constructed on similar principles. This is a good example of Cranmer's confident naturalizing of a Latin rhythmic movement into English idiom. The succeeding phrases may at first glance seem the same: 'We worship thee, we glorify thee'. What makes all the difference is the so slight change, with the beat-word getting longer by minimal increments, so that the stress is followed in its word first by one unstressed syllable, then two. When we get to 'We give thanks to thee for thy great glory' Cranmer has brought off a crescendo that is also a fitting climax of sense for this opening phrase. 'We praise thee, we bless thee' obviously work as single-beat *commata* organized round the beats on *praise* and *bless*, but with the last longer phrase we find additionally a greater closeness to verse.

We give thanks to thee   for thy great glory

is again quite close to an (a x / a a) alliterative line (on *g*, but with displacement of the first alliterating syllable one syllable ahead of first beat) and it is only the difference between aspirated and unaspirated *th* away from being regular on *th*, and so is almost a line with cross-alliteration. But it is quite close as well to iambic pentameter, with rather regularly spaced stresses on *thanks*, *thy*, and the first syllable of *glory*: in other words it belongs within the Chaucerian tradition too. I do not mean to suggest that the verse-like movement is insistent; it is combined with the more basic stress-cluster in which there is ascending stress from *thy* through *great* to *glory* (a three-beat phrase), before the crescendo goes even further into the superb 'O Lord God, heavenly King, God the Father Almighty'—again with the repeated two-stress pattern, the stresses on *O* (and a lesser one on *Lord*) being intensified in the stresses on the first syllable of *heavenly* and on *King* before Cranmer so to speak takes the roof off with a three-stress phrase expanded by the unstressed syllables *the* and the second syllable of *Father* and the last syllable of *Almighty* to end in the *cursus* form *planus*. The art is such that a phrase which can imaginably be inert, 'God the Father Almighty' is indeed a great climax of praise and thanksgiving; the words become through the poetry very full of their own meaning. That this is the opposite of rhetorical embellishment is suggested by the experience that it is actually hard to use these words without meaning them: the rhetoric is put to the work of *doing* something. And so to the turn into the section about the only-begotten Son, which you don't need any musical markings to take much more *piano*.

There is a whole range in Cranmer between on the one hand the great public things like the Gloria in Excelsis and on the other the more intimate moments that may (by modern instinct therefore) seem to invite us all to join in, but which in fact often go far better in the single voice of the priest. The Prayer of Humble Access[33] includes verse runs like the regular trochaic tetrameter 'Grant us therefore, gracious Lord' and the full pentameter 'And our souls washed through his most precious blood.'[34] This is nevertheless, to repeat an essential remark, a true prose, better taken as such than as *vers libre*. The churches that use a form of the text with the sentences chopped up into a line a phrase, actually do it a disservice. The weightiness and formality introduced by things like these verse runs is counterbalanced by runs of short unstressed syllables such as every choir dreads, like 'to this thy table, O merciful Lord' or 'so much as to gather up the crumbs'.

Cranmer's mastery of prose rhythm appears to be one of the very few matters in literary criticism that are beyond serious dispute. His prose is nevertheless decisively post-medieval in a way that Tyndale's transla-

---

[33] This is a text sometimes thought not to be Cranmer's own, though Peter Newman Brooks declares it to be 'pure Cranmer' (*Thomas Cranmer's Doctrine of the Eucharist*, 2nd edn, 1992, p. 116). Whether or not, the alterations made in 1552 are all improvements and do suggest the master's hand.

[34] Blank verse in Cranmer's day was in its infancy and it is possible that the presence of Shakespeare between us and Cranmer makes a difference to the reading of this phrase.

tions are not. The Prayer Books are composed in a prose to which the syntax of the well-formed complex sentence is as necessary as the phrasal rhythms of sound.

It was in the Litany of 1544 that Cranmer, already in his mid fifties, first showed his hand as a liturgist and developed his sense of the rhythms of spoken English. ('Graciously hear us, O Christ, graciously hear us, O Lord Christ'—where the small variation in the repetition makes a great difference.) The probability is that Cranmer completed his discovery of modern liturgical prose when, five years later, he was making the Collects (the set of short prayers that vary with each Sunday and feast day), often translating from the Sarum Missal. Here he accepted the challenge to retain a Latin form in English.

The Collect in Sarum Latin or the English of 1549 is a quite closely defined form. According to Procter and Frere, the Roman and English Collects generally consist of

(i) an introductory address and commemoration, on which is based (ii) a single central prayer: from this in turn (iii) other clauses of petition or desire are developed, and (iv) the whole concludes with some fixed form of ending.[35]

Sometimes this is discussed with the learned terminology of *protasis* for (i), an invocation and 'relative predicate', *apodosis* for (ii) and (iii) and *doxology* for (iv). The form contrasts for instance with Litany, but the Eucharistic Prayer seems to have been influenced by it.

The form of the Latin Collect can hardly be imitated in English without the production of complex sentences, and it has long been recognized that each of the Prayer Book Collects consists of one sentence. Professor Mueller rightly observes that

this unusual provision in natural language—the provision for an exact coincidence between the limits of a discourse and the boundaries of a sentence— materially facilitates the task of a writer who seeks to engraft Latinisms within English syntax.[36]

Even this underestimates the momentousness of Cranmer's maintaining the Collect syntax while being as well aware as Tyndale of the need to make the prayers genuine English, for (as we have seen) Mueller did not realize how original idiomatic sentence-syntactic writing was in English in 1549. Cranmer might well have either stuck to the Latin form without making it idiomatic in English, or abandoned the Latin shape altogether for paratax. The grammatical achievement on which the success of his

---

[35] Procter and Frere, *New History of the Book of Common Prayer*, p. 524.
[36] Mueller, *The Native Tongue and the Word*, p. 227.

liturgical work depends was in making a genuinely complex sentence fully at home in English.

The composition of the Collects drilled Cranmer simultaneously in the making of one sort of complex syntactic structure and in the rhetoric of the period. Mueller informatively explores the different syntactico/rhetorical varieties of Collect produced by reordering the elements—always within one sentence—but it is worth reiterating that this does not mean leaving behind either English idiom or the sound of periodic prose. For instance, as Lewis shows well,[37] the English frequently gives doublets like *sins and wickedness, mortify and kill* for one Latin polysyllable: this at once enters into the spirit of a language descended from Anglo-Saxon, where doublets are second nature, and imitates a rhythmic movement for which Latin uses longer words and inflections.

Cranmer's Collects are *syntactically* superior to modern reworkings. Notoriously, the second-person-singular 'relative predicate' of the *protasis*, forms like 'who hast made all men, and hatest nothing that thou hast made, nor wouldest the death of a sinner',[38] has given much trouble to modern revisers without Cranmer's syntactic confidence, who usually render them by main clauses. The ASB revisers of 1980 did retain the first two relatives just quoted but then continue

> you desire not the death of a sinner
> but rather that he should be converted and live.

The full point destroys the syntactic unity of the Collect; the sense of this well-formed sentence is bound to be that after reminding ourselves of two of the attributes of God we go on as the main clause of the sentence to present Him, as news, with the logical conclusion we have reached about Himself. The Church in Wales book often renders these relatives by third-person formations (whether purposely I will not speculate), again removing us out of prayer into report. It was the only-just-post-medieval liturgist of the sixteenth century who had a better grasp of syntax, as well as of rhythm.

At this stage of our discussion it will come as no surprise that much can be learned from the punctuation of the editions of the first Prayer Book of 1549 and the second of 1552. The punctuation settles any question there may still be about the modern syntax of the Collects.

Whatever the reason for the use of three printers for the 1549 Prayer Book, whether the wish to distribute patronage, haste, or both, Grafton

---

[37] Lewis, *English Literature in the Sixteenth Century*, pp. 217–21.
[38] Good Friday third Collect.

and Whitchurch were employed in London, as well as Oswen in Worcester. Ayris and Selwyn list eleven editions of the Book of Common Prayer dated 1549 (STC 16267–16277) and fourteen of the Book of Common Prayer and Ordinal dated 1552 (STC 16279–16290.5).[39] I have been able to consult about two thirds of these in the original; several are available on microfilm. So I have not made a comprehensive bibliographic study, but have seen enough to be confident in making a few significant generalizations. The indispensable Everyman reprint of *The First and Second Prayer Books of Edward VI* says that 'These editions are not identical in detail.'[40] This is a comical understatement. In fact the 1549 books vary even as to whether to give texts of the ancient hymns and canticles. This Everyman text of Whitchurch, 7 March, like Whitchurch in May, has the Gloria in Excelsis, Magnificat and Nunc Dimittis; John Oswen's first issue, May, has none of them and gets Evensong into one and a half pages, after which the Athanasian Creed continues without a break. Texts of the Magnificat and Nunc Dimittis were added in a later edition. Grafton, March, has no Te Deum, Magnificat or Nunc Dimittis, but a later Grafton issue also declaring itself to be March has them all.[41] Not all the first issues even give a text of the Lord's Prayer.

They vary as to punctuation of the texts they have in common, and also within the same copy between different quotations of the same text.[42] Oswen (May) gives this text in Euensong: 'Glory to the father, and to the sonne, and to the holy ghost. As it was in the begynnynge, is now, & euer shalbe world without end. Praise ye the lorde.' But in the same copy Mattyns gives a comma after 'shalbe' and ends 'worlde without ende Amen'. Whitchurch (May) at Mattyns begins 'Glory to the father, and to the sonne,' but in June reads 'Glory be to the father, and to the sonne:'. Grafton (March) at Mattyns has no comma after *father* but a colon after *sonne*. And so on.

There are some significant agreements, however; for instance in the tricky Second Collect at Evening Prayer the great majority put a comma

---

[39] Ayris and Selwyn, *Thomas Cranmer, Churchman and Scholar*, p. 288.
[40] 'Historical and Bibliographical Note' by E. C. Ratcliff in the 1949 impression, p. xvi. This means that the claim on the same page that 'the text of both Prayer-Books is strictly followed' needs some modification, since in 1549 and 1552 there was no unitary text.
[41] Cambridge University Library shelfmarks Young 239, SSS.14.13.
[42] I do not know how significant the differences are between copies of the same edition, but it is well known that early printers ordinarily made alterations during a print run. My authorities are copies in Cambridge University Library and the British Library. I have noticed different spellings in different copies of the same edition, but in the ones I have been able to inspect no variation in punctuation.

into the phrase 'and also that by thee, we being defended' plainly indicating a pause to avoid a possible trap.

All the editions of 1549 and 1552 are in black-letter, with which the vernacular and the older punctuation is associated. The prayers are nevertheless punctuated with commas, colons and full points evidently used as the end of a unit in the modern way, and not with virgules. The syntactic punctuation is not quite modern in that it is still more a matter of taste than it would be for us. Different printers will have different ideas about what to put in a parenthesis, not counting outright mistakes;[43] this varies more than the phrase-boundaries in psalms and hymns. The establishment of a fairly precise *correctness* in punctuation was still over a century in the future. The principle of predominantly syntactic punctuation, varied by traditional phrase-marking for the places where that is obviously more appropriate is, however, clear in all the variety of the Prayer Book editions of 1549 and 1552.

The decisive evidence of syntactic punctuation comes, naturally, from the one-sentence Collects. Some of the Collects are long enough to make it unrealistic to expect an elderly priest to speak them in one breath; they can nevertheless be seen as periods each having a complete stress-contour. Unlike some earlier periods I have quoted, however, the stress contours are within one clearly pointed syntactic structure.

The editions of 1549 and 1552 vary (of course) in their punctuation of the Collects. Fourth in Advent, for instance, has copious parentheses in Whitchurch, 1552, but none in Grafton, 1552. But in all the copies of the Prayer Books of 1549 and 1552 I have been able to see, though I cannot guarantee that copies of 1549 and 1552 cannot be found with other examples, I have found full points within the texts of only three Collects, and then not in all editions.

The Collect for the second Sunday after Trinity is a curiosity of anomalous form, was rewritten for 1662, and in some of the 1549 books has an internal full point. For the third Sunday after Easter Grafton in one of the March 1549 issues prints a full point between 'righteousness' and 'Grant' but not in the other issue; two editions of Whitchurch 1552 similarly vary, but all other copies I have seen use the proper colon. I only know of one other exception to the rule of not using a full point within the Collect. This is the Good Friday Collect in which I have shown the modern revisers losing their way, the prayer to 'haue mercy upon all Jewes, Turkes, Infidels, and heretikes, and take from them all ignoraunce, hardnes of heart, and contempt of thy word: and so fetch them home'. Here some editions put a full point between *word* and

43 E.g. 'And to (thende the people may the better heare)' (Oswen, July 1549, f. i v.): should have been 'And (to thende . . .)'.

and.[44] At a time of such variety of punctuation, this counts as an exception to a very strong rule.

It is a rule new with the Prayer Book. King Henry's Primer of 1545 has the Apostles' Creed, the Lord's Prayer and the ancient hymns and canticles virtually in the 1549 form. But the Primers (which do not give a full set of Collects) frequently use full points within a Collect.

Most of the 1549 Collects, as complex sentences, would by modern standards be incorrectly punctuated if any full point appeared within them; but some have more than one main clause, making a period which it would not be incorrect for us to take as more than one sentence, as

LORD we beseche thee, assoyle thy people from their offences, that through thy bountiful goodnes we maye bee delyuered from the bandes of all those synnes, which by our frayltye we haue committed: Graunt this, &c.[45]

Such constructions are *always* in 1549 and 1552 punctuated by colon not by full point. Cranmer invented the English text sentence as a bye-product of the complex sentence.

The punctuation of the epistles and gospels is likewise that of Coverdale, syntactic, not Tyndale's virgules.

In 1549, however, *all* issues of the Prayer Book point the Psalms used at the Lord's Supper by lineation for verse and colon (or occasionally comma) for the not necessarily syntactic mid-verse division. This follows the practice of the Psalter of 1548, which announces itself as 'after the translacion of the great Bible, poincted as it shalbe song in Churches'.[46] The ancient hymns and canticles are also generally punctuated with lineation for verse end and medial pause-mark, though not so consistently.

This pointing/punctuation is the kind of division of the psalms into verses and phrases with which we are still familiar, obviously into *cola* not clauses. The parts meant for singing were punctuated in the old fashion, the parts for the priest to read in the new.

The division between syntactic and rhetorical punctuation is similarly easy to understand in the *Catechismus*, which came out the year before

---

44 'word. And' (variant spellings) 1549 Oswen, May; 1552 Whitchurch two issues (Cambridge University Library shelfmarks Sel.3.139, Sel.3.220): 'word: And' 1549 Grafton, March (two issues), Whitchurch, May and June; 1552 Whitchurch BL shelfmark C.21.d.14 (the one without the 'black rubric') and BL shelfmark G 12099: 'word: and' 1552 Grafton all issues.

45 24th after Trinity. So the Everyman version of 1549. The ordinary modern Prayer Book goes '. . . committed: Grant this, O Heavenly Father, for Jesus Christ's sake, our blessed Lord and Saviour. *Amen*.'

46 Cf. Charles C. Butterworth, *The Literary Language of the King James Bible*, p. 153. The practice was maintained in the psalters accompanying the Elizabethan prayer books; the Barker edition of the Psalter (printed by John Day, 1579) retains 'pointed as it shalbe sung or said in churches' from 1548.

the First Prayer Book. The Preface uses parentheses and, sparsely, commas; the annexed sermons use comma and full point predominantly, with an occasional colon after *sayeth*, which seems to be syntactic in a quite modern way, for there need not always be a pause there in speech. The Ten Commandments, though, are set in large type and use the virgule evidently as rhetorical phrase-marker in the old way: 'Thou shalt not take the name of the Lord thy God in vayne / for he shal not be gyltles before the Lorde / that taketh hys name in vayne.'

Cranmer's later Prayer of Consecration (as 1662 but not 1552 calls it) has provoked more controversy than any other work of his. He determined to incorporate the narrative of the institution of the Lord's Supper into the prayer. The words of the 1662 text are the same as those of 1552 except that an archaic *which* becomes a *who* and 'most humbly' is inserted: in an ordinary modern edition the prayer looks like this:

Almighty God, our heavenly Father, who of thy tender mercy didst give thine only Son Jesus Christ to suffer death upon the cross for our redemption; who made there (by his one oblation of himself once offered) a full, perfect, and sufficient sacrifice, oblation, and satisfaction, for the sins of the whole world; and did institute, and in his holy Gospel command us to continue, a perpetual memory of that his precious death, until his coming again; Hear us, O merciful Father, we most humbly beseech thee; and grant that we receiving these thy creatures of bread and wine, according to thy Son our Saviour Jesus Christ's holy institution, in remembrance of his death and passion, may be partakers of his most blessed Body and Blood: who, in the same night that he was betrayed, took Bread; and, when he had given thanks, he brake it, and gave it to his disciples, saying, Take, eat, this is my Body which is given for you: Do this in remembrance of me. Likewise after supper he took the Cup; and, when he had given thanks, he gave it to them, saying, Drink ye all of this; for this is my Blood of the New Testament, which is shed for you and for many for the remission of sins: Do this, as oft as ye shall drink it, in remembrance of me.

The whole prayer appears thus as two sentences, which must surely make the first the longest English sentence in common use. Like a Collect, this prayer begins by addressing one Person of the Trinity, our heavenly Father, using the following second-person-singular relative clause to remind us of the property or action relevant to the present prayer ('who . . . didst give'); but then the complications start, for we go on to a relative clause within the relative clause, referring to the Son ('who made there . . . ') at which point the editions of 1552 have the parentheses for an adverbial phrase before the direct object retained by the modern text; the narrative within the relative clause then continues by reminding us that the action instituted the 'perpetual memory' to be continued until his coming again. It is not fanciful to see the syntax as expressing the unity of our 'memory' with the original event. Then comes a colon—as syntactically it has to be, for so far all the relative clauses and the clauses within them are subordinated not to a main clause but to the opening vocative of the naming of the Father, and it is only after the colon that we get the main clause of the sentence, the imperative 'Hear us' followed by the parallel 'grant'. The object of the 'grant' is 'that we [separated from its verb by another quite long string of clauses, "according to . . . "] may be partakers of his most blessed body and blood'. It is worth remarking that by the standards of modern prose this is rightly the main clause, being what in fact we are praying for. We then come to the really daring and decisive syntactic continuation: instead of an anticipated full point, the colon followed by 'who'. Though the 1552 punctuation differs elsewhere, this 'who' in all the 1552 issues I have seen follows a colon not a full point. Any modern writer would end a sentence here. Cranmer continues the sentence with the narrative of institution as a series of relative clauses, which brings the narrative into the present address to the Father, a syntactic unity. The union of complex syntax with perfectly judged rhythm saves the prayer from being the wander any other writer of the age would have made it. As meaningful re-enactment the 1662 rite is nearly perfect! and is made so by (amongst other things) this particularly daring use of an extremely long complex sentence, ending with a creation in language, for the faithful, of the real presence of the body of the Lord.

There was a story circulating amongst the exiles of Queen Mary I's reign that at the time of his arrest Cranmer was working on another revision of the Prayer Book. Whether or not, the punctuation of this great prayer was not quite complete either in 1552 or 1662.

The one modern-text-1662 stop might be defended on liturgical grounds. In many churches to this day there is a ringing of bells at this point which takes up to half a minute. It would not be right to suspend the same sentence over such a long pause. But the connective word *likewise* is right, for it expresses continuity from, and conjunction of sense (including syntactic shape) with, what precedes the full point. Burkitt's opinion was that the only improvement it would be desirable to make in the 1662 rite is the substitution of 'and' for 'or' between the alternative post-communion prayers;[47] I would just add the replacement of this, the only surviving full point in the Prayer of Consecration, by a semicolon—and if this helps us not to venerate the elements in themselves it would be thoroughly in the spirit of Cranmer. 1552 went far

---

[47] F. Crawford Burkitt, *Eucharist and Sacrifice*, 2nd edn, 1927; repr. Gringley-on-the-Hill, 1990, p. 26.

enough in the direction to give to those with the benefit of hindsight an invitation to go a little further.

The 1552 books did not, however, go quite as far as the modern text. Before and after 'Do this in remembrance of me' 1552 puts a full stop, the second of which 1662 retains. Moreover the Whitchurch editions of 1552 put a full point before 'Heare'. This latter victory of the periodic over the syntactic, I think, just has to be seen as wrong, though I think it is true that the voice sinks and pauses at this point; the mistake was not made in the Grafton editions, which print a colon. Surprisingly enough, however, this full point can still be found post-1662.[48]

The syntactic confidence of 1552–1662 nevertheless stands out by comparison with the work of modern revisers. Of the many new prayer books, the only one I know that tries to retain some of Cranmer's eucharistic prayer is that of the Church in Wales. What, in the modern world of complex sentences, this does not do, is to keep his syntactic grasp. I have heard the objection from Romanizers within the Church of England that Cranmer's is not a prayer at all, but a narrative.[49] That misses the point of the syntactic subordination of the last relative clause, but can be justly objected to the Church in Wales book, which puts a full stop and starts a new sentence at 'Who made there . . .' ('There he made . . .') and thereby moves from prayer to third-person narrative, only clearly recovering the status of prayer with the 'Wherefore', taken from 1549, that later rather desperately tries to gather everything we have to keep in mind.

Cranmer developed a sense of what needed to be kept strictly unified, and what could be recurred to after breaks. I concur with Burkitt in taking the Our Father as the final act of Cranmer's eucharistic prayer, after communion. Here the unity is quasi-dramatic, as Dix pointed out, that of an unfolding action, but one which (*pace* Dix) need not be disunified by act and scene divisions.[50] Cranmer did need, though, to unify this prayer syntactically as well as rhythmically, by putting it into as few sentences as possible, in the modern sense of sentence.

---

[48] 1552 'again. Hear' Whitchurch, BL shelfmarks C.21. d. 14, C. 25. h. 5 (perhaps 1553), C. 36. l. 16, G 12099. An edition of 1671 ('In the Savoy, Printed by the Assigns of John Bill and Christopher Barker, Printers to the Kings most Excellent Majesty', the nearest to 1662 handily available to me), keeps this Whitchurch full point after 'coming again'.

[49] Basil Hall, however, rightly observes 'a major difference from all the other Protestant liturgies in the words of Institution being said over the bread and wine in the course of a prayer' ('Cranmer, the Eucharist and the Foreign Divines in the Reign of Edward VI', in Ayris and Selwyn, *Thomas Cranmer, Churchman and Scholar*, p. 241).

[50] Cf. my discussion of Gregory Dix, *The Shape of the Liturgy* (repr. 1949), in *Prayers for the New Babel*, ch. 4. John Wesley too understood the unity of Cranmer's eucharistic prayer, I think—or whoever it was who modified the 1662 eucharist for the Methodists.

What a pity he did not have the same confidence with the Nicene Creed, where the proliferation of sentences and the repetition of 'I beleue' gives periodic shape at the expense of syntactic unity, a mistake aggravated by the revisers of 1980.

Cranmer developed an English prose syntax, the first time this had been done anew since King Alfred the Great insisted that translations from the Latin must be into genuine English. To know in one's bones that the syntax of Latin is no substitute for a true English prose, and to carry the knowledge into extensive, determined practice, was in both cases a sign of the sort of union of intelligence with force of character that one may well wish to call genius. The rarity of the achievement can be seen by comparing Cranmer with his contemporaries, which we shall do.

Cranmer's Prayer Books are true prose in being quite steadily reliable, though of course there are places that need care with phrasing and stressing. ('Drink ye all of this' must not be taken to mean 'quaff the lot!') Cranmer's feat is the perfect unification of the new Renascence syntactic organization with the old tradition of the phrasal movement of the human voice. I think the word *wonderful* is called for.

There is a good book waiting to be written on Cranmer's own English prose. I do not promise not to try myself when I have time, though I would rather supervise somebody else. There is plenty of surviving material to support a discussion of the *details* of the emergence of the Cranmerian style.[51] Topics would include the overlap and difference from his Latin, beginning with the Preface to the Prayer Book that survives in a Latin original,[52] and his ways of introducing subordination into fluent English prose. The *Determinations of the most Famous and most Excellent Universities* of 1531 would be compared both with the Latin original and with the prose of a few years later. The 1538 translation of Luther on the Donation of Constantine would come in, and Cranmer's probable contributions to the Primers. There would be some detailed comparisons within the *Homilies* between writing properly ascribed to Cranmer and writing by his contemporaries, and comparisons between Cranmer's writing and his reported speeches. This would of course be made much easier if we could have a good modern edition. What other major English writer has gone a century and a half without new editing? Here I can only give a few hints.

I had been hoping to find that Cranmer taught himself English prose in the course of his liturgical work. This is possible, because nobody

---

[51] The most up-to-date bibliography of Cranmer's writings is in Ayris and Selwyn's appendices to *Thomas Cranmer, Churchman and Scholar*.
[52] Cf. J. W. Legg, (ed.), *Cranmer's Liturgical Projects*, Oxford, 1915.

knows when he began the English liturgy,[53] and in any case the composition of the English Collects was, as argued above, a drilling in complex sentences. But he was already an outstandingly competent writer of English prose well before the King in 1544 commanded him to make 'processions' in English, and even before his 1540 Preface to the Bible. The likelihood must be that it was the pressure of public affairs and role of propagandist in English for the King's cause that drove Cranmer into modern prose, even more than the liturgical work; though why similar pressures did not, for instance, have the same effect on Thomas Cromwell is not explained.

Cranmer himself wrote an unusually legible small secretary hand; his own punctuation is consistently modern in all the documents I have seen (though he followed the inconvenient custom of not indenting paragraphs) from Letter I in the *Miscellaneous Writings* to Letter CCCXI more than twenty years later.[54]

Cranmer's prose, however, was not an inborn gift. In this Letter I, 12 June 1531, he does make a period in the midst of a (well-formed) sentence:

As concernynge the Kynge hys cause, Mayster Raynolde Poole hath wrytten a booke moch contrary to the Kynge hys purpose, wyth such wytte that yt appeareth that he myght be for hys wysedome of the cownsel to the Kynge hys grace. And of such eloquence, that yf yt were set forth & knowne to the common people, I suppose yt were not possible to persuade them to the contrary.[55]

The first paragraph of this letter to Thomas Boleyn, Earl of Wiltshire, is remarkably plain and workmanlike for its date, with many short sentences, two in a row starting with *But*; but Cranmer could not at that date summarize the contents of a book without an ominous syntactic over-complexity which drove the nineteenth-century editor to the use of parentheses not found in the manuscript. The near contemporary report to the King of his affairs in Germany avoids such large structures but only by being a very plain, paratactic narrative.[56]

It may be that as a writer of English prose Cranmer started rather close to Tyndale's translations. But the letter to the King of 11 April 1533, just after Cranmer became archbishop,[57] kicks off with a More- or

---

[53] MacCulloch reinterprets one text to support the case that Cranmer was already at work on an English liturgy in 1539 (*Thomas Cranmer*, p. 224).
[54] For letters discovered since Cox was doing his editorial work in the 1840s, see Ayris and Selwyn's bibliography. My numbers are those of the *Miscellaneous Writings* edition.
[55] British Library Lansdowne 115, f. 1 r., renumbered p. 2.
[56] British Library Cotton Vitellius B xxi, ff. 89 ff; Cranmer, *Miscellaneous Writings*, pp. 232–6.
[57] Cranmer, *Miscellaneous Writings*, Letter v, pp. 237–8.

Wolsey-like monstrous sentence perhaps to be explained by the emulation of the new office-holder ('high style, as men to princes write'). Whether or not, the traditional syntactic ponderousness does occasionally occur in the earlier letters.

The contemporary *Determinations* is not at all bad for its date but not free of the clumsinesses natural to a man translating from Latin into a language without an ordinary prose of scholarship and argument; it includes the occasional wander. MacCulloch quotes an edited text of part of a sentence that is not even well-formed:

it shall be the duty of a loving and a devout bishop not only to withstand the Pope openly to his face, as Paul did resist Peter, because the Pope verily is to be reprehended and rebuked, but also with all fair means and gentleness, and learning, in time and out of time ought to cry upon him to rebuke, reprove, beseech, exhort him that the persons so coupled together may forsake such marriages.[58]

'Ought' is either redundant or needs a subject 'he'.

The three or four following years made a great difference. Letters IV, 8 February 1533, and CLXXII, 22 April 1536, are both short requests to Thomas Cromwell for favour to an individual, but the later is so much more fluent and less cumbersome that it seems to move us into a different age.

As an example of good non-liturgical prose from Cranmer's prime here is bit of the opening of *Agaynst the Articles of the Devonshire Men* of 1549:

To whom [James and John] Christ answered, you aske you wot not what. Even so thought I of you, as sone as euer I harde your articles, that you were deceyued by some crafty Papistes, which divised those articles for you, to make you aske you wist not what.

As for the devisers of [these *deleted*] your articles (if they vnderstode theym [*deleted* there selfes]) I may not cal theym ignorant parsons, but as they be in dede most ranke papistes, and wilful traitors [& adversaries *inserted*] both to god, to our souerayngne lorde the kynge, & to the hole realme. But I can not be persuaded so to thynk of you, that in your hartes willyngly you be papistes & traitores, but that those that be such, haue craftely seduced you [being symple & vnlerned people *inserted*] to aske you wit not what.

Wherefore my dewty vnto god, & the pitie that I haue of your ignorance, moue me [now *inserted*] at this tyme, to open playnly & particulerly your own articles vnto you, that you may vnderstande theym, & no longer be deceyued.[59]

The rhetoric of the repeated plain phrase is simple and effective. Equally

---

[58] MacCulloch, *Thomas Cranmer*, p. 56.
[59] Corpus Christi College, Cambridge, 102, pp. 337–8; a manuscript extensively corrected by Cranmer; cf. Cranmer, *Miscellaneous Writings*, p. 163.

authoritative, from the Sermon against Rebellion in the same manuscript:

The generall cause [of al thies commotions *inserted*] is synne, and vnder christiann profession vnchristian lyving but there be also [certen *inserted*] speciall causes, of the whiche somme pertayne [both *inserted*] to the higher and lower sorte, aswell to the governours, as to the common people, somme appertayne only to the people, and somme agayne, only to the governours and rulers, [of the whiche *deleted*] And of theym I will firste begynne to speake.[60]

I think this has the prose virtues we might expect in the principal architect of the Prayer Books: the style is often pithy and forthright and quotable, but Cranmer is not afraid of complex sentences.

From the Preface to the Bible of 1540, at latest, Cranmer's prose is *consistently* good, so exhibiting the first prose virtue of reliability. The opening paragraph, for instance, is fully characteristic in its simultaneous management of syntax, rather witty antithesis, metaphor (the spur, the bridle, short shooting and overshooting the game) and closeness to racy speech. In the last fifteen years of his life Cranmer wrote no *bad* prose; some knowledge of his contemporaries is necessary for appreciating the gravity of this compliment, and of course it is meant as a challenge.

I do want less faint praise for him, however; I have to dissent from Lewis's judgement that More and Tyndale 'can be loved and [Cranmer] cannot'.[61] That Cranmer can be loved is a fact I know from experience: I don't even find it very difficult. The letter which he dared to address to the King on the occasion of the fall of Queen Anne in 1536 (3 May) is punctuated in a more modern way—essentially syntactic but less fussy— than the Parker Society edition of 1846. It is also very moving and full of character. The original holograph manuscript suffered badly, presumably in the fire of 1731, and in the following extract the text between square brackets is supplied from the *Miscellaneous Writings*: but enough survives to substantiate my claims both about punctuation and about character:

And I [am in such a perplexity, that my mi]nde is clene amased.[62] For I neuer [had better opinion in woman,] than I had in her, which mak[eth me to think, that she should n]ot be culpable, & agayne[63] I t[hink your highness would not] haue gone so farre excep[t she had surely been culpable. Now I thin]ke that

---

[60] *Ibid.*, pp. 415–16; cf. Cranmer, *Miscellaneous Writings*, p. 191.

[61] Lewis, *English Literature in the Sixteenth Century*, p. 195.

[62] The *Miscellaneous Writings* text puts a semi-colon here: Cranmer's full point is surely better!

[63] Cranmer, *Miscellaneous Writings*: 'culpable. And again,': Cranmer preferable as including the toings and froings of anxious thought in the same sentence.

your grace [best knoweth, that next unto your] grace I was most bounde vnto her of al creatures lyvynge.

Wherfore I most humbly besech your grace, to suffre me in that which both goddes lawe, & nature & also her kyndnes byndeth me vnto: that is, that I may with your graces favour wyssh & pray for her, that she may declare her selfe inculpable & innocent. And if she be fovnde culpable, considerynge your graces goodnes towardes her, and from what condition your grace of your only mere goodnes toke her, & set the crowne opon her heade, I repute hym not your graces f[aithful] seruant and subiecte, nor true vnto the realme, that wolde [not desire] the offence without mercy to be punnyshed to the example of [all other].[64]

I agree with MacCulloch that in context this was courageous. From prison he wrote a truly comfortable letter to Mrs Wilkinson[65] beginning

The true comforter in all distresses is onlie god thorow his sonne Jesus Christ. And whosoeuer hath hym, hath company enough: althoe he were in a wildernes all alone. & he that hath 20 thowsand in his companye, if god be absent, he is in a miserable wilderness & desolason [?]. In hym is all comfort & without him is none. Wherfore I besech yow: seke youre duelling there, as you maye trulye & rightlye serue god, & duell in him & have hym ever duelling in you.[66]

He was not always solemn. In the following, there is an element both of the man-of-the-world and of wry humour:

As for your admonition, I take it most thankfully, as I have ever been most glad to be admonished by my friends, accounting no man so foolish as he that will not hear friendly admonishments. But as for the saying of St Paul, 'Qui volunt ditescere, incidunt in tentationem,' I fear it not half so much as I do stark beggary. For I took not half so much care of my living, when I was a scholar of Cambridge, as I do at this present. For although I have now much more revenue, yet I have much more to do withal; and have more care to live now as an archbishop, than I had at that time to live like a scholar. I have not so much as I had within ten years passed by 150*l* of certain rent, besides casualties. I pay double for every thing that I buy. If a good auditor have this account, he shall find no great surplusage to wax rich upon.[67]

To make the minimal claim: this is just what we expect good forthright idiomatic prose to be; but there is no tension between the businesslike approach to the things of this world and the steady realization that they cannot be carried away. In this case I have not been able to collate the printed text with any manuscript. I predict that the original is very close but if anything more lightly punctuated. Criticism is not restricted to

64 British Library Cotton Otho C.x, f. 226 r.–v. (Cranmer wrote on both sides of the paper); cf. Cranmer, *Miscellaneous Writings*, p. 324.

65 For Mrs Wilkinson, see MacCulloch, *Cranmer*, pp. 548–9.

66 MS Emmanuel College, Cambridge, 262, f. 214 r.; Cranmer, *Miscellaneous Writings*, p. 444.

67 Cranmer, *Miscellaneous Writings*, p. 437.

technicalities, and so I say further that only a real man could have written this.

As to the non-liturgical prose works: for instance his reply to Gardiner is as effective in style as in argument, if the two can be separated. Gardiner is not bad by the standards of the age, but does tend towards the sixteenth-century wander. Cranmer begins characteristically: 'Here before the beginning of your book you have prefixed a goodly title; but it agreeth with the argument and matter thereof, as water agreeth with the fire.'[68] And he keeps it up. Gardiner's text up to the first full point, as quoted by Cranmer, is:

F OR AS MVCHE as amonges other myne allegacions for defence of my selfe in this matter, moued against me by occasion of my sermon made before the kynges most excellent maiestie, touching partely the Catholike fayth of the most precious sacrament of thaultare, which I see now impugned,[69] by a booke set forthe, vnder the name of my lord of Cantorburyes grace: I haue thought expedient for the better openynge of the matter, and consydering I am by name touched in the sayde booke, the rather to vtter partely that I haue to say by confutacion of that booke, wherein I thynke neuerthelesse not requysyte to dyrecte any speache by specyall name to the person of him that is entyteled author, because it may possible be that his name is abused, wherwith to sette forth the matter, beyng hym selfe of suche dignity and auctoryty in the common wealth, as for that respecte shoulde be inuiolable. For whiche consideracion [. . .]

We shall need two or three sentences of Cranmer's reply:

The fyrste entrye of your booke sheweth to them that bee wise, what they may looke for in the rest of the same, except the beginning vary from al that foloweth. Now the beginning is framed with such sleight and subtilty, that it may deceiue the reader notably in .ii. things: The one, that he shulde thinke you were called into iudgement before the Kynges maiesties Commyssioners at Lamhith for your catholike faith in the sacrament: The other, that you made your boke for your defence therin. which be both vtterly vntrue.[70]

This is simply the difference between an unidiomatic prose and a good

---

[68] The titles of Reformation books are normally too long to quote: I mean here the first work in the Parker Society *Cranmer on the Sacrament of the Lord's Supper*, quoted from the 1st edn, Wolfe, 1551, p. 9.

[69] Copy used actually reads *impugued*.

[70] Cranmer, *An Answer . . .* , 1551, p. 2. The text of the original edition of Gardiner's *Explication and assertion of the true Catholique fayth . . .* , 1551, differs much from this quotation in spelling and sometimes in word-breaks, but its punctuation is quoted exactly and doesn't change much in the nineteenth-century edition.

   The full point before lower-case *w* of *which* is probably a mistake, but the colon followed by capital is not uncommon, e.g. in the Prayer Book Collects, as the maximum division within a sentence. This survived into Scott's *Waverley*.

modern prose. Cranmer is hardly any simpler, syntactically, than Gardiner, but is the assured master of a prose that is at once genuinely syntactic and genuinely phrasal, close to English idiomatic speech. This difference is quite consistently maintained throughout the three hundred and sixty-seven big Parker Society pages. I leave the reader to test this assertion, with the opinion that Cranmer is well worth the effort.

The one and only contemporary peer of Cranmer I have found is Nicholas Ridley. For instance here is a fragment of a letter Ridley wrote to Mr West 'from Bocardo in Oxfourde the first of Aprill [1554]':

yow desire me for goddes sake to remember my selfe. / Indede for now it is tyme for me so to do: ffor so farre as I cann parceive, it standith me vpon no lesse daunger, then of the losse bothe of bodie & soule, and I know, then it is tyme for a man to awake, if any thing wyll awake hym./[71]

The letters of farewell Ridley wrote in the first fortnight of October, 1555, are all beautifully written as well as wonderful records of the human spirit. *Beautiful* means style not handwriting, to show which I will give as a footnote a text unedited except for the expansion of abbreviations:

O London London to whom now may I speak in thee or whom shall I byd farewell? shal I speak to the prebendaries of powles? alas al that loved goddes word & was true setterforth therof ar now as I hear say some brent & slaen some exiled & banished & some holden in hard prison & appoynted dayly to be put to most cruel death for Cristes gospelles sake. As for the rest of them I know they cold neuer brouk me well nor I cold neuer delite in them / Shal I speak to the sea therof whearin of layt I was placed almost or not fully by the space of 3 years / but what may I say to it beyng as I hear say I am deposed & expulsed by Juggement as an vniust vsurper of that roome / O Juggement Juggement can this be juste Juggement to condemn the chefe minister of goddes word the pastor & byshop of the Diocese & neuer bryng hym in to Juggement that he mythe haue hard what crimes was laid to his charge nor neuer suffer hym to haue any place or tyme to answer for hym self, thynkest thow that hereafter when true Iustice shal have place that this Juggement can euer be alowed eyther of god or of man?[72]

[71] Corpus Christi College, Cambridge, 105, p. 323; cf. *The Works of Nicholas Ridley D.D.*, ed. Henry Christmas, Cambridge, 1843, p. 338 for a substantially different text.

[72] Emmanuel College, Cambridge IV. 1. 17 ff. 98 v.–99r.; unedited:

O London London to whom now may [I speak *inserted*] in thee or whom shall [I *inserted*] byd farewell? [if *del.*] shal I speak to the prebendaries of powles? alas al that loved goddes [word *inserted*] & was true setforth [?] therof ar now as I hear [say *inserted*] some brent & slaen [?] some exiled & banished & some holden in hard prison & appoynted dayly to be put to most cruel death for Cristes gospelles sake. As for the rest of them I know they cold neuer brouk me well nor I cold neuer delite in them / Shal I speak to the sea therof [wherof I had *deleted*] whearin of layt I [was *inserted*] placed [almost or *inserted*] not fully by the space of 3 years / but what may I say [that place

This manuscript was written very hastily. It is the mildest of compliments to say that only someone genuinely competent in English prose could have written like this at a time when he knew he had only a few days to live.

Ridley's name gives the occasion just also to mention Cranmer's doctrine of the Real Presence of the Lord in the eucharist, for he acknowledges that his later understanding was much indebted to Ridley—how much so, how much to Ratramnus, how much to mainstream Protestantism, and how much to his own frequentation of the Bible and the Fathers we need not inquire. Cranmer is commonly reported, for instance by Jasper Ridley[73] and now by MacCulloch, to have changed his mind between the catechism of 1548 and the controversial writings of 1550–1 and in the latter to have denied the Real Presence. Cranmer's notion of reality seems to me much subtler and philosophically sounder than that of his modern biographers. He not only never denied that the Lord is present to the faithful in the eucharist, he positively insisted on the presence, and 'real' quite accurately reports his position, provided only one acknowledges that the word has occasioned some philosophical discussion. Cranmer depends on an understanding of signs resembling the views on language I have found in Wittgenstein. How far Cranmer differed from Zwingli we need also not inquire, but Zwingli's understanding of *hoc est corpus meum* was *est* = *significat*, and his understanding of *signifies* was Aristotelian: on one of the Marburg Articles offered as a common agreement between Reformers, Zwingli wrote, 'Sacramentum signum est veri corporis etc., non est igitur verum corpus.'[74] Cranmer's doctrine allows the signified and the signifier to be one. Cranmer is then accused of treating the elements as *only* signs, and the presence as *only* spiritual, and so certain theologians find themselves in the surely odd position of acknowledging that God is spirit, but arguing that Cranmer was a believer in what is sometimes called the Real Absence because the presence he asserted

wherof as it *deleted with more words illegible*] to it beyng as I hear say I am deposed & expulsed by Juggement as an vniust vsurper of that roome / O Juggement Juggement can this be juste Juggement [to condemn ama *deleted with another deleted phrase above the line*] to condemn the chefe [minister of goddes word the *inserted*] pastor & byshop of the Dioceses & neuer bryng hym in to Juggement that he mythe haue hard what crimes was laid to his charge [nor *deleted then above the line* nor neuer suffer hym to haue] any place or tyme to answer for hym self, thynk[est *added*] thow that hereafter when true Iustice shal have place that this Juggement can euer be alowed eyther of god or [of *inserted*] man?

73 Jasper Ridley, *Thomas Cranmer*, Oxford, 1962, p. 283.
74 Peter Newman Brooks, *Thomas Cranmer's Doctrine of the Eucharist*, 2nd edn, 1992, pp. 90, 61. Cf. my 'Thomas Cranmer on the Real Presence'.

was only spiritual. It seems to me the question is whether he believed in the *reality* of the spiritual presence, and that the only possible answer is that he did, simultaneously defining *faith*. I asserted that a word and its sense are the same thing in the understanding; substitute faith for understanding and Cranmer's doctrine frees the real presence from the impossible physics of transubstantiation and the equally impossible linguistics of the separate signified. The bread and the wine are signs, but not of anything anywhere else. A word is sound but at the same time *really* sense when taken as a word. The Word is what the bread and wine really are when eaten and drunk by faith, though remaining bread and wine as the word remains sound. Though one must not confuse faith and poetry, both are makers. Cranmer's and Ridley's really wonderful achievements in English prose are internally related to their theology.

The decisive difference between Cranmer and Tyndale as prose writers is that Cranmer learned his own lesson. Was the *Defence of the True and Catholic Doctrine of the Sacrament* first thought in Latin, like the Preface to the Book of Common Prayer? What we can know, for sure, is that it reads perfectly idiomatically in English, though it is a work of intellect of the kind you do not expect to have been written at that date in English. It has the strengths, rhetorical and uncerebral, that one sees in the Prayer Book: but it's a work of often subtle theology. We have to make a conscious effort to see how extraordinary an achievement of *language* as well as of argumentation this is.

And for this cause Christ ordeyned baptisme in water, that as surely as we se, fele and touch water with our bodies, and be washed with water, so assuredly ought we to beleue, whan we be baptised, that Christ is veryly present with vs, and that by him we bee newly borne agayn spiritually, and washed from our synnes, and grafted in the stocke of Christes own body, and be apparailed, clothed, and harnessed with hym, in such wise, that as the dyuel hath no power agaynst Christe, so hath he none against vs, so long as we remayne grafted in that stocke, and be clothed with that apparel and harnessed with that armour. So that the washyng in water of baptisme, is as it wer shewyng of Christ before our eyes, and a sensible touchyng, feelyng, and gropyng of hym, to the confirmation of the inward faithe, which we haue in hym.[75]

Cranmer will occasionally write a sentence without a finite verb, for rhetorical effect, but this is still very decisively post-medieval and syntactic. Like the Prayer Book, the *Defence* can also rise to splendour and fervour, as at the end, which rightly concludes with a doxology:

[75] Cranmer, *Defence of the True and Catholic Doctrine of the Sacrament*, Reynold Wolfe's 1st edn, 1550, f. 10 r.–v. The second, corrected Reynold Wolfe edition of 1550 punctuates with parentheses (frequent), comma, colon, question mark and full point. Both differ little in punctuation from the nineteenth-century texts.

Who is before vs entred into heauen, and sitteth at the right hand of his father, as patron, mediatour and intercessour for us. And there hath prepared places for all them that be liuely membres of his body, to raigne with him for euer, in the glory of hys father, to whome with hym, and the holy ghoste, bee glory, honor and praise for euer and euer. AMEN.[76]

Cranmer is here doing just what we demand of prose, conducting an argument, albeit an argument that like Anselm's in the *Proslogion* constantly moves towards prayer. All the same, it isn't a John-Stuart-Mill or Bentham kind of argument. I believe Cranmer's manner is really more intellectual, more truly a work of mind. If modern prose is expected to convey information briskly and efficiently along its metalled ways, Cranmer is not less efficient but is more whole. Cranmer's prose does not need to exclude so much of the human psyche as Mill's.

The Cranmer achievement, in one word, is to be undissociated. I have in mind, of course, the work done by Eliot and Leavis on what the former called 'dissociation of sensibility', the unwholeness that came into the language with Restoration sense at the very same moment as modern prose, and which makes us tend to separate the logical mind from emotion or from the spiritual. In Prayer Book prose, emotion may come naturally, and stateliness, but also physicality, and also figurative language. Some of the things in heaven and earth denied by Lockean philosophy are there in Cranmer, and held in a unity. The language that came in with Locke and the Royal Society, for all its necessity and its fluency, is a comparatively narrow room. Cranmer developed in his prose a better mode of thought. This is part of what I mean by appealing to another well-known dictum of T. S. Eliot's, 'Sensibility alters from generation to generation in everybody, whether we will or no; but expression is only altered by a man of genius.'[77]

This is a prose in which arguments can be conducted and information conveyed *and* which without any discontinuity can invite us, quite realistically, in Cranmer's supreme improvement of 1552 at the beginning of Morning Prayer, to approach the throne of the heavenly grace:

And although we ought at al times humbly to knowledge our synnes before God: yet ought we most chiefly so to doe, when we assemble and mete together, to rendre thanks for the great benefytes that we have receyved at his hands, to set foorth hys moste worthy prayse, to hear his most holy word, and to aske those things which be requisite and necessarye, as well for the body as the soule.

---

[76] *Ibid.*, 2nd edn, 1550, f. 117 r.; it differes from the first edition only in spelling. As the fashion was, this is printed as an inverted pyramid.

[77] T. S. Eliot, Introduction to Johnson's 'London' and 'The Vanity of Human Wishes', 1930; repr. as 'Poetry in the Eighteenth Century' in *The Pelican Guide to English Literature*, ed. Boris Ford, vol. 4, 1957, p. 271.

Wherfore I praye and beseche you, as many as be here present, to accompany me wyth a pure heart and humble voyce, unto the throne of the heavenly grace.

Cranmer has provoked fierce controversy from his day to our own. The mild Anglican *via media* seems to be the one frame of judgement impossible to bring to his life, though he has some claims to be its originator. I confess that I find the age of Henry VIII extremely hard to understand: the intense moral seriousness and gross cynicism, the sycophancy and courage to the death exhibited by the same courtiers. The age, even the revolution Thomas Cromwell carried through for King Henry VIII, may be opaque, but there is no difficulty at all in finding one's way into the world of the Prayer Book, which is the same age seen in a different way. As Bishop Buchanan well says, of Cranmer's last Prayer Book, '1552 itself yields up its secrets best if it is approached from the centre outwards.'[78] The Book of Common Prayer is wonderfully lucid and an embodiment of a particular conception of the kingdom of heaven, being made here in earth, even under King Henry VIII. That conception needed the prose style of Cranmer.

The word whose re-glossing allows MacCulloch to argue for an early date for Cranmer's work on English liturgy is none other than our old friend *orationes*, which he takes to mean *prayers*. We have at last arrived at the moment when *oratio* and *well-formed sentence* coincide, but the coincidence is not for the sake of conveying information or describing the external world. The main clause of these well-formed sentences of the Collects is not indicative, but imperative.[79] So the well-formed sentence was developed in English not as a result of the activities of the Royal Society, to purify the language and make it fit for science, but to approach God.

---

[78] Colin Buchanan, *What did Cranmer Think he was Doing?*, Grove Liturgical Study 7, Bramcote, 1976, p. 21.

[79] Some grammarians use the term *precative* for the petitions of prayer, presumably because *imperative* suggests commands and it is thought improper to give orders to God. The N.E.D. cites James Harris, *Hermes* (1751):

The Requisitive . . . hath its subordinate Species: With respect to Inferiors, 'tis an Imperative Mode; with respect to equals and superiors, 'tis a Precative or Optative.

This is plainly sociolinguistics not grammar. Precatives and the like do exist in some languages. (In Sanskrit, I am told by Professor Susan Tripp, there is a grammatically definable though rare precative based on the subjunctive.) The only formal difference between the ordinary English imperative and the 'precative' is that exclamation marks are not used for the latter. This *is* a difference, but not a syntactic one.

5   Shakespeare *versus* the wanderers
(home win)

i   The worst English prose

A change of expression is communal; the Edwardian books were *common* prayer, and Cranmer did make a new English prose possible to others. The authorship of some parts of the Homilies is still disputed, which is the mark of a number of authors practising a common style, one of the signs, along with reliability and consistency, of an age of prose. But there are still obvious differences between Cranmer's change of expression and Dryden's. The prose of much scholarly writing, much that was intended to be businesslike and even much offered as entertainment, was unaffected by Cranmer.

The long complex prose sentence, and the long text sentence, are developments of the Renascence. But the modern sentence did not carry a general style with it. The more established prose sentences became, the more prose writers wandered. The English wandered right into the Civil War.

Contempt for the 'barbarous' or 'rude' English language was widespread amongst the scholars of the sixteenth century. It is true that work had to be done on developing a modern syntactic prose in English. But it never seems to have occurred to the learned writers that the badness of much English prose was their own responsibility.[1]

So in the sixteenth century we had the paradoxical situation of a true ordinary prose, that of the Bible, the liturgy, and works of their tradition, which stands out in its age as extraordinary. The extraordinary English sixteenth century! the age of the best prose in the language—and, far exceeding it in quantity, the worst prose I have ever seen in any language but German!

During the Renascence in England important and urgent business was often conducted in prose any modern editor would judge unreadable. This was already true a hundred years before Shakespeare. King

---

[1] Cf. 'The Inadequate Language' in R. F. Jones, *The Triumph of the English Language*, Oxford, 1953.

Richard III summoned his friends to his immediate aid in a Latinate prose, neither well-formed modern sentences, nor periods, nor pithy Anglo-Saxonate phrases, that seems simply uninterested in communication:

> We greet you well, and as ye love the weal of us, and the weal and surety of your own selves, we heartily pray you to come unto us to London in all the diligence ye can possible after the sight hereof, with as many as ye can defensibly arrayed, there to aid and assist us against the Queen, her blood adherents, and affinity, which have intended, and daily doth intend, to murder and utterly destroy us and our cousin the duke of Buckingham, and the old royal blood of this realm, and as it is now openly known, by their subtle and damnable ways forecasted the same, and also the final destruction and disinheriting of you and all other inheritors and men of honour, as well of the north parts as other countries, that belong to us; as our trusty servant, this bearer, shall more at large show you, to whom we pray you give credence, and as ever we may do for you in time coming fail not, but haste you to us hither.[2]

The writs of the eleventh century were much more businesslike, as well as livelier—some of them quite rollicking, in fact.[3] Richard III's trouble, or his secretary's, is a failure of correspondence between syntax and rhythm. This is to politics what Bishop Pecock is to theology. The men of York do seem to have taken the point on that occasion, but I wonder how far the poor turnout at Bosworth Field is attributable to the King's failure to get his message across.

Forty or so years and two reigns later, English prose is often even worse. Look at the difference between Cranmer's prose of the 1540s and what came out under his master's name twenty years earlier. King Henry VIII, a prolific author for a monarch, published in 1528 a little *Answere unto a Certaine Letter of Martyn Luther*. We need a rather long quotation to get the feel of this prose. The following begins with the beginning of the preface. Take a deep breath and—

> It hath semed to vs alwayes / our entierly beloued people / that lykewise / as it apperteyneth to the offyce and estate of a kyng / dilygently to procure the temporall welth / and commodyte of his subiectes: So dothe it of dewtie / more especially belonge to the parte and offyce of a christen kynge / ouer and besydes / his labour / payne / and traueyle / bestowed vpon the prouysyon of worldly welth and quyete for his people: farre yet more feruently to labour / trauayle and studye / by all the meanes and wayes to hym possible / howe he maye surely kepe / establysshe and confyrme / and spyritually set forthe and forther / the hertes and myndes of his subiectes / in the right relygion of god / and trewe faythe of Christ / by whose highe prouydence & especiall bounte / they were for that

---

[2] Quoted in Paul Murray Kendall, *Richard the Third*, 1955, pp. 205–6. This text, which I have not been able to check against a source, is not very authentic, but good enough to make the point.

[3] Examples in F. E. Harmer, *Anglo-Saxon Writs*, Manchester, 1952.

purpose / chefely commytted vnto his gouernaunce. For albeit so / that our sauyour Christ hath in his ecclesyasticall hierarchy moost ordinately set & prouyded / and apoynted the spyrituall fathers and curates / most especially to solycite / procure / and haue in charge / those thynges that apperteyne by faithe or other spyrituall vertues / to the weale and saluation of his chosen chyldren / whiche ben christen men: yet is there no man but he well wotteth / that the temporall princes / concurryng with them and setting their handes therto / and ouerseyng and orderynge them to execute the charge / whiche god hath elect them to / euery prince in his o wne [*sic*] realme / the mater shall bothe moche better & moche faster come forwarde. The profe wherof / hath euydently appered in tymes past / for soone after the begynnynge of Christes churche / the conuersyon of kynges to the faithe / breuely tourned all their realmes with them: And where the opposyte was vsed / there neither grace / vertue / nor other gode worke coude florisshe or encrese / but alwayes where lacked faythe / there raigned heresies / sensualyte / voluptie inobedyence / rebellyon / no recognytion of superiour / confusyon / and totall ruyne in the ende. Whiche thynges / by the great wysedome of oure noble progenitours well parceyued / they haue of their vertuous mynde and princely corage / as well by the makyng of good and sharpe lawes / requisite for that entent / as by due executyon of the same / nat without the puttyng of their owne bodies / somtyme in the auenture of bataile / done their effectuall deuoyre to withstande and represse from tyme to tyme / the pernicious errours and heresyes / that els had of lykelyhode / as well by Wycclyffe / as other abhomynable heretikes / ben depely roted in this realme.[4]

There are plenty of complications of syntax here ('For albeit so' pointing forward to a 'yet' in the middle distance; 'Whiche thynges . . . well parceyued' an absolute phrase, and so on) but for the most part King Henry's prose is governed (if that is the right word), as English prose had been for a thousand years, by phrase rhythms, rightly punctuated by virgules. The Anglo-Saxon two-beat doublets are frequent: 'trauayle and studye . . . meanes and wayes'. The virgules are obviously phrase-boundaries, sometimes of *cola*, more often of *commata*: hints to the voice about where to pause. The colons mark the limits of something bigger, indicating as well as a pause some sort of rounding-off of sense, of which the full point is a further degree. So the punctuation is still periodic, but vaguely: the periods do not achieve the original aim of periods, to make nicely rounded units of sense. The punctuation is also vaguely syntactic. But though the full points have some tendency towards a grammatical function, it is still only a tendency, and the syntactic clauses are not clearly bounded. Most of what we would regard as sentences end with a virgule, which also frequently represents our comma, but which also appears at some places where it would for us be incorrect to put any

---

[4] King Henry VIII, *Answere unto a Certaine Letter of Martyn Luther*, facsimile repr., Amsterdam, 1971, ff. A ii r.–A iii v. The non-appearance of an expected virgule may sometimes be explained by a word's place at a line end, e.g. 'voluptie'.

punctuation at all. This prose, in the old way, is still not really written in sentences; the trouble is, it isn't really written in anything else either. After major punctuation the King habitually continues indifferently with what in modern English might well have been a relative clause taken into the previous sentence ('For angre and furye whereof . . .', just after the quoted passage) or an *And*. The complications of syntax are pointing in a new direction, but without getting there. There is no unifying principle; which is just to say that the rhythm is ineffective.

A little lower:

So came it than to passe / that Luther at laste / parceyuyng wyse men to espye hym / lerned men to leaue hym / good men to abhorre hym / and his frantyke fauourers to fall to wracke / the nobles and honest people in Almaygne / beynge taught by the profe of his vngratyous practyse / moche more hurt & myschefe to folowe therof / than euer they loked after / deuysed a letter to vs written / to abuse them and all other natyons / in suche wyse / as ye by the contentes therof / herafter shal well parceyue.[5]

Henry VIII was quite capable of speaking his mind plainly in public; many of these *commata* individually sound good, often, not surprisingly, as two-beat alliterative phrases like 'lerned men to leaue hym'. They certainly come from a speaker of idiomatic English. But it would not be possible to think of the whole extract as part of a speech, and almost as impossible to imagine it read aloud. Nothing is clear apart from his anger. It's all blurry: not of the old age and not of the new.

A simple threefold division is very useful for thinking about the English prose of the sixteenth century. Leaving Cranmer and Tyndale out of it, prose is either speech (real or imaginary) written down, or writing intended to be delivered as a speech, or what we think of as ordinary prose, intended for the page and the inner not the outer voice. The first class is frequently pithy, idiomatic, well done; the second often falls between the two stools of the first and the third but has its good moments, as in some sermons. (I can't honestly join in Lewis's compliments to Latimer, however, whose fame rests on the one immortal sentence to Ridley at the stake.) The third division, the prose of history, argument, narrative, controversy, always excluding Cranmer and the minority who benefited by his example, is normally *intolerable*.

Sir Thomas Wyatt, accomplished courtier, fluent lyrist and effective public speaker, as a *writer* of prose was downright incompetent:

And what is more vncomly/ than that in suche plays we syt with suche pertynax scylence doyng nothing els (as they say) (for there is no man that lamenteth or

[5] *Ibid.*, f. A v r.

wepeth/ whan he seith Pythia begyn/ no more than he is hungry after the feest) and those good lynesses wherof god hym selfe is auctor vnto vs/ and in maner player/ with lamentyng and sowernesse of mynde/ ledying a dolorous lyfe/ we defile and make soroufull.[6]

Wyatt is translating an argument about the mistakenness of enjoying ourselves at plays but not in church: with an effort one can follow it. But the second parenthesis ought surely to have been worked in in some other way, and he should have avoided what is plainly the pitfall of putting the adverbial phrase *with lamentyng* before its verb. The quotation ends with a periodic movement based on three three-stress phrases and some play with alliteration of *l* and *f*, but the syntactic shape trips the reader. It may be thought that Wyatt was here constrained by his *matere*, but the Epistle to 'the most excellent and most vertuous princes Katheryn', where Wyatt was writing for himself, is not much better:

Altho/ as me semeth/ and as sayth thisPlutarch [*sic* no space]/ the plentuousnesse and faire diuersyte of langage/ shulde nat so moch be desyred in suche thynges/ as the frutes of the aduertysmentes of them/ whiche in my opinyon/ this sayde Plutarch hath handsomly gadred togyder/ without tedyousnesse of length/ contaynyng the hole effect/ of that your hyghnes desyred of Petrarch in his lytell boke/ which he wrate to one of his frendes/ of the Quiete of mynde/ nerawhyt erryng from the purpose of the sayd Petrarch.[7]

This is just the primeval wander. The punctuation by virgules does not fit the ponderous syntactic structure. Contrast it with the much racier Defence written when Wyatt was on trial for his life, and plainly intended to be spoken:

/ Come on now my lorde of Londone what is my abhominable and viciouse livinge. Do ye know yt or have ye harde yt? I graunte I do not professe chastite, but yet I vuse not abhomination / yf ye knowe yt tell yt here with whome and when yf ye harde yt. who is your autor? have you sene me have anye harlet in my howse whylst ye were in my companie. Dyd you euer see woman so myche as dyne or suppe at my table. none but for your pleasure the woman that was in the gallie which I assure you may be well seen for before you came nether she nor anye other came above the maste / but by cawse the gentell men toke pleasure to see you intertayne here therfore theie made her dyne and suppe with you and theie leked well your lokes your carvinge to Madona your drynkinge to here and your playinge vnder the table / Aske Masone, aske Blage, Rowes is dede, aske wolf that was my stuarde.[8]

---

[6] Sir Thomas Wyatt, *Tho. Wyatis translatyon of Plutarckes boke/ of the Quyete of mynde*, [probably 1528], facsimile repr. ed. Charles Read Baskervill, Cambridge, Mass., 1931; no foliation but this is the last but one leaf r.–v.; cf. the conservatively edited text in Muir, *Life and Letters of Sir Thomas Wyatt*, p. 11.

[7] *Ibid.*, ff. a ii r.–v.

[8] Harley 78, f. 14 r. This MS is not Wyatt's autograph but certainly closer to what he wrote than any edition: cf. Muir, *Life and Letters of Sir Thomas Wyatt*, p. 206. Muir alters

One can sometimes see quite precisely where Sir Thomas More goes over from keeping in mind what something sounds like in a public world of which the centre is a lawcourt to being more concerned with what it will look like on the printed page. The awareness of print is always fatal.

For instance this from the early *Life of Richard III* gives more than a suggestion of why Shakespeare was able to do so much with the scene of the dying Edward IV's efforts to reconcile his factious nobles. More's version of the King's speech includes:

> My lordes, my dere kinsmenne and allies, in what plighte I lye you see, and I feele. By whiche the lesse whyle I looke to lyue with you, the more depelye am I moued to care in what case I leaue you, for such as I leaue you, such bee my children lyke to fynde you. Whiche if they shoulde (that Godde forbydde) fynde you at varyance, myght happe to falle themselfe [*sic*] at warre ere their discrecion woulde serue to sette you at peace.[9]

I think this is very good. The confident handling of what might have been clumsy in the second sentence is well done; the forensic antithetical style is present but not done to death. This style lies behind euphuism and Bacon's essays, without obtruding itself as in them. But on the same page, just before the quoted passage, is:

> But in his laste sickenesse, when hee receiued [*sic*] his naturall strengthe soo sore enfebled, that hee dyspayred all recouerye, then hee consyderynge the youthe of his chyldren, albeit hee nothynge lesse mistrusted then that that happened, yet well foreseynge that many harmes myghte growe by theyr debate, whyle the youth of hys children shoulde lacke discrecion of themself and good counsayle, of their frendes, of whiche either party shold counsayle for their owne commodity and rather by pleasaunte aduyse too wynne themselfe fauour, then by profitable aduertisement to do the children good, he called [. . .][10]

The habit of Greek is to form long sentences (though not often as long as this) by participial constructions, but it just can't be done in English without an embarkation on a horizonless wander. This is just trying to incorporate too much information within the subordinate clauses of one sentence.

If I had thought the indispensable Chambers right all the way through I would hardly have needed to add anything; at this point I have to part company with Chambers.[11] I want, I hope not for partisan reasons, to substitute 'Tyndale and Cranmer' for 'More' in Chambers's title.

---

the syntax by punctuating 'Yf ye knowe yt, tell yt here, with whome and when. Yf ye harde yt, who is your autor?' The original punctuation is syntactically vaguer but gives a text that sounds to me more like a speaking voice.

[9] *The Workes of Sir Thomas More*, p. 38, col. b.

[10] *Ibid.*, cols. a–b. We take leave of the second passage at the main verb. I do not know whether the punctuation is More's or Rastell's.

[11] I am not alone here. Cf. Mueller's citations of criticism of More in *The Native Tongue*

More's wandering prose, as against his speech-aimed prose, has no continuity from King Alfred or from Ælfric or the *Ancrene Riwle*. His syntactic complication is not a development of the tradition.

To establish that the proposed threefold division can be consistently applied to More is beyond the scope of this brief discussion. But for instance the *Dialogue of Comfort* is often very well done especially when More remembers he is writing a dialogue. On the other hand, the controversy with Tyndale is unreadably ponderous. Pages of sometimes well-judged ridicule built on the paragraph-start 'Then have we' are followed by this:

Nowe seinge the kynges graciouse purpose in this point: I reken that being hys vnworthy chancellour, it appertayneth as I saied vnto my parte and dewtye, to folowe the ensample of hys noble grace, and after my pore wyt and learning, wyth opening to hys people the malice and poyson of those perniciouse bokes, to helpe as muche as in me is, that his people abandoning the contagion of all suche pestilent wrytyng, maye be farre from infeccion, and thereby from al such punishement as folowing therupon, doth oftentimes rather serue to make other beware that are yet clere, then to cure and hele well those that are al ready infected: so harde is that carbuncle, catching ones a core, to bee by any means well and surely cured. Howebeit God so worketh, that sometime it is. Towarde the helpe whereof, or if [. . .][12]

Like his royal master, More is quite capable of producing pithy, alliterative-like phrases:

For so helpe me god as I nothynge fynde effectuall amonge them all, but a shamelesse boldenesse and vnreasonable raylynge, wyth scryptures wrested awrye, and made to mynyster them mater vnto theyr iestynge, scoffynge, and outragyouse rybaldry/ not onely agaynste euery estate here in erth, & that agaynst them moste that be moste relygyouse in lyuynge, but also agaynste all the sayntes in heuen, and agaynste the blessed body of Cryste in the holy sacrament of the aulter. In whyche thynges they fare as folke that truste in nothynge elles, but to wery all wytes at last with endlesse and importune babelynge, & to ouerwhelme the hole worlde wyth wordes.[13]

It is worth remembering that More was a younger contemporary of Skelton, who might well have written 'wyth scryptures wrested awrye' as one of his short lines.[14] But inevitably one turns More's words against himself. One feels overwhelmed in this case at the proliferations

---

and the *Word* and trenchant remarks in Lewis's *English Literature in the Sixteenth Century*.

[12] More, *The Confutacion of Tyndales Aunsvvere made anno 1532*, *The Workes of Sir Thomas More*, p. 351, col. b. The original edition of 1532 uses some virgules.

[13] More, *Confutacion*, 1532 edn, f. 13 v.

[14] Cf. Robinson, *Chaucer's Prosody*, pp. 216–23.

introduced by 'not onely'. This is all just too ponderous in its syntax for the forceful phrases to tell as they should.

More's letters to the King and Wolsey, and the replies, are just about impossible to read.[15] The King had a notoriously large appetite, an absolute necessity for him to have had any chance of digesting his state correspondence. Not being himself an artistic genius (though some of his songs are enjoyable) it is not surprising that the King then replied in kind.

What I have objected to in More would have been unobjectionable if he had been writing Latin as usual. When the writing was in English, efforts were made simply to reproduce in English the syntactic structures of Latin or, less frequently, Greek. The real English monster sentence is a sixteenth-century phenomenon, caused by the unsuccessful grafting of Latin syntax on to English.

The fashion came in of linking sentences with relatives in a way that for us calls for semi-colons not full-points, i.e. marking major clause divisions within what for us is the same sentence. So Roper or Harpsfield will go on page after page without getting anywhere we should think a full point proper, even on the infrequent occasions when they use one.

Perhaps their biographies of More may be deliberately unCranmerian, disdainful towards the vernacular. In Roper's Life of More the gap between reported speech and writing is still very noticeable. When More's conversation is reported, the book comes to life, evoking a living, pious, humorous man. But 'Son Roper' writes the narrative framework as if he is learning English as a foreign language, without any enthusiasm, and will get back to Greek and Latin as soon as possible:

Assone as she sawe him, after his blessing on her knees reuerently receaued, Shee hastinge towards him, and, without consideracion or care of her self, pressinge in amonge the middest of the thronge and company of the garde that with halberdes and bills wente round aboute him, hastely ranne to him, and there openly, in the sight of them all, imbraced him, toke him about the neck, and kissed him. Who, well liking her moste naturall and deere daughterlye affection towardes him, gaue her his fatherly blessinge and many godly wordes of comforte besides. From whom after she was departed, she, not satisfied with the former sighte of him, and like one that had forgotten herselfe, being all ravished with the entyre loue of her deere father, having respecte neyther to her self, nor to the presse of the people and multitude that were there aboute him, sodainely torned back againe, ranne to him as before, tooke him about the neck, and divers tymes together most lovingly kissed him; and at last, with a full heavy harte, was fayne to departe from him: The beholding whereof was to many of

15 State Papers vol. I, King Henry the Eighth Parts I and II, 1830.

them that were present thereat so lamentable that it made them for very sorowe therof to mourne and weape.[16]

The strings of participial clauses would run quite well if rendered word for word into Greek, and the absolute phrase in the first sentence if rendered into Latin. As it is, the good feeling, which I am ready to credit Roper with, gets tangled up in the expression. Tyndale's, Coverdale's, Cranmer's various avoidance of the syntax of the learned languages stands out from their contemporaries as scholarly boldness.

In the sixteenth century whole libraries were printed of books whose prose varies between basic incompetence and unreadable syntactic complication. Even the *titles* of books could wander. A sixteenth-century title: *The Defence of the Answere to the Admonition against the Reply by T.C.* Little TC in a prospect of animadversion! This was apparently intended for a polemic. (Martin Marprelate makes fun of long involved titles, but in that as in so much else is very unusual.)

The wanderers did not have the non-Cranmerian field to themselves, but the reaction by those who wanted to make artistic use of prose was not towards Cranmer, but away from the huge-sentence Latinate into something equally extraordinary, a set of artifically pointed sententious or precious styles.

And though women haue small force to ouercome men by reason, yet haue they good fortune to vndermine them by pollicie. The soft droppes of raine perce the hard Marble, many strokes ouerthrow the tallest Oke, a silly woman in time may make such a breach into a mans heart, as hir teares may enter without resistaunce: then doubt not, but I wil so vndermine mine olde father, as quickly I wil enioy my new friend.[17]

It hardly needs demonstrating that the prose of John Lyly is extraordinary, and dependent on the perpetual manipulation of rhythmic phrases. Lyly's is more engaging, but no more a true prose than Roper's. Nor yet is that of the racy pamphleteers of the end of the century. I would rather have Nashe's frothy confections than Roper's pseudo-Latin, but only on condition of not being required to read more than a page a day. Neither has the basic prose mark of sounding natural. Wanning cites this from Dekker:

A stiffe and freezing horror sucks up the rivers of my blood: my hair stands on ende with the parting of my braines: mine eye balls are ready to start out, being

---

[16] William Roper, *The Lyfe of Sir Thomas Moore, knighte*, ed. Elsie Vaughan Hitchcock, EETS, Oxford, 1935, pp. 98–9. This text is edited from manuscripts and the punctuation is editorial, but the passage makes my point.
[17] John Lyly, *Euphues*, ed. Edward Arber, Birmingham, 1 October 1868, p. 81.

beaten with the billows of my teares: out of my weeping pen does the ink mournfully and more bitterly than gall drop on the palefac'd paper.[18]

Wanning calls this 'solemn'. Whether or not, it is certainly ridiculous and, from our point of view, *not prose*, more like what Chaucer called 'cadence', one mark of which is the drop into verse at the end and the incorporation of a nearly regular alliterative line in the middle.

Greene is of the precious school. *A Groatsworth of Wit* might as well have been written by Lyly. A working dramatist, albeit from Cambridge, should have done better. I hope to make a point by choosing this as the moment just to mention the sermons of Donne. These virtuoso prose performances, so full of pyrotechnical vocal effects, are so much less natural-sounding than the equally virtuoso verse. Ordinary prose does not demand the presence of the speaker.

This suggests the formula for the English prose of the end of the sixteenth century: when it was not monstrous or sprawling it was precious—always with the exception of the happy few able to learn from Cranmer.

The more or less Latinate prose went on being common. Sir Walter Raleigh, man of affairs, author of large books, still can't write a competent narrative.

Syr *Richard* finding himselfe in this distresse, and vnable anie longer to make resistance, hauing endured in this fifteene houres fight, the assault of fifteene seuerall Armadoes, all by tornnes aboorde him, and by estimation eight hundred shot of great artillerie, besides manie assaults and entries. And that himselfe and the shippe must needes be possessed by the enemie, who were now all cast in a ring round about him; The *Reuenge* not able to moue one way or other, but as she was moued with the waues and billow of the sea: commanded the maister Gunner, whom he knew to be a most resolute man, to split and sinke the shippe; that thereby nothing might remaine of glorie of victorie to the Spaniards: seeing in so manie houres fight, and with so great a Nauie they were not able to take her, hauing had fifteene houres time, fifteene thousand men, and fiftie and three saile of men of warre to performe it withall.[19]

The *that* of 'And that' is grammatical, though awkwardly so, if taken to be following from *finding*, but the full points are a fairly desperate expedient to introduce periodic structure into this monstrous and repetitive sentence. The subject does come first, and the main verb *commanded* is all right; Raleigh also produces a pithy alliterative phrase for the decisive action. But an English complex sentence cannot be

---

[18] Thomas Dekker, *The Wonderfull Years*, 1924, p. 36; Andrews Wanning, *Some Changes in the Prose Style of the Seventeenth Century*, Cambridge PhD, 1938, p. 397.

[19] Sir Walter Raleigh, *A report of the truth of the fight about the Iles of Açores, this last Sommer. Betvvixt the Reuenge, one of her Maiesties Shippes, and an Armada of the King of Spaine*, 1591; repr. 1901, ed. Edward Arber, pp. 21–2.

made to incorporate Grenvill's reasons into a narrative of action without an intolerable sprawl. This is just not how to write English prose.

The good prose writers stand out as extraordinary, and so even do the ordinary ones. There was some survival in the sixteenth century of the workaday prose of the late Middle Ages, in Thomas Deloney's tales for instance, though they occasionally rise into pseudo-euphuism and rhetorical effects.

I will just mention a couple of the more interesting prose writers. Sidney's prose at best is better than competent—but not when he is on his mettle as an artist. In both versions *Arcadia* is sometimes very rhetorical, at others, or simultaneously, wandering, even to the point of ungrammaticality. 'Unrelated participles abound; the main clause sometimes gets lost, the subject changes, and pronouns which form the object of one sentence find themselves the subject of the next.'[20] In all its styles *Arcadia* is a sort of manifesto against the ordinariness of prose, except when Sidney makes a similar point with the deliberately paratactic prose he writes as comic relief.

The *Apologie for Poetrie* is different. The peroration exhorting the reader to honour poetry takes the almost necessary step of making fun of the huge sentence. Writing one that could so easily have become cumbersome, but is perfectly well managed, Sidney naturally gets to irony and humour:

> Thus doing, your name shal florish in the Printers shoppes; thus doing, you shall bee of kinne to many a poeticall Preface; thus doing, you shall be most fayre, most ritch, most wise, most all, you shall dwell vpon Superlatiues.[21]

This leads on to an equally well-managed if simple long structure made out of a 'But if (fie of such a but)' leading to a *then* complicated by a *though* and *yet* formation. The rhythmic run is good at the end:

> then, though I will not wish vnto you, the Asses eares of *Midas*, nor to bee driuen by a Poets verses (as *Bubonax* was) to hang himselfe, nor to be rimed to death, as it is sayd to be doone in Ireland: yet thus much curse I must send you, in the behalfe of all Poets, that while you liue, you liue in loue, and neuer get fauour, for lacking skill of a *Sonnet*: and when you die, your memory die from the earth, for want of an *Epitaph*.

This is complex syntax rhetorically well-managed for comic effect.[22] The two last *members* both have *cursus* forms and end with respectively a

---

[20] Sir Philip Sidney, *The Countess of Pembroke's Arcadia*, ed. Maurice Evans, 1977, pp. 48–9.

[21] Sidney, *An Apologie for Poetrie*, 1595; facsimile repr. Amsterdam, 1971.

[22] Sidney's syntax is not carried through with complete consistency: a sentence about *Gorboduc* is not well-formed, beginning with a subject 'Our Tragedies and Comedies' that never gets to a main verb.

planus and a *tardus*, but of course unlike so many of the Latinate monstrosities the whole is not meant solemnly. The combination of syntactic competence, familiar style, raciness and occasional rhetoric is unlikely to have been hit on by Sidney in complete independence of Cranmer.

'Martin Marprelate', on the other hand, may owe more to Tyndale's translation style. It is extraordinary enough to find puritan criticism proceeding by way of sometimes scabrous fun about the Fyckers of the Confocation House; even more extraordinary is the self-consciousness of the stylistic rejection of the Latinate prose justly associated with the prelates.

'Martin Marprelate' proves that as late as Armada Year, when in all probability Shakespeare was already hard at work writing for the London stage, the old phrasal prose not only survived but could be consciously adopted by an intelligent polemicist for cultural/political reasons. The series of pamphlets up to and including *Hay any Worke for Cooper* is printed in black-letter and uses punctuation by virgules because the writer is conscious more of the voice than of the syntactic structure, though the syntax is far more secure than it would have been in medieval prose.[23] This comes straight down from Tyndale, who was known to Marprelate as a theologian as well as translator.[24]

'Marprelate' starts in the second paragraph of the first pamphlet with criticism from the most traditional rhetorical standpoint, that of the reader anxious to take a breath: 'Most pitifully complayning therefore/ you are to vnderstand/that D. Bridges hath written in your defence/ a most senceles book/ & I cannot very often at one breath come to a full point/when I read the same.'[25]

He maintains an effective sniper fire of comment in the margins and running titles, often stylistic and specifically aimed at the wander of 'brother' Dean Bridges in such quotations as:

Yea some of them haue for a great part of the time,continued euen till our times, & yet continue, as the operation of great workes, or if they meane miracles, which were not ordinary no not in that extraordinary time,and as the hipocrites had them,so might and had diuers of the papists , & yet their cause neuer the better,& the like may we say of the gift of speking with tongs which haue not bin with studie before learned, as Anthonie, &c. [. . .]

---

[23] Very occasionally major punctuation comes within a complex sentence; examples from the *Epitome* (the second pamphlet of the series), ff. D i r. and D iii v. (*The Marprelate Tracts*, facsimile, Menston, 1967).

[24] Tyndale is cited in the last pamphlet of the series, the *Protestatyon*, pp. 12 and 16.

[25] *Oh read ouer D. Iohn Bridges / for it is a worthy worke* ('The Epistle to the terrible Priests of the Confocation House': the next tract begins with the same title!), 1588, p. 2.

The marginal (black-letter) comment at this point reads: 'who who [= Ho ho] / Dean take thy breath and then to it againe.'[26] Black-letter is associated with colloquial force and syntactic clarity, roman with the unreadable wander. The explanation is not that the clandestine printer had no other fount; Dean Bridges is quoted in roman. It may even be that the roman of the later pamphlets, after the 'surprising of the printer', is so explained. (The *Protestatyon* is rather desperately printed.)

Marprelate's own punctuation really does divide up the discourse differently from syntactic punctuation:

You see therefore my friendes/ that M. Deane in this point/will haue nothing to do with you/ or Paules testimonie. And you are not ignorant I am sure/ howe soone all lordes would be out of the ministerie/ if we had none in England/but the pastors spoken of by Paule/ & therefore M. doctor hath prayed against this order. Yea/ and he hath brought such a reson [no virgule but wider than usual space] against this your platform of gouernment/ as is iust [roman] Secundum vsum Sarum.[27]

The gouerment of the church of Christ/ is no popular gouernement/ but it is Monarchicall/ in regarde of our head Christ/ Aristocraticall in the Eldership/ and Democraticall in the people.[28]

This is not a matter of where pauses *naturally* come, but of the survival of a tradition of rhetorical/periodic phrasing. After centuries of syntax it may seem downright unnatural to insert a pause between *Christ* and *is* or after *Monarchicall*: but such was the old periodic habit, which the learned Martin is following here, surely on purpose.

I think this is good stuff, if rowdy (other influences from earlier in the century must include Skelton, for instance in the uses of countrified speech). These tracts are for us much more like vigorous ordinary prose than their targets, but their punctuation as much as the absence of decorum from their comments declares them to be deliberately out of the late-sixteenth-century mainstream. They support the case that what we think of as good ordinary prose was then anything but ordinary.

The earlier seventeenth century, though the crowning achievement of Bible translation came in 1611, was still not an age of good prose. I long ago pointed out that the 1611 translators themselves wander when

---

[26] 'The Epistle to the terrible Priests of the Confocation House', p. 12; Scolar facsimile margin is illegible at this point and I quote a copy from Cambridge University Library, shelfmark Syn. 7. 60. 115/3.

[27] *Oh read ouer D. Iohn Bridges / for it is a worthy worke* (The Epitome; second in the series), f. F 2 r.

[28] *Hay any worke for Cooper . . .* Penned and compiled by Martin the Metropolitane, 1589, p. 26; facsimile 1967.

they are not translating; in this way they are of the tradition of Tyndale.[29]

What I rudely call 'wandering' Croll calls 'baroque'; Croll and the scholars write learnedly about the Senecan *versus* the Ciceronian, and have some useful things to say. Barish's account of the difference between Shakespeare's prose and Jonson's under these heads makes some sharp observations. Most English sixteenth-century prose of either kind, however, remains unreadable, whether by its syntactic and/or rhythmical cumbrousness or its rapidly wearying artificial pointedness —as Croll virtually admits.[30] I think it is most unfair to Cicero to apply his name to the English wanderers.

Similarly: Bacon goes down in Crollian history as the 'Senecan' reaction against the 'Ciceronian' prose of the long sentences. I will not spring to the defence of Seneca, but on the other hand I don't think Tacitus (the other name invoked as anti-Ciceronian) would have tolerated Bacon's essays. Like all labourers in this vineyard I am much indebted to Professor Vickers. But I have much sympathy with what Vickers reports as T. S. Eliot's 'one reference only', to 'the heavy sententiousness of Francis Bacon'.[31] The generalization that when non-Cranmerian prose was not speech-based (as at best Bacon, another lawyer, is) it was wandering or precious, still applies to Bacon, who is alternately both. The descent of Bacon's *Essays* of 1597 is at least as much from Ascham as from Seneca. But the effort at expository prose in the English version of *The Advancement of Learning* seems to me far too close to its Latin origins. For instance here is Bacon declaring his intention of not offering an opinion:

So vnto Princes and States, and specially towardes wise Senats and Councels, the natures and dispositions of the people, their conditions, and necessities, their factions and combinations, their animosities and discontents ought to be in regard of the varietie of their Intelligences, the wisedom of their obseruations, and the height of their station, where they keepe Centinell, in great part cleare and transparent; wherefore, considering that I write to a king that is a maister of this Science, and is so wel assisted, I thinke it decent to passe ouer this part in silence, as willing to obtaine the certificate, which one of the ancient Philosophers aspired vnto, who being silent, when others contended to make demonstration of their abilities by speech, desired it mought be certified for his part, *that there was one that knewe how to hold his peace.*[32]

[29] Cf. any of the twenty-eight pages of Miles Smith, *The Translators [of the 1611 Bible] to the Reader*, repr. Lewes, n.d.
[30] E.g. Croll, *Style, Rhetoric and Rhythm*, pp. 273, 278.
[31] Brian Vickers, *Francis Bacon and Renaissance Prose*, Cambridge, 1968, p. 265.
[32] Francis Bacon, *The Twoo Bookes of the Proficience and Advancement of Learning*, 1605, facsimile Amsterdam, 1970, The Second Booke f. 106 v.

In a very public document, when Bacon was attacking duelling as weightily and lucidly as he knew how, he produced this:

For, if one iudge of it truely, it is noe better then a sorcery that enchanteth the spirits of young men, that beare great myndes, with a false shew, *species falsa*; and a kind of satanicall illusion and apparition of honour; against religion, against lawe, against morall vertue, and against the presidents and examples of the best times, and valiantest Nations, as I shall tell you by and by, when I shall shew you that the law of *England* is not alone in this poynt.[33]

This is just a rather unwieldy period forced into the syntax of a complex sentence at the usual price of wandering.

So: can one find ordinary prose anywhere in English between Cranmer and Dryden? I shall continue to limit the discussion by concentrating on the prose apparently intended for silent reading, but it would not be sensible to ignore altogether everything intended for public performance, and the one-word answer to this question brings us to the stage. The Prayer Book itself was primarily intended to be read aloud. By far the numerically largest surviving prose *genre* from Shakespeare's day is the sermon. The published English sermons of the late sixteenth and early seventeenth centuries are stylistically very various, ranging from what looks like speech written down to what one can hardly believe was ever spoken.[34] As far as one can generalize, the pre-civil-war sermons still follow the distinctions I drew in sixteenth-century prose: that when they are simply intended for oral delivery they are often fluent and racy, whichever party they come from, but when the preacher remembers the page he frequently wanders.

The sermons are, however, sometimes perspicaciously written in ways we expect of prose. I do not claim to have read even most of the 1,353 pages of Joseph Hall's *Works* (1634) but where I have sampled it I would have happily accepted much of the prose as post-Restoration. It is true that Hall's Characters are rather artificially pithy-pointed, as the manner of this insignificant *genre* was, and that his Centuries of Meditation are closer to Bacon than to Traherne. But for instance this from a sermon said to have been preached at Paul's Cross on 24 March 1613 could have been, apart from the spelling, fifty years later:

---

[33] Bacon, *The Charge of Sir Francis Bacon Touching Duells*, 1614, facsimile repr. Amsterdam, 1968, p. 12.

[34] There is a well-established difference between puritan and Anglican styles (cf. Perry Miller, 'The Plain Style', repr. Fish, *Seventeenth-Century Prose* pp. 147–86). I shall not challenge the consensus that the puritans disapproved of rhetorical flights in their sermons, though I do not know how consistently their disapproval was carried into practice.

This is the feare of the Lord. There is nothing more talkt of, nothing lesse felt. I appeale from the tongues of men to their hands; the wise Heathen taught mee to doe so, *Verba rebus proba*. The voice of wickednesse is actuall, saith the Psalmist, wickednesse saith there is no feare of God before his eyes. Behold wheresoever is wickednesse, there can be no feare of God; these two cannot lodge under one roofe, for the feare of God drives out evill (saith *Ecclesiasticus*.) As therefore *Abraham* argues well from the cause to the effect: Because the feare of God is not in this place, therefore they will kill me: So *David* argues back from the effect to the cause, *They imagine wickednesse on their bed, &c. therefore the feare of God is not before them*. I would to God his argument were not too demonstrative. Brethren, our lives shame us.[35]

The use of short phrases and monosyllables is well-judged but the presence of words like *demonstrative* avoids any hint of levelling. Greek and Hebrew are both quoted on the same page of this open-air sermon. I don't think it is at all fanciful to see here a direct descent from Cranmer.

T. S. Eliot's late promotion of George Herbert from the rank of minor to major poet was, I think, one of the few errors of judgement he made under the influence of Anglican orthodoxy; nothing can make it not ridiculous to mention Herbert in the same breath as Shakespeare and Milton, or even of Donne and Marvell. So I hope it is some compensation that I admire Herbert's prose very much. The University Orator might have been expected to write very Latinate English, but his letters are genuine English prose. *A Priest to the Temple* is better than that.[36] There is perhaps a touch too much influence from the Character *genre* and also from Bacon's essays, but this writing is plain, authoritative, manly, serious, as well as lively—or, one might say, centrally of the tradition of Cranmer. Herbert of course used the Prayer Book daily. Just one snatch, about 'processions', i.e. the beating of the parish bounds on Rogation Day as the Litany is chanted:

Particularly, he [the Countrey Parson] loves Procession, and maintains it [. . .] Nay, he is so farre from condemning such assemblies, that he rather procures them to be often, as knowing that absence breedes strangeness, but presence love. Now Love is his business, and aime; wherefore he likes well, that his Parish at good times invite one another to their houses, and he urgeth them to it: and somtimes, where he knowes there hath been or is a little difference, hee takes one of the parties, and goes with him to the other, and all dine or sup together. There is much preaching in this friendliness. Another old Custome there is of

---

[35] *The Works of Joseph Hall*, 1634, p. 437.
[36] Herbert's *Remains* were not published until 1652, nineteen years after his death. The manuscript of *A Priest to the Temple* has presumably been lost, as Hutchinson does not mention its fate after transmission by the Revd Edmund Duncon, Rector of Fryarn-Barnet, to the Stationer (*The Works of George Herbert*, ed. F. E. Hutchinson, Oxford, 1941; repr. 1967, p. 556). It is reasonable, however, to assume that the text is pretty close to what the author wrote.

saying, when light is brought in, God send us the light of heaven; And the Parson likes this very well; neither is he affraid of praising, or praying to God at all times, but is rather glad of catching opportunities to do them.[37]

Martin Marprelate was no more representative of puritan style than Herbert of Anglican, but on the other hand Herbert was not a sport. I would say something similar to what I said about Hall, and more confidently, of another bishop, John Bramhall, one of Marvell's targets in *The Rehearsal Transpros'd*. Bramhall writes consistently clear, forthright prose wherever I have sampled him, though I confess that his pages too are copious enough (1,021 pp.) for it to be quite possible that they may contain a wander or two. But it is a real achievement that the second paragraph of the *Just Vindication of the Church of England*, thirty lines long, is not the hopeless wander it would have been in Roper, but a very well-managed and clear rhetorical *tour de force*. If the mark of ordinary modern prose is the easy management of the syntactic subordination of complex sentences for the fluent articulation of thought without loss of contact with speech, there may be a good case to be made for Bramhall as Dryden's principal forerunner. He has a good sense of rhythm and bold turn of phrase. This, from a characteristic attack on 'Scottish Discipline' is typical: in Scotland,

The King hath no more Legislative power in Ecclesiastical causes, than a Cobler, that is a single vote in case he be chosen an Elder, otherwise none at all. In *Scotland* Ecclesiastical persons make, repeal[,] alter their Sanctions every day, without consent of King or Council. King James proclaimed a Parliament to be held at *Edenburgh*, and little before by his letter required the Assembly *to abstain from making any innovations in the Policy of the Church, and from prejudicing the decisions of the States by their conclusions and to suffer all things to continue in the condition they were until the approaching Parliament.* What did they hereupon? They neglected the Kings letter, by their own authority they determined all things positively, questioned the Archbishop of St. *Andrews* upon their own Canons, *for collating to benefices, and voting in Parliament*, according to the undoubted Laws of the Land. Yea to that degree of sawciness they arrived, and into that degree of contempt they reduced Sovereign power, that twenty Presbyters, (no more at the highest sometimes but Thirteen, sometimes but seven or eight) dared to hold and maintain a General Assembly, (as they miscalled it,) after it was discharged by the King, against his Authority, an insolence which never any Parliament durst yet attempt.[38]

The difference is plain enough between the style of King James's letter, even in this short quotation, and the lively and fluent prose that surrounds it. The syntactic *confidence* is noticeable: the parentheses do

[37] George Herbert, *Herbert's Remains*, 1652, pp. 157, 158–9; *The Works of George Herbert*, ed. Hutchinson, p. 284.

[38] John Bramhall, *The Works of the Most Reverend Father in God, John Bramhall D.D.*, Dublin, 1677, p. 495.

not clot, and this is good pamphleteering style in the alliteration on King and Cobler, King and Council, in varied sentence-length, and the use of a word as colloquial as *sauciness*. I think it's good! though not quite with the intimate weightiness of Cranmer. All the same, Bramhall has a genuine religious feeling that divides him decisively from Dryden.

Bramhall, who did not die until 1663, may be compared with writers from the other side in the Civil War who might be expected to be plainer. I will mention the most august of them first, because he seems to me to be the very last of a line in prose as well as verse.

Fifteen years younger than Bramhall, Milton wrote large amounts of very convoluted prose, very oddly described as Ciceronian, on purpose, as a subscriber to the belief that the reader's obligation to join the author in making sense should be brought home to him by the labour of unravelling the author's sentences. Critics who, as Leavis said of Saintsbury, have read everything, may relish the exercise; personally I am disinclined to accept this sort of invitation, whether it be from Milton or *Finnegans Wake*.

Which makes me wonder much that many of the Gentry, studious men, as I heare should engage themselves to write, and speak publickly in her defence, but that I beleeve their honest and ingenuous natures coming to the Universities to store themselves with good and solid learning, and there unfortunately fed with nothing else, but the scragged and thorny lectures of monkish and miserable sophistry, were sent home again with such a scholastical burre in their throats, as hath stopt and hinderd all true and generous philosophy from entring, crackt their voices for ever with metaphysical gargarisms, and hath made them admire a sort of formal outside men prelatically addicted, whose unchast'nd and unwrought minds were never yet initiated or subdu'd under the true lore of religion or moral vertue, which two, are the best and greatest points of learning, but either slightly trained up in a kind of hypocritical and hackny cours of literature to get their living by, and dazle the ignorant, or els fondly overstudied in uselesse controversies, except those which they use with all the specious and delusive suttlety they are able, to defend their prelatical Sparta, having a Gospel and Church government set before their eyes [. . .][39]

—and so on with the next full point still well in the future and followed by a 'Which . . .'. The individual phrases are so strong! whether polysyllabically as in *metaphysical gargarisms* or the Anglo-Saxonate *scragged and thorny*.[40] A century and a half after King Henry VIII Milton's individual phrases can be even more telling than the King's but like Henry's there is

---

[39] Milton, *The Reason of Church Government urg'd against Prelaty*, 1641, pp. 61–2; facsimile repr. *Prose Works of John Milton*, vol. I, Menston, 1968.

[40] This is so English that it doesn't convey the impression of a *cursus* form, though if *cursus* in English is marked only by stress this is an ordinary *planus*.

no way of putting them together. The rhythm here is just that of the individual phrases, without anything whole for them to make or derive from. In the absence of the metre which keeps the phrases in order in *Paradise Lost* it is difficult not to make jokes about *in*subordinate clauses, the freedom having escaped from the author and running wild in the fissiparous phrases. Reading the mixture in, say, *Areopagitica*, of very strong Anglo-Saxonate phrases with a sentence-structure that may well span several pages, is too much of an intolerable wrestle between reader and syntax. Who but Milton would have argued for the liberty of unlicensed printing in a prose which is itself a sort of inhibition?

What Milton did defiantly and on principle many of the English prose writers of the century preceding him, and even of his contemporaries, did without anything of Milton's force, because they couldn't help it. Let us, however, before further supporting the contention, allow ourselves some refreshment.

ii   Shakespeare's prose

It is hardly surprising that we think of Shakespeare as a poetic dramatist; and so, without contradicting that at all, it can be useful to remind ourselves that he was the leading practitioner of the *mixed play* of verse and prose. This, like the English history play,[41] is an achievement essentially of Shakespeare alone. The mixed play had both a pre- and post-Shakespearean existence: but not very much of one. The pre-Shakespeare mixture is always crude and unassimilated. Marlowe may well not have bothered to write his own comic prose scenes. They have at least none of the characteristic Marlovian verse onrush. The editor or printer left them out of the text of the two parts of *Tamburlane*, which therefore, accidentally, does not count as mixed play. Ben Jonson, with his instinct of decorum and classicality, did not much care for the mixed play, though he did write Volpone's most exuberant scene in prose.

The inventor of the mixed tragedy (for want of a better phrase), the tragedy that essentially, and not only to provide relief to the groundlings, incorporates a great deal of comedy, naturally also developed a form to which both verse and prose were necessary. But this is certainly not to suggest any simple correlation between prose and humour.

We may suppose too easily that prose writing for the stage must be easy and fluent. That is no truer than that popular blank verse must be easy and fluent. (Look at Kyd!) Prose in Elizabethan drama first becomes remarkable in the very opposite of ordinary writing, that is to

[41] Cf. my *'Richard II' and 'Woodstock'*. The excellence of the prose in *Thomas of Woodstock* is not the least of the reasons for ascribing it to Shakespeare.

say in the plays of John Lyly. This begins a sort of microcosmic re-enactment of the usual history of prose in accordance with the principle that ordinary prose is normally a late development, and that prose originates as the precious. Lyly's prose is very much more extraordinary than the verse with which Shakespeare was beginning his career a few years afterwards. But only twenty or so years later, prose is reserved for the ordinary; prose moves towards what we expect prose to be. Beaumont and Fletcher are prosaic, deliberately, when they contrast the verse and the prose in *The Knight of the Burning Pestle*. That play is almost as prophetic of the Augustan age of prose as Jonson's all-prose *Epicoene, or The Silent Woman*. Much of the verse in *The Knight of the Burning Pestle*, spoken by Ralph as Knight, is in any case parody, but the verse of the serious love plot, that nobody could possibly remember, is (often deliberately) parody too, leaving prose to do the duty we expect of it in the modern world, of representing the commonsense of the citizens.

Jonson's prose is not reductive in the same way, but with a few exceptions comparably expresses a restriction. The oddity in Jonson is that the verse of so classically inclined a moralist should create for his villains so superabundant an energy of imagination. They have the life of the plays, even as they are always condemning themselves. As Barish puts it, of two of Jonson's characters, 'In these cases Jonson was trying to *suppress* the undercurrent of absurdity, and could not. The language seemed to go on leading a life of its own, outside the conscious control of its maker.'[42] But *The Silent Woman* has much more of the controlled sharpness that, as Dryden discerned,[43] pointed the way to restoration comedy and, through it, to Augustan prose in general. The restriction in *The Silent Woman* is beautifully intentional, and from a writer who produced other and different things; but it is unShakespearean. This all-prose play is quite unlike Shakespeare's mainly-prose *Merry Wives of Windsor*.

Shakespeare's prose can have a poetic abundance which in Jonson is associated with verse. It is nevertheless a true prose, not precious; very various,[44] but quite reliable. The immediate mention of Cranmer is again necessary. If we look at what Shakespeare managed to do with prose, I don't think we shall find any other exemplar.

Shakespeare is, firstly, and right from the beginning of his career, a

---

[42] Barish, *Ben Jonson and the Language of Prose Comedy*, p. 279.
[43] Cf. the 'Examen' of *The Silent Woman* in the *Essay of Dramatic Poesy*.
[44] Barish oversimplifies the periodic tendency of Shakespeare's prose, and its dependence on Lyly. Shakespeare can certainly make both shapely periods and sharp antithetical phrases. Polonius thinking aside (*Hamlet*, II. ii. 66) is speech-like; Hamlet's reply is very periodic, with sarcastic intent. But Shakespeare does so many other things as well.

very competent writer of prose, which is rather more than one can say for him as a writer of verse. The prose of the early history plays has none of the stiffness of the early blank verse. What differentiates Shakespeare's from our modern prose, but not from Cranmer's, is that it is not, in the Dictionary phrase, opposed to poetry.

Shakespeare *often* uses prose to upstage blank verse, but not just reductively, though he does that too, for instance at the beginning of *Troilus and Cressida* and in the comments of Goneril and Regan on the action of the first scene of *King Lear*. But so much of Shakespeare's prose is just not prosaic.

My leading example must be Falstaff. The political contest in *1 Henry IV* is not so much between the King and Worcester as between the whole political establishment, including the opposition, on one side, and Falstaff on the other. The former, in all their varieties, from the King to Northumberland to Glendower, speak blank verse as part of their membership of the club. There need not be anything precious or poetical about the blank verse; Hotspur gives Glendower a splendid practical lesson in how to speak blank verse without being merely beautiful, and the King's verse is a suitable vehicle for majesty even, I think, in the end, in face of the challenge from Falstaff. But that is a deadly serious challenge. Falstaff speaks a couple of lines of verse, plainly as parody, but his use of a true, not precious prose constitutes a claim to represent the real world. Though Falstaff can be deliberately reductive, however, one would never call him in the modern sense prosaic. The challenge Falstaff's prose makes to the values by which both the monarch and the rebels live is not the challenge of mere flat commonsense. Falstaff's prose is so effective because of its poetic seductiveness.

Shakespeare naturally gives us a leading example as soon as we meet Falstaff, in act one scene two. The Prince leads the way in speaking prose (going into verse for the chilling soliloquy at the end of the scene), lively enough; but it is the style of Falstaff's answer that gives the audience his powerful fascination:

Marry then, sweet Wagge, when thou art King, let not vs that are Squires of the Nights bodie, bee call'd Theeues of the Dayes beautie. Let vs be *Dianaes* Forresters, Gentlemen of the Shade, Minions of the Moone; and let men say, we be men of good Gouernment, being gouerned as the Sea is, by our noble and chast mistris the Moone, vnder whose countenance we steale.[45]

This is as poetic as the beautiful use of the moon in act five of *The Merchant of Venice*. The almost exact rhythmic repetition of *Squires of the Nights bodie* in *Theeues of the Dayes beautie* (trochee iamb trochee with

[45] I. ii; Folio facsimile, p. 351.

antithesis of *night* and *day* and close similarity of sound from *body* to *beauty*) is evidently prose as a kind of free verse, and something similar could be said of *Gentlemen of the Shade, Minions of the Moone* two identically constructed phrases with stress at each end separated by runs of (actually four) unstressed syllables. 'Prose poetry', even a hundred years after Pater and Wilde, must still suggest the late-Victorian purple patch, which is not what I mean at all, and why I insist that this is a true prose. It is still the *making* of something infinitely tempting, a real siren's song.

But this is still no more enticing than some of the phrases in the Psalms or the Book of Common Prayer. 'O pray for the peace of Jerusalem : they shall prosper that love thee. Peace be within thy walls : and plenteousness within thy palaces!' I do believe that the Prayer Book is Shakespeare's take-off point.

Falstaff's manner reaches its supreme sustained moment in the Boar's Head scene. The severity of the test Falstaff sets the King is shown when the King has to undo Falstaff's work in the long succeeding verse scene. Readers and audiences will no doubt differ as to who wins this contest. It is noticeable that Falstaff is a much better prose-speaker than the Prince. In this scene many of Falstaff's funniest lines are (like Malvolio's, but Falstaff is doing it on purpose) parody, of Lyly or Bacon, but when the Prince comes to make his formal charge against 'that swolne Parcell of Dropsies, that huge Bombard of Sacke' etc. etc., his hitting off of the Falstaff manner loses that corrupt charm and becomes merely bombastic and offensive. Falstaff's reply has all the force of Cranmer:

My Lord, the man I know . . . But to say, I know more harme in him then in my selfe, were to say more then I know. That hee is olde (the more the pittie) his white hayres doe witnesse it: but that hee is (sauing your reuerence) a Whoremaster, that I vtterly deny. If Sacke and Sugar bee a fault, Heauen helpe the Wicked: if to be olde and merry, be a sinne, then many an olde Hoste that I know, is damn'd: if to be fat, to be to be hated, then *Pharaohs* leane Kine are to be loued. No, my good Lord, banish *Peto*, banish *Bardolph*, banish *Poines:* but for sweete *Iacke Falstaffe*, kinde *Iacke Falstaffe*, true *Iacke Falstaffe*, valiant *Iacke Falstaffe*, and therefore more valiant, being as hee is olde *Iack Falstaffe*, banish not him thy *Harryes* companie, banish not him thy *Harryes* companie; banish plumpe *Iacke*, and banish all the World.[46]

Falstaff is a traditional *rhetor*, with the beautifully placed stress on *old* after the repeated *valiant*, and the whole repeated phrase 'banish not him thy *Harryes* companie'. It is by way of a rhetoric that does not deny the nature of prose that Falstaff succeeds in being all the world (that

---

[46] II. iv; Folio, p. 361.

world the catechism associated with the flesh and the devil), infinitely tempting in a way ordinary modern prose could hardly permit.

The high moral moment of Hamlet's life comes in a prose unmistakably Cranmerian.

> *Hor.* If your minde dislike any thing, obey. I will forestall their repaire hither, and say you are not fit.
> *Ham.* Not a whit, we defie Augury; there's a speciall Prouidence in the fall of a sparrow. If it be now, tis not to come: if it bee not to come, it will bee now: if it be not now; yet it will come; the readinesse is all, since no man ha's ought of what he leaues. What is't to leaue betimes?[47]

Though this is a genuinely syntactic prose I note as usual the rhetorical, not syntactic, punctuation which suggests here a different syntax from that of some modern editions that end a sentence at *all* and unnecessarily relate the following *Since* to the last clause. This has a simplicity and gravity we rightly associate with prose but there is no sense here of cutting off the upper or lower registers. Again, though epithets like *grave* are fair enough, traditional rhetoric is not excluded, with stress-balances and cross alliteration in *special providence . . . fall of a sparrow*; obvious isocolon, homoteleuton, and a figure for which there is, as one might expect, no exact classical name, the exact repetition of a syntactic structure in the string of constructions beginning *If it be now*.

When Gloucester bemoans the degeneracy of the world he is already speaking prose, and one might expect the Bastard's comment (one phrase of which we glanced at as an example of rhythmic contour in prose) to be, so to speak, even more prose, reductive in a Swiftian way. Not so. His prose sense is as creative as Falstaff, and more unanswerable:

> This is the excellent foppery of the world, that when we are sicke in fortune, often the surfets of our own behauiour, we make guilty of our disasters, the Sun, the Moone, and Starres, as if we were villaines on necessitie, Fooles by heauenly compulsion, Knaues, Theeues, and Treachers by Sphericall predominance. Drunkards, Lyars, and Adulterers by an inforc'd obedience of Planatary influence; and all that we are euill in, by a diuine thrusting on. An admirable euasion of Whore-master-man, to lay his Goatish disposition on the charge of a Starre,[48] My father compounded with my mother vnder the Dragons taile, and my Natiuity was vnder *Vrsa Maior*, so that it followes, I am rough and Leacherous. I should haue bin that I am, had the maidenlest Starre in the Firmament twinkled on my bastardizing.[49]

---

[47] v. ii; Folio, p. 770.
[48] Comma *sic*, though I have not checked other copies.
[49] *King Lear*, I. ii; Folio, p. 776.

As usual with Cranmerian prose the syntax is as important as the periodicity, but the latter is splendid, the *not*-isocolon of the expanding series of members beginning 'villaines on necessitie' coming down to the short phrase 'diuine thrusting on'. The sarcasm of 'so that it follows' is syntactic as well as logical.

Not that all Shakespeare's periods are shapely. It is almost a matter of course that Shakespeare can give a disjointed period when the drama demands it. Benedick, easily gulled into thinking that Beatrice is in love with him, says:

This can be no tricke, the conference was sadly borne, they haue the truth of this from *Hero*, they seeme to pittie the Lady: it seemes her affections haue the full bent: loue me? why it must be requited: I heare how I am censur'd, they say I will beare my selfe proudly, if I perceiue the loue come from her: they say too, that she will rather die than giue any signe of affection: I did neuer thinke to marry, I must not seeme proud, happy are they that heare their detractions, and can put them to mending: they say the Lady is faire, 'tis a truth, I can beare them witnesse: and vertuous, tis [*sic*] so, I cannot reprooue it, and wise, but for louing me, by my troth it is no addition to her witte, nor no great argument of her folly; for I wil be horribly in loue with her, I may chance haue some odde quirkes and remnants of witte broken on mee, because I haue rail'd so long against marriage: but doth not the appetite alter? a man loues the meat in his youth, that he cannot indure in his age.[50]

This has fragmentary elements of period, but the trains of thought are going in several directions and will not be periodized, so that the *cola* just jumble together. It is almost the period used for stream-of-consciousness.

I am of course not saying that Shakespeare's prose is the same as verse, or that it can do everything he does in verse. Lady Macbeth's verse speech immediately following her reading of her husband's prose letter takes us into a concentration of passion and will that would not go into the letter itself. Edmund's quoted soliloquy is rightly in prose, but Hamlet's soliloquies have to be in verse. Edmund is more analytic, as befits prose.

It would not have been right to leave Shakespeare out of this discussion though of course almost all Shakespeare's surviving prose except his will is dramatic dialogue or monologue, including the letters and proclamations in the plays, for even they have to be read aloud on stage. It may nevertheless be useful to differentiate the prose of spoken dialogue and the prose supposed to be imitating written documents. I will just use three examples of his *written* range.

---

[50] *Much Ado about Nothing*, II. iii; Folio, p. 109.

Hamlet to Horatio, Macbeth to his Lady, are much better at *writing* than most of Shakespeare's contemporaries. Hamlet writes rather short sentences, not periods, rather Tyndale-like. Macbeth is more syntactically complex:

> *They met me in the day of successe: and I haue learn'd by the perfect'st report, they haue more in them, then mortall knowledge. When I burnt in desire to question them further, they made themselues Ayre, into which they vanish'd. Whiles I stood rapt in the wonder of it, came Missives from the King, who all-hail'd me* Thane of Cawdor, *by which Title before, these weyward Sisters saluted me, and referr'd me to the comming on of time, with haile King that shalt be*[.] *This haue I thought good to deliuer thee (my dearest Partner of Greatnesse) that thou might'st not loose the dues of reioycing by being ignorant of what Greatnesse is promis'd thee. Lay it to thy heart, and farewell.*[51]

At the other end of the scale, the oracle in *The Winter's Tale*, quite unlike any expectations we may have of a riddle, is startlingly plain:

> Hermione *is chast,* Polixenes *blamelesse,* Camillo *a true Subject,* Leontes *a iealous Tyrant, his innocent Babe truly begotten, and the King shall liue without an Heire, if that which is lost be not found.*[52]

This still makes a periodic structure (tricolon followed by tetracolon, I would say, though again it fits Cicero's reservation of *commata* for this sort of effect). The gradual increase of length in phrases all of rising rhythm is not artless: cf. remarks on Cranmer's Gloria in Excelsis, above. The simple power of this could not have been as well done in verse.

The exception to the rule that all Shakespeare's prose is meant to be spoken on stage is the stage directions. One of the reasons for supposing that Shakespeare wrote many of the stage directions himself is the excellence of the prose. Put the direction for the dumb show in the play-within-the play in *Hamlet* beside Sir Walter Raleigh's sea-fight quoted above, and one notices how nicely succinct a narrative Shakespeare's is:

> *Enter a King and Queene, very louingly; the Queene embracing him. She kneeles, and makes shew of Protestation vnto him. He takes her vp, and dcclines* [sic in cited copy] *his head vpon her neck. Layes him downe vpon a Banke of Flowers. She seeing him a-sleepe, leaues him. Anon comes in a Fellow, takes off his Crowne, kisses it, and powres poyson in the Kings eares, and Exits. The Queene returnes, findes the King dead, and makes passionate Action. The Poysoner, with some two or three Mutes comes in againe, seeming to lament with her. The dead body is carried away: The Poysoner Wooes the Queene with Gifts, she seemes loath and vnwilling awhile, but in the end, accepts his loue.* Exeunt[53]

---

[51] I. v; Folio, p. 724.   [52] III.ii; Folio, p. 287.
[53] *Hamlet*, Folio, p. 757 (no act and scene divisions, now III. ii).

A rather more syntactically complex example from the same author:

Enter certaine Reapers (properly habited:) they ioyne with the Nimphes, in a gracefull dance, towards the end whereof, Prospero *starts sodainly and speakes, after which to a strange hollow and confused noyse, they heauily vanish.*[54]

Crane[55] informs us that one well-established conventional use of prose in earlier Elizabethan drama is for mad scenes. This is in itself curious and one should beware of supposing that all these mad scenes, because they are not written in verse, should be thought of as prose. It may be more convincing to see them as fragments of language that are neither verse nor prose, though it is also true that the inveterate human habit of making sense does drive even mad speeches in the direction of prose, and the Elizabethans, like the Victorian novelists, found it hard to write madly enough. Howbeit, Crane is certainly right that the earlier plays used what looks like prose to express madness.

Shakespeare makes Malvolio write a letter in prose to prove his sanity. Malvolio proves that he is *not* a madman not so much by what he says as by writing a good prose letter:

By the Lord Madam, you wrong me, and the world shall know it: Though you haue put mee into darkenesse, and giuen your drunken Cosine rule ouer me, yet haue I the benefit of my senses as well as your Ladieship. I haue your owne letter, that induced mee to the semblance I put on; with the which I doubt not, but to do my selfe much right, or you much shame: thinke of me as your please. I leaue my duty a little vnthought of, and speake out of my iniury. *The madly vs'd Maluolio.*[56]

Elsewhere Malvolio is a parody of the Baconian-sententious ('Some are born great . . .'); here, the accent of a man with a real grievance is expressed in very well-shaped sentences. The *though . . . yet* formation can be a lure into infinitely proliferating syntax or artificial antithesis— Falstaff's parody of euphuism uses a *though . . . yet*—but is here perfectly controlled as well as expressing fury. This is just what we expect of a prose writer, the sane participation in common life. Prose is the sanity of the modern world. Malvolio, sick of self-love and spleen, yet uses prose to demonstrate a genuine spiritual wholeness. But the notions both of common life and sanity may still be different in Shakespeare's world from ours.

Later again, in *The White Devil*, madness is represented *in verse*. Webster is nevertheless the most interesting successor of Shakespeare as

---

[54] *The Tempest*, IV. i; Folio, p. 15. How do you vanish heavily? This is poetic language not stage-effect!
[55] Milton Crane, *Shakespeare's Prose*, Chicago, 1951.
[56] *Twelfth Night* V. i; Folio, p. 274.

user of prose in a mixed play, in his case a virtuoso decadent mixture, as in the final scene between Bosola and the Duchess of Malfi.[57]

Shakespeare's prose does mix with his verse within a whole language. In this his prose is quite unlike Dryden's, between whose prose sense and the flights of passion in the verse dramas there is a great gulf fixed.

iii Puritan pamphleteers

We look round the Commonwealth period for signs that Restoration good sense did not suddenly spring fully armed from the head of the King on his return from his travels. Cranmer's liturgical work being my central point, it seems natural to try first the Puritan replacements of the Prayer Book. Comparisons are not straightforward, however, because the Presbyterian *Directory for Public Worship* of 1644 is strongly against all set prayers and refrains even from giving a text of the Lord's Prayer. 'The Minister is to pray to this or like effect' or 'to this or the like purpose'; the third-person outlines do not give us much to go on. But I chanced upon a pamphlet called *A Supply of Prayer for the Ships of this Kingdom* which I think more informative. The preaching ministers could not be aboard every vessel every sabbath, and so actual written-out prayers had to be 'supplied'. Perhaps this little book is a high-church spoof, a sort of Peter Marpreacher? The first long item is a confession:

O Great and gracious Lord, we acknowledge before thee our sinfulnesse, first, by reason of Originall sin, which (besides the guilt of it, which makes us lyable to eternall damnation) is the seed of all other sins, and hath depraved and poysoned all the faculties and powers of soul and body, and doth defile our best actions, and (were it not restrained, or our hearts renewed by Grace) would break forth into innumerable Transgressions, and the greatest Rebellions against the Lord, that ever were committed by the vilest of the sons of men. And next, [. . . for $2\frac{1}{2}$ more pages; Cranmer is sometimes accused of overdoing confession.][58]

In a later terminology this is called 'preaching the prayers', but to try to keep my remarks stylistic, I just notice that it has lost Cranmer's simultaneous syntactic grasp and rhythmic shape. What the sailors made of it, let us not speculate.

Ordinary prose is more likely to be found in pamphlets, and it is often

---

[57] Massinger, Shakespeare's official successor, otherwise a journeyman of Shakespeare's *atelier*, tends towards the pure verse play. Were there but world enough and time Middleton, Ford and Tourneur could be discussed.

[58] *A Supply of Prayer for the Ships of this Kingdom . . . Agreeable to the Directory*, Iohn Field, London, n.d., pp. 5–6.

supposed that the efforts of the Puritan pamphleteers and the first English journalists, of the 1640s and 1650s, were a necessary trailblazing for the prose age of the 1660s. What I have seen does not support the position. We are looking for some consistently easy, natural-sounding prose, with the reasonable expectation that it is more likely to come from the Roundheads than the Cavaliers, but I have not found this. We have already seen the most famous Puritan not writing anything like modern prose, and two well-known royalists doing so. Some of the Puritan pamphlets are, however, clearly as well as forcefully written. What I have not found is any consistent level of clarity such as one can hardly miss in the prose of forty years later.

This is even true of the first English newspapers and newsletters; in fact *all* the ones I have seen still wander. Nigel Smith gives a photograph of the first page of *A Perfect Diurnall of the Passages in Parliament* which according to the illustration though not its caption is no. 25, 1642. It begins:

There was Information given to the House of Commons by Letters from Glocester-shire, That there is great opposition in that County betweene the ordinance for the Militia, and the Commission of Array, whereby the County is much disturbed; that many able men in that County stand up for the Array, and 4. of the Members of the House of Commons, viz. Sir *Ia. Lucy,* sir *Robert Pyne*[?], sir *Tho. Deane* and *Humphrey Hooke* Esquire, who are the chief causers of the disturbance there; whereupon the House of Commons have agreed upon a Vote, that the said 4. Members shall be expelled the House, disabled for being members during this Parliament, and to be sent for as delinquents.

This just should not have gone into one sentence. Lord Beaverbrook would have improved it. A few pages earlier Smith says, of an account of the storming of Berkeley Castle in 1645, 'Equally speedy is the narrative itself, which runs detail and analysis together'—in this way, as quoted by Smith:

The same day col. *Rainsborough* with his forces before *Barkley-castle* stormed the out-works and the Church, which were the main strength of the castle, with Scaling-ladders, performing the service with so much resolution & gallantry (both Officers and Souldiers) as quickly made them masters of the place; wherein were taken 90 prisoners, besides 40 put to the sword, amongst whom were a Major and a Captain. This was such a terror and discouragement unto the Enemy within the Castle, to see the resolution of our souldiers, and the execution done upon theirs in the Church and out-works, that the Governour, Sir *Charles Lucas* (who returned answer to the first Summons, that he would eat horse-flesh before he would yield, and mans flesh when that was done: and upon a second Summons sent as peremptory an answer;) yet now perceiving the planting of our ordnance against him upon his own Works (which we had newly gained) whereby we had a great advantage to play into the castle; and sensible what he was to expect if he came not to present tearms, was glad to sound a Parley, which was yielded to, and Commissioners sent out to treat, and the Castle was surrendered upon these Articles.[59]

Detail and analysis are indeed run together, but not by syntax that is the internal organization of thought. The syntax here rather permits the insertion of the main pieces of information as afterthoughts, for which my technical term is still 'wander'. For this to be published as news means that there was still no accepted sense of what counted as prose. It needs untangling, not necessarily into shorter sentences:

The main strength of the castle was its outworks and the Church. Col. Rainsborough stormed them the same day. Officers and men fought with such resolution that they were soon masters; they took 90 prisoners and put 40 to the sword, including a major and a captain. The Governor, Sir Charles Lucas, had answered to the first summons to surrender that he would eat horse flesh rather than yield, and men's flesh when the horseflesh was done, and had sent as peremptory an answer to a second summons; but seeing our guns directed against him on his own earthworks newly gained by us, and realizing what he had to expect if he did not surrender on the present terms, he was glad to sound a Parley. This was agreed to, Commissioners sent to negotiate, and the Castle was surrendered on these terms.

It isn't much of a boast to say my version is better. The point is that *anyone* thirty years later would have made something more like my version.

Well into the second decade of the Commonwealth the wander continued. A sort of pamphlet sketch-history gives an excited account of the events of Tuesday 22 November 1653 in this way:

THis night was a great Mutiny at the *New Exchange* in the Strand, such, as hath scarce ever been the like: The businesse upon the best information that I can have from those who were present in part of the businesse, and have conferred with others upon the whole, is this:

On Mundaynight (which was the night before) three of the Portugall Ambassadours family, whereof his brother was one, being at the New Exchange, they talking in *French* spake of such discourse of Transactions of some English Affaires, which Col. *Gerhard*, Sir *Gilbert Gerhards* brother, understanding the French tongue, hearing, told them very civilly, that they did not represent the stories they spake of right; [. . . → sentence and paragraph end 20 lines][60]

The Greek-like string of participles, hopelessly awkward in English, might have come from Roper a hundred years earlier.

---

[59] Nigel Smith, *Literature and Revolution in England 1640–1660*, New Haven, 1994, pp. 55, 51–2.

[60] *The Names of the Members of Parliament begun on Munday the Fourth of June, 1653 . . . with the severall Transactions since that time*, Tho. Jenner, 1654, pp. 9–10.

The pamphleteers vary very much, and not consistently with faction. For instance, more or less at random, *A Pack of old Puritans maintaining the Unlawfulnesse & inexpediency of subscribing the new Engagement*[61] is brisk and neat, at least in parts. Robert Greville Lord Brooke's *Discourse opening the Nature of Episcopacie*, 1641, is pithy and racy with a good sense of a rhetorically effective phrase. But the moderate royalist Dr Fern's *Resolving of Conscience* is also well and competently written:

To this purpose shall you have this Treatise speaking to you for the direction of your Consciences. If you think it strikes too boldy upon any thing concerning the Parliament, I desire yours and their favourable interpretation, fain would I silence every thought and word that may seem to reflect upon that high Court; but what is necessary, I must speak for truth and conscience sake, from which neither King nor Parliament should make us swerve. We are taught that Kings must not be flattered; and the people ought to learn, that Parliaments must not be Idolized [. . .][62]

On the other hand Dr Hen. Hammond's *View of the New Directory . . .*, Oxford, 1646, wanders: but no more than many of the Puritans. It is still surprising that so many of them are evidently either not trying for, or unable to achieve, anything like a brisk pamphleteering style.

Along with Gerard Winstanley, the Leveller John Lilburne exemplifies in R. G. Cox's useful survey a movement towards a 'plainer prose'.[63] I am afraid I can't see it. Winstanley is rustic, which is not what is meant by the simplicity of modern prose. Lilburne, Leveller by reputation, shows no sign of stylistic levelling, at least in the 1640s. As a young man Lilburne wrote prose that is the graphic equivalent of shouting. (Shouting is not ordinary prose.) By 1646 he had matured, but not into modern prose:

It is wonderfull, that the failings of former Kings, to bring our Fore-fathers into bondage, together with the trouble and danger that some of them drew upon themselves and their Posterity, by those their unjust endevours, had not wrought in our latter Kings a resolution to rely on, and trust only to Justice and square dealing with the People, especially considering the unaptnesse of the Nation to beare much, especially from those that pretend to love them, and unto whom they expressed so much hearty affection, (as any People in the world ever did,) as in the quiet admission of King *James* from *Scotland*, sufficient, (if any Obligation would worke Kings to Reason,) to have endeared both him and his

---

[61] *A Pack of old Puritans maintaining the Unlawfulnesse & inexpediency of subscribing the new Engagement*, London, printed by the Company of Covenant-Keepers, dwelling in Great Brittain, 1650.

[62] H. Fern DD, *The Resolving of Conscience . . .*, Cambridge, 1642, f. 3 r.

[63] R. G. Cox, 'A Survey of Literature from Donne to Marvell', *The New Pelican Guide to English Literature* 3, 1982, p. 85.

sonne King *Charles*, to an inviolable love, and hearty affection to the *English Nation*; but it would not doe.[64]

This is only twenty years before *Grace Abounding to the Chief of Sinners*, but there is still no marriage between syntactic structure and rhythmic phrasing. The syntactic complication does not justify itself in the sense made. From being a shouter Lilburne matured into a sprawler. T. B. Tomlinson makes a persuasive case for William Walwyn,[65] but Walwyn too can sprawl in a way that would have been unimaginable in the 1670s:

I might insist here upon a Booke called *The Confutation of Anabaptists* lately set forth, which saies, *They are absolute and professed enemies to the essentiall Being of Civill Government*, but I find people so little regard the Booke, it being so full of non-sence, and in this particular so evidently contrary to truth, and the experience of every man, that lookes abroad, and knowes any thing of the Anabaptists; that it will be but losse of time to take notice of it, only it were worth observation to see how easily it obtained an *Imprimatur*, and how open the Presse is to any thing true or false, sence, that tends to the Anabaptists scandall or disgrace.[66]

Meanwhile John Goodwin leads off his *Theomachia; or The Grand Imprudence of men running the hazard of fighting against God* . . . (1644) with this as his first sentence:

When the Children of *Israel*, in the progresse of their Warres upon the *Canaanites*, wherein God had promised to be with them, and to give them successe, and that a man of their enemies should not be able to stand against them: notwithstanding they fought under the protection of many such promises as these, yet met with a disaster and losse, thirty six of them being slaine by the men of *Ai*, and the rest of the partie ingaged in that service put to rout, and chased by their enemies: God himselfe upon the great dejection and solemne humiliation of the Elders of *Israel*, and *Joshua* their Generall, was pleased to make knowne unto him by speciall revelation, what root of bitternesse it was that brought forth this fruit of death, what sin by name it was amongst them, that had separated between him and them in their late sad miscarriage, yea, and would separate still, to their further and greater misery, except they took a course to make an atonement for themselves, by purging and clensing themselves from it.[67]

This has not even the excuse, which Rastell might have used for his epistles dedicatory, of an appropriately lapidary occasion, but appears to

---

[64] John Lilburne, *A Remonstrance of Many Thousand Citizens, and other Free-born People of England, To their owne House of Commons* . . ., 1646, p. 4; Haller III, p. 354.

[65] T. B. Tomlinson, 'Seventeenth-Century Political Prose: William Walwyn', *The Critical Review*, Canberra, 1989, pp. 25–41.

[66] William Walwyn, *The Compassionate Samaritane*, 1644, pp. 70–1; Haller, *Tracts on Liberty*, III, pp. 99–100.

[67] Haller, *Tracts on Liberty*, III, pp. 7–8.

have originated as a sermon, complete with text. Could it imaginably be preached?

However many writers of decent prose the Puritans had, decent prose was not *normal* in Puritan pamphlets. That is to say, the Puritan pamphleteers were still without the first mark of a prose age, reliability and consistency.

There may be many other examples of good ordinary prose from the Puritans, but the author I am surest of is the Protector himself. It would have been nice at this point to have had a set-piece contrast between Oliver and Charles. Unfortunately *Eikon Basilike* seems most unlikely to have been the King's and is in any case written just in the ordinary moderately turgid prose of the age. The King's authentic prose is quite unremarkable.[68] Cromwell's individuality stands out if one puts him next to his colleague, Marvell's patron Fairfax.

And though (had we (upon our first addresses) for our undoubted Rights and Dues) bound or free, a candid reception, with a just consideration, and a reasonable satisfaction, or at least a free answer therein, wee should have been easily perswaded to have abated or forborne much of our Dues, and not to have enquired into, or considered (so farre as we have) either the possibilities there are for more present satisfaction of Arreares, or the credit of future securities proposed; yet since [. . . → paragraph/sentence end ten lines][69]

Two years earlier had been published *Three Letters* about Naseby, of which the first is by Fairfax and the second Cromwell. Fairfax is steadily turgid, as above. This is part of Cromwell's account:

[W]e after three howers fight, very doubtfull, at last routed his Army, killed and tooke about five thousand, very many Officers, but of what quality we yet know not, we tooke also about two hundred Carriages all he had, and all his Guns, being twelve in number, whereof two were Demie-Cannon, two Demie-Culverins, (and I thinke) the rest Sacres, we persued the enemy from three miles short of Harbrough *to nine beyond, even to sight of* Leicester *whether the King fled. Sir this is none other but the hand of God, and to him alone belongs the Glory, wherein none are to share with him, the Generall served you with all faithfullnesse and honour, and the best commendations I can give him is, that I dare say he attributes all to God, and would rather perish than assume* [sic] *to himselfe, which is an honest and a thriving way, and yet as much for brauery may be given to him in this action, as to a man. Honest men served you faithfully in this action, Sir they are trusty, I beseech you in the name of God not to discourage them, I wish this action may beget thankefullnesse, and humility in all that are concerned in it, he that venters his life for the liberty of his Country I wish he trust*

---

[68] Cf. *The Letters Speeches and Proclamations of King Charles I*, ed. Sir Charles Petrie, 2 vols., 1935. This is an edited text, but nothing could make the prose distinguished.

[69] Thomas Fairfax, *A Declaration or Representation . . . from his Excellency, Sir Thomas Fairfax*, 1647, p. 3.

God for the liberty of his conscience, and you for the liberty he fights for, in this he rests who is,

Your most humble Servant,

14 *Iune* 1645   Oliver Crumwell[70]

The responsibility for the punctuation in this official publication cannot be Cromwell's, still in the field. If properly stopped and paragraphed, the Churchillian ring would be clearer. It is not a technical observation, though I think it is one about style, to say that here is a formidable man one would not wish to have for an enemy.

I am unable to give a very authentic text of the letter Cromwell wrote two days after the decisive battle of Marston Moor to give his brother-in-law a compound of private grief and public joy, but though well-known it is too good not to quote.

It's our duty to sympathise in all mercies; that we may praise the Lord together in chastisements or trials, that so we may sorrow together.

Truly England and the Church of God hath had a great favour from the Lord, in this great victory given unto us, such as the like never was since this war began. It had all the evidences of an absolute victory obtained by the Lord's blessing upon the godly party principally. We never charged but we routed the enemy. The left wing, which I commanded, being our own horse, saving a few Scots in our rear, beat all the Prince's horse. God made them as stubble to our swords, we charged their regiments of foot with our horse, routed all we charged. The particulars I cannot relate now, but I believe, of twenty-thousand the Prince hath not four-thousand left. Give glory, all the glory, to God.

Sir, God hath taken away your eldest son by a cannon-shot. It brake his leg. We were necessitated to have it cut off, whereof he died.

Sir, you know my trials this way; but the Lord supported me with this: that the Lord took him into the happiness we all pant after and live for. There is your precious child full of glory, to know sin nor sorrow any more. He was a gallant young man, exceeding gracious. God give you his comfort.[71]

The lack of polish is a sign of good true prose: the man is writing fast and fluently, allowing himself inelegant freedoms though within the limits of a very good sense of how to write English sentences. 'Principally' is an afterthought that would not have appeared in anything revised or studied, but the clause structure is well in hand. The freedom with Latinate diction shows in 'necessitated' but the Saxon monosyllabic plainness needs no remark. This is competent prose in going straight to the point and doing what has to be done.

[70] *Three Letters from the Right Honourable Sir Thomas Fairfax, Lieut. Gen. Crumwell and the Committee residing in the Army . . .*, 1645, pp. 2–3.

[71] Howard Erskine-Hill and Graham Storey, (eds.), *Revolutionary Prose of the English Civil War*, Cambridge, 1983, pp. 33–4. The credit for drawing our attention to Cromwell's letters and speeches belongs, of course, to Thomas Carlyle.

The Lord's name is frequently on Cromwell's lips, for which A. L. Rowse (for instance) can hardly mention him without accusing him of hypocrisy. This doesn't sound like the style of a hypocrite. But nor does it sound quite like modern prose, though not for any technical reason. Neither unembarrassed emotion nor a sense of the presence of God are associated with modern prose. Cromwell is a world away from Restoration prose, a thousand miles from the coffee house and quite without the bows and scrapes Addison manages to set down on paper. The connection with the Bible is the reverse of a weakness. Cromwell really did pant for happiness in the Lord! No writer at the court of Charles II could have used *glory* so without embarrassment and so convincingly.

I think all I mean about Cromwell (though to hear the opinion would not have pleased any of the parties) is that he is more of a successor of Cranmer than a forerunner of Dryden.

6   Dryden's democracy

More useful than trying to contrast King and Protector is to move from Cromwell to the King's stylist, Clarendon, or Edward Hyde as he then was. Dr Hartman calls one of her quotations from Clarendon 'rhetorically effective'.[1] Whether or not, *both* sides seem to me to be serious but still ponderous. Here is a part of a Parliamentary document, as quoted by Clarendon:

The Lords and Commons, in Parliament assembled, having receiv'd your Majesties Message of the 25th of *August*, do with much grief resent the dangerous and distracted State of this Kingdom; which We have by all means endeavour'd to prevent, both by Our several Advices and Petitions to your Majesty; which hath been not only without success, but there hath followed that which no ill Counsel in former times hath produced, or any Age hath seen, namely those several Proclamations and Declarations against both Houses of Parliament, whereby their Actions are declared Treasonable, and their Persons Traitors.[2]

On both sides men knew they were engaged on no trivial matter; but this is not (if we think for instance of Churchill three hundred years later) a *prose* way of conducting public affairs. I can't see that on the King's side, either.

Clarendon not only survived into what I think of as the age of Dryden, but had a late heyday at the beginning of the Restoration. When he fell in August 1667, the year of Sprat's *History of the Royal Society* and the year before Dryden's *Essay of Dramatic Poesy*, his prose and his world fell with him.

Put Clarendon and Dryden side by side and see two worlds:

He had been, by the extraordinary favour of King *James* to his Person (for he was a very handsome Man) and his parts, which were naturally great, and had

---

[1] Joan E. Hartman, 'Restyling the King: Clarendon Writes Charles I', repr. in James Holstun, (ed.), *Pamphlet Wars: Prose in the English Revolution*, 1992, p. 48. 'Clarendon . . . was chiefly responsible for the style in which Charles, his station challenged by Parliament, addressed his subjects,' she says (p. 45).

[2] Edward Hyde, Earl of Clarendon, *The History of the Rebellion*, Oxford, 1706, vol. II, Part I, p. 11.

been improv'd by good Education at home and abroad, sent Embassadour into *Spain*, before he was thirty years of Age; and afterward in several other Embassies; and at last, again into *Spain*; where he Treated, and Concluded the Marriage between the Prince of *Wales* and that Infanta; which was afterwards dissolved. He was by King *James* made of the Privy Council, Vice-Chamberlain of the Household, an Earl, and a Gentleman of the Bed-Chamber to the Prince, and was then crush'd by the power of the Duke of *Buckingham*, and the prejudice the Prince had himself contracted against him, during his Highness's being in *Spain*; upon which he was imprison'd upon his return; and after the Duke's death, the King retain'd so strict a Memory of all that Duke's Friendships and Displeasures, that the Earl of *Bristol* could never recover any admission to Court; but liv'd in the Country, in ease, and plenty in his Fortune, and in great Reputation with all who had not an implicit Reverence for the Court; and before, and in the beginning of the Parliament, appear'd in the head of all the discontented Party; but quickly left them, when they enter'd upon their unwarrantable Violences, and [. . . six more lines before the next full point.]³

Clarendon's *History* occupied a privileged place throughout the eighteenth century as the authorized version of the Great Rebellion. Perpetual copyright was given by Act of Parliament to Oxford Univerity, a division of whose press still bears the name, though they have let the great work go out of print. By 1750 Clarendon must surely have been one of the great unreadables. The quoted passage is syntactic with a vengeance, actually dividing the auxiliary and participle of the pluperfect passive of the first quoted verb by (on my count) an adverbial phrase containing within itself a parenthesis and a relative clause which itself includes a complete pluperfect formation. At any subsequent date of English history it would nevertheless just have been called a muddle. When the wandering sentence does come to an end the end takes us by surprise. The dissolution of the contracted marriage between Prince Charles and the Infanta must to our ears, coming last in the sentence, seem to be making the final point the sentence is leading to, but in Clarendon it is just a diminuendo after the not very intelligible roll of the preceding clauses.

Clarendon took his prose with him into exile in 1667, to finish his history. Here is Dryden:

But while I was thus employ'd about this Impression,⁴ there came to my hands a new printed Play, called, *The Great Favourite, or the Duke of* Lerma. The Author of which, a noble and most ingenious Person, has done me the favour to make some Observations and Animadversions upon my *Dramatique Essay*. I must confess he might have better consulted his Reputation, than by matching himself with so weak an Adversary. But if his Honour be diminished in the choice of his Antagonist, it is sufficiently recompens'd in the election of his

³ *Ibid.*, pp. 201–2.
⁴ He is talking about correcting the printing of a play for a new edition.

Cause: which being the weaker, in all appearance, as combating the received Opinions of the best Ancient and Modern Authors, will add to his glory, if he overcome; and to the opinion of his generosity, if he be vanquished, since he ingages at so great odds; and, so like a Cavalier, undertakes the protection of the weaker party. I have only to fear on my own behalf, that so good a cause as mine may not suffer by my ill management, or weak defence; yet I cannot in Honour but take the Glove when 'tis offer'd me: though I am only a Champion by succession; and no more able to defend the right of *Aristotle* and *Horace*, than an infant *Dimock* to maintain the Title of a King.[5]

It would be absurd to say that this is not close to speech: its relation to the urbane talk of Dryden's circle is clearly necessary. The feat of manners of paying compliments to his opponent in the act of insinuating that he has obviously the worse argument and all authority against him comes from a writer in no danger of forgetting that he is a member of a social world, to whose members he is talking. All the same, this is true *writing*. In Dryden we find, dependably, a union of rhythm and syntax that we may recognize (however we envy Dryden's fluidity and mastery) as our own. The periodic phrasing, still important, is the obedient servant of syntactic structure.

Dryden's style is actually not 'plain' if by plain one means the works of modern exponents like Ernest Hemingway or Lord Beaverbook. Dryden's sentences are often long. They are nicely various in construction. Never, never do they give us the old sensation of the wander. We never have to ask why his sentences are shaped as they are, why they end as they do, for the shape always seems so beautifully that of the sense. Dryden has really mastered a way of acclimatizing complex syntactic structures in English, without any tension between grammar and rhythm.

This is not to say that his punctuation would always satisfy a Victorian schoolmaster. The second sentence of the Epistle Dedicatory of this same *Indian Emperor* in both the first and second edition has no finite verb! Sentences without finite verbs are not uncommon in Dugdale and as late as Berkeley's *Principles of Human Knowledge* (1710). There is even one in *Middlemarch*.[6] I think they show *security*: Dryden is so sure of the well-formed sentence that he can take liberties with it.

Dryden's change of expression was not quite like Cranmer's: Dryden was not a great technical innovator in prose or verse, and plenty of others began writing modern prose at about the same time. I think it is fair to take Dryden as the key prose influence, however, for much the

5 John Dryden, Preface to 2nd edn of *The Indian Emperor*, 1668.
6 A paragraph beginning 'Especially from Mr Borthrop Trumbull' halfway through ch. XXXII starts in mid-sentence.

same reason that he is more obviously the founder of a long-lasting style of verse: he was the nearest his age came to having a literary dictator, and his prose set the fashion. Dryden managed to seize a moment and make a style out of it—unlike Abraham Cowley, a writer perhaps of greater genius, equally well thought of by the Royal Society, and for a few years of greater fame. The contrast between the imaginative excesses of Cowley's verse and the restraint of his prose is very remarkable. As poet, for a very few years at the beginning of the 1660s, he continued the metaphysical tradition uninhibited by the restraints of taste to be found even in Donne, but his prose Essays (he wrote essays in verse as well) belong to the new age after the feeling had decisively changed. The two Cowleys fit together only awkwardly.

Much use is made by scholars of the term *Ciceronian* to characterize some of the English prose of the Renascence. My view is that Dryden is the real English Cicero, not by direct imitation of Cicero's long periods, and certainly not in putting periodic structure before syntax, but in showing and establishing once and for all how the 'text' sentence should be easily and fluently written in English. When in his first considerable prose work, the *Essay of Dramatic Poesy*, Dryden displays his learning, the Latin runs with the English like an elder brother. Dryden is not the first author to take Cicero as the great exemplar of civility, of good manners in the conduct of the state, but he is the first really to establish a way of doing likewise in English:

And yet, My Lord, this War of Opinions, you well know, has fallen out among the Writers of all Ages, and sometimes betwixt Friends. Only it has been prosecuted by some, like Pedants, with violence of words, and manag'd by others like Gentlemen, with Candour and Civility. Even *Tully* had a Controversie with his dear *Atticus*; and in one of his Dialogues makes him sustain the part of an Enemy in Philosophy, who in his Letters is his Confident of State, and made privy to the most weighty Affairs of the Roman Senate. And the same respect which was paid by *Tully* to *Atticus*, we find return'd to him afterwards by *Cæsar* on a like occasion, who answering his Book in praise of *Cato*, made it not so much his business to condemn *Cato*, as to praise *Cicero*.[7]

Only a genius capable of seizing a historic moment could write with such fluent naturalness.

Taking then a Barge which a Servant of *Lisideius* had provided for them, they made haste to shoot the Bridge, and left behind them that great fall of waters which hindred them from hearing what they desired: after which, having disingag'd themselves from many Vessels which rode at Anchor in the *Thames*,

---

[7] *Of Dramatick Poesy an Essay* by John Dreyden [*sic*], Henry Herringman, 1684, Epistle Dedicatory unfoliated; the first item collected in *The Works of Mr John Dryden*, Tonson, 1691—the earliest edition I could handily find.

and almost blockt up the passage towards *Greenwich*, they order'd the Watermen to let fall their Oares more gently; and then every one favouring his own curiosity with a strict silence, it was not long ere they perceiv'd the Air to break about them like the noise of distant Thunder, of or Swallows in a Chimney: those little undulations of sound, though almost vanishing before they reach'd them, yet still seeming to retain somewhat of their first horrour which they had betwixt the Fleets: after they had attentively listned till such time as the sound by little and little went from them; *Eugenius* lifting up his head, and taking notice of it, was the first who congratulated to the rest that happy Omen of our Nations Victory: adding, that we had but this to desire in confirmation of it, that we might hear no more of that noise which was now leaving the English Coast.[8]

The punctuation here is not strictly modern: perhaps the semi-colon after 'went from them' enacts a little pause, though more likely it is arbitrary; and all modern editors end a sentence at 'betwixt the Fleets'. It is nevertheless surely beyond dispute that these are complex, even Ciceronian sentences (the 'having disingag'd' coming before the subject 'they' makes a lengthier sentence than modern journalism would approve) but managed with an ease quite beyond the reach of Croll's 'Ciceronians' of earlier in the century.

I shall explore the belief that Dryden is especially Ciceronian in making a particular public world by a particular prose style. In the last quotation this is true even geographically: I find the evocation of this very civilized little group having their discussion during the most recent enemy incursion up the Thames vivid and delightful. This is an epitome of what in its own day was called 'good sense'. It need not follow that Dryden's (or Cicero's) is the best kind of prose, sense or world.

Dryden's being at home in the new world he was helping to create went much deeper than his opinions. He had a genuine regard and occasional envy for the kind of genius represented by Shakespeare, from whom he knew himself to be so different. In religion he ended up in what must have seemed to his sensible contemporaries a position of extremism and obscurantism, as an active Roman Catholic. The style, however, is the man himself and his world, and the style is never Shakespearean and never obscure and, except when he is being deliberately wild for some would-be tragic moment, never extreme.

The most recent biographer argues that Dryden's 'complexity of . . . inventions in [*The Hind and the Panther*] should stand as a powerful counterargument to those critics who still describe his work as a "poetry of statement".'[9] As one such, I regret I am unconvinced. Dryden is so consistently competent as almost to be wonderful. *All for*

[8] *Ibid.*, p. 2.
[9] James Anderson Winn, *John Dryden and his World*, New Haven, 1987, p. 427.

Love is the best pastiche of Shakespeare I know. The blank verse does not attain Shakespeare's fluidity, but who else's does? There is even imagery. Nevertheless the play's characteristic mode is statement as Shakespeare's is not. 'My love's a noble madness,' states Dryden's Cleopatra, though it is not altogether clear why she thinks it either mad or noble. She is not averse to the idea of doing 'some wild extravagance / Of love in public'. Antony rather coarsely reminisces about orgasm 'now and then', and states his eagerness for the next:

> I'm eager to return before I go
> For, all the pleasures I have known beat thick
> On my remembrance.—How I long for night!

This is gusto not passion, as in Dryden's emotionally coarse lyrics. The innocent Juliet gives a wonderful contrast in the real passion of the 'Gallop apace ye fiery-footed steeds' speech.

Leaving out of the present discussion all consideration of Dryden's great discovery of the Augustan back door into art by way of mock, burlesque, satire, it is true to say that the alternative to the 'sense' of Dryden's prose and verse statements is not Shakespearean imagination or passion but going crazy. Cleopatra asserts that

> Moderate sorrow
> Fits vulgar love, and for a vulgar man:
> But I have loved with such transcendent passion,
> I soared, at first, quite out of reason's view,
> And now am lost above it.[10]

But even this, unlike some of the flights in the heroic plays, when Dryden has followed his own prescription, 'loos'd the Reins, and bid his Muse run mad,'[11] is a rational description, not itself an expression of being beyond reason.

If rhythm is the joining of parts, Dryden's whole *oeuvre* has no rhythm. Shakespeare's verse belongs with his prose in the whole Shakespeare; Dryden's prose, along with what must seem the more characteristic part of his verse, demolishes the passionate-heroic efforts. As Purvis says, of *Marriage à la Mode*, 'It is not surprising, given their unconsciousness of how the other half lives, that the characters of the elevated action should frequently and solemnly employ the hyperboles

---

[10] All quotations from II. i; *Restoration Plays*, introd. Sir Edmund Gosse, new edn 1932.
[11] Cited C. J. Purvis, *The Offensive Art*, Gringley-on-the-Hill, 1991, p. 24. I gratefully acknowledge a large debt to this book and recommend this chapter, 'The Divided Sensibility: Dryden's Plays—and Shakespeare'. Cf. Fielding's *Tragedy of Tragedies or Tom Thumb the Great* for the riposte by the spirit of the age to Dryden's flights of tragedy. If it were not for Shakespeare I would say *Tom Thumb* is the funniest play in English.

and archaic conventions of love-making which the comic action treats with matter-of-course levity.'[12] This is what Eliot called the 'dissociation of sensibility'. It can be seen just by putting passages from Dryden's plays together and seeing that they *won't* be put together.

Dryden's prose is to Cranmer what his heroic or narrative couplets are to Shakespeare's blank verse. To say so is to suggest possible indebtedness, and I think this very likely. An Augustan writer who managed not only to salute *Paradise Lost* but to turn it, rhyming, into a libretto, would surely have been able to take the much more usable prose hints of Cranmer. It is not in doubt that Dryden often heard the Prayer Book, and he was a writer who would learn where he could. The basic similarity to Cranmer is in the perfect naturalness of the complex sentence in an English prose that is at the same time close to speech. The differences, however, are equally remarkable.

Dryden is so fluent, in prose or verse, that one has to make an effort to remember how much all his prose, and most of his couplets, leave out, even of John Dryden the man. *Sense* becomes an exclusive and reductive positive. Must it have been like this in the Restoration?

Andrew Marvell gives hints of what a genuine prose different from the Restoration establishment's might have been like. At best Marvell's prose bears the same relation to Dryden's prose as his verse to Dryden's verse. Marvell is not polite like Dryden, and in particular not like Addison. Marvell's defence of Calvin has the Augustan virtues of good sense and moderation, but with a not-always-genteel life that may remind one of the seriousness of Martin Marprelate:

and like a raging *Indian* (for in *Europe* it was never before practised) he[13] runs a *Mucke* (as they cal it there) stabbing every man he meets, till himself be knockt on the head. This here is the least pernicious of all his mischiefs: though it be no less in this & all his other Books, than to make the *German Protestancy* a reproachful Proverb, and to turn *Geneva* and *Calvin* into a Common-Place of Railing. I had always heard that *Calvin* was a good Scholar, and an honest Divine. I have indeed read that he spoke something contemptuously of our Liturgy: *Sunt in illo Libro quædam tolerabiles ineptiæ.* But that was a sin which we may charitably suppose he repented of on his death-bed. And if Mr. B*ayes* had some just quarrel to him on that or other account, yet for *Divinity's sake* he needed not thus have made a constant Pissing-place of his Grave.[14]

The mention of pissing does not suit that element within the Augustan

---

[12] Purvis, *The Offensive Art*, p. 31.

[13] This is the wretched Parker, who seems on my sampling to be as conceited and foolish as Marvell makes him.

[14] Andrew Marvell, *The Rehearsal Transpros'd*, [first part], 1672, p. 59; facsimile repr. Farnborough, 1971.

sensibility, later also offended by Pope, that tends towards the genteel. Marvell's syntactic management is that of the new world, but Marvell is even closer to speech than Dryden.

But it isn't a secure achievement. Marvell had difficulty in hitting on a prose mode. Though page by page he is a very entertaining and natural-sounding writer I confess I read his prose, most unlike his verse, with decreasing impetus. It is clear that Marvell was not himself altogether happy about his levity of tone, which contrasts remarkably with that of the very businesslike letters he wrote to the Corporation of Hull as their MP. It also contrasts with his last work of political controversy, *An Account of the Growth of Popery and Arbitrary Government in England*, of which Salgādo rightly says, 'The raillery and banter of the earlier pamphlets have disappeared.'[15] It is in *The Growth of Popery* that Marvell's contemporaneity with Bunyan is clearest, but the reaction into gravity seems as much an expression of strangeness in the new world as the earlier badinage. Marvell was irrepressible (some of his best parliamentary effects were practical jokes) but not really naturalized in the Restoration.

Marvell was not altogether alone, though. I will just mention a writer in whom I declare an interest, for I was his first modern publisher. Thomas Burnet, *The Remarker* as he called himself, is perfectly well mannered but shows an easy raciness in the pamphlets against Locke which reminds me of Marvell:

> Your general Principle of picking up all our Knowledge from our five Senses, I confess does not sit easily in my Thoughts, tho' you joyn Reflection to help us. I think the illiterate part of Mankind (which is far the greatest part) must have more compendious ways to know their Duty, than by long and obscure Deductions.
> . . . .
> I proceed now to another Difficulty in your Doctrine of the Soul, which I mentioned formerly. You think the Soul, when we are asleep, is without any Thoughts or Perceptions. I am still at a loss, I confess, how to frame any Idea of a *thoughtless, senseless, lifeless soul.* This Carcase of a Soul I cannot understand: If it neither have Cogitation, nor Extension, as you suppose, what Being or manner of Being it hath, I am not able to comprehend [. . .] However, you ought to tell us, how you bring the Soul out of this unintelligible State. What Cause can you assign able to produce the first Thought at the end of this Sleep and Silence, in a total Ecclipse and intermission of Thinking? Upon your Supposition, That all our Thoughts perish in sound Sleep, and all Cogitation is extinct, we seem to have a new Soul every Morning.[16]

---

[15] Marvell, *An Account of the Growth of Popery and Arbitrary Government in England*, 'Amsterdam', 1677; facsimile repr. introd. Gāmini Salgādo, Farnborough, 1971, unfoliated Introduction.

[16] Thomas Burnet, *Remarks upon an Essay concerning Humane Understanding in a Letter Address'd to the Author*, 1697, p. 4; *Second Remarks . . .* , 1697, pp. 16–17; cf. Thomas Burnet, *Remarks on John Locke*, ed. George Watson, Gringley-on-the-Hill, 1989.

The Remarker, Master of the Charterhouse and a very serious scholar who is said to have missed the archbishopric of Canterbury because of some unorthodoxies about hell, is racy enough not to care about an occasional anacoluthon. This is the very opposite of the loss of syntactic shape in sixteenth-century writers: they wander because they can do no other, Burnet is so confident in his speech-like grasp of syntactic structure that the occasional deviation matters to him no more than it did to Jane Austen writing her letters. Burnet can evidently write the beautifully clear prose of philosophical argumentation that one finds in Berkeley or David Hume, but he has a shade less decorum and more idiosyncratic insolence than either.

The Remarker seems to me a much more impressive prose writer than, for instance, Saintsbury's favourite Sir Thomas Browne. Browne, whose best-known work came out in 1643, survived into the age of the Royal Society, and writes with syntactic confidence, but overloads his prose with beauty of sound in a way that must be against the spirit of the new age without really offering to replace it. The *savouring* of sound-rhythms cannot be good in a prose-writer, even if done within the new syntactic control. One would not confuse Browne with the purple patches of Oscar Wilde, but his relation to ordinary prose is comparable.

I have not discovered whether Bunyan knew Cranmer's theological works. He certainly learned the lesson of Cranmer and Tyndale so effectively that he continued their tradition into a new age, and was for hundreds of years the most important channel leading from Cranmer to the prose of art.

Bunyan himself records that before his conversion he frequented his parish church;[17] it is indisputable that he was well enough acquainted with the Prayer Book to disapprove of it.[18] And of course his whole work hinges on quotations from the 1611 Bible.[19] One might have expected

---

[17] John Bunyan, *Grace Abounding to the Chief of Sinners*, para. 12. The possibility that Bunyan may have been writing of a non-Prayer-Book church of the Commonwealth seems to be denied by 'I adored, and that with great devotion, even all things (both the High-place, Priest, Clerk, Vestments, Service and what else) belonging to the Church.'

[18] 'The Common Prayer Book . . . a thing . . . patched together one piece at one time and another at another; a mere human invention and institution, which God is so far from owning of, that he expressly forbids it . . .' (Bunyan, *A Discourse touching Prayer*, *Works*, I, p. 628 b): and 'antichristian' (p. 640 b).

[19] He also knew the Geneva Bible, but seems to have had no scruples about using the version authorized by the monarch and used by the bishops. Surprisingly, Bunyan does not worry overmuch about absolute verbal accuracy. The most-used quotation in *Grace Abounding to the Chief of Sinners* appears on my count five times, complete or in part (paras. 113, 117, 131, 151, 180). There are numerous minor variations of wording, spelling and punctuation, but all the punctuation is quite correct by modern standards.

that if the tinker managed to avoid the Lilburne wander he would do so by way of being thoroughly Bible-based and paratactic. In fact Bunyan's prose is not simple if the standard of simplicity is, say, the Parker Chronicle. He consistently manages long complex sentences without strain.

Bunyan seems to have taken to a modern style without any great labour. His first publication, *Some Gospel Truths Opened according to the Scriptures* (1656), is not as fluent or as powerful as *Grace Abounding to the Chief of Sinners*, but at the least, beside the Puritan wanderers who survived into the same decade, or his learned contemporary Milton, is very competent. I have not been able to consult the first edition, but am confident of the general observation. The closeness to the speaking voice is the safeguard; much of the treatise is cast into a question-and-answer form:

But, perhaps thou wilt say, I am not only convinced of my sins against the law, but I have also some power against my sins, so that I do in some considerable measure abstain from those things that are forbidden in the law.[20]

No doubt the fluency came from Bunyan's extensive experience of preaching, though not all popular preachers are also fluent with the pen. The end of *The Doctrine of the Law and Grace Unfolded* (1659) is that of a hell-fire sermon:

Canst thou hear of Christ, his bloody sweat and death, and not be taken with it, and not be grieved for it, and also converted by it? If so, I might lay thee down several considerations to stir thee up to mend thy pace towards heaven; but I shall not; there is enough written already to leave thy soul without excuse, and to bring thee down with a vengeance into hell-fire, devouring fire, the lake of fire, eternal everlasting fire; O to make thee swim and roll up and down in the flames of the furnace of fire![21]

There is no difficulty in seeing the simple rhetorical force of the repeated *fire* as the last syllable of four *commata* and the rising rhythm (emphatically not *cursus*[22]) of the end, iamb plus two anapaests. This is already, however, a genuine syntactic prose ('not only . . . but also . . . so that'), and not a speech written down. Much of Bunyan's best prose was written in prison when the speaking voice at best had presumably to be imagined—unless he composed aloud like Yeats.

I think it is *Grace Abounding to the Chief of Sinners* that establishes

---

[20] Bunyan, *Works*, II, p. 153 b.   [21] *Ibid.*, I, p. 575 b.
[22] Bunyan did of course produce *cursus* forms '. . . bound down with the chains and bonds of eternal darkness' (*velox*: *Grace Abounding to the Chief of Sinners* para. 5). An interesting experiment would be to discover whether any of the recognized *schemes of words* are, despite the declaration of plainness quoted below, *not* found in *Grace Abounding to the Chief of Sinners*.

Bunyan's critical importance in the history of English prose—not just technically: I would not make the claim if I did not also believe that the book is the best autobiography in English. *Grace Abounding to the Chief of Sinners* is magnificent in its Cranmer-like mastery of simultaneous syntactic and periodic structure. The paragraphs are numbered; many of them consist of one sentence:

Having thus in few words given you a taste of the sorrow and affliction that my Soul went under by the guilt and terror that this my wicked thought did lay me under; and having given you also a touch of my deliverance therefrom, and of the sweet and blessed comfort that I met with afterwards, (which comfort dwelt above a twelvemonth with my heart, to my unspeakable admiration) I will now (God willing) before I proceed any further, give you in a word or two, what, as I conceive, was the cause of this Temptation; and also after that, what advantage at the last it became unto my Soul.[23]

Bunyan's syntactic competence does not explain his power as a prose writer, though it is one of the necessary conditions. I need the old word *enactment* for Bunyan's prose. The frequent well-rhythmized images of physical movement are no more the sign of an unintellectual mind than the similar things in Cranmer; rather of a writer who has a Shakespearean capacity for expressing the spiritual by way of the physical. Imagining during his imprisonment the possibility of being hanged, and fearing how he would conduct himself on the occasion,

Wherefore, thought I, the point being thus, I am for going on, and venturing my eternal state with Christ, whether I have comfort or no; if God doth not come in, thought I, I will leap off the Ladder even blindfold into Eternitie, sink or swim, come heaven, come hell; Lord Jesus, if thou wilt catch me, do; I vvill venture for thy Name.[24]

The imagined leap is at the same time literally a physical one and a leap of faith into eternity. The energetic physical imagery used in genuine thinking is very Cranmerian.

At the beginning Bunyan makes a remark about style:

I could have enlarged much in this my discourse of my temptations and troubles for sin, as also of the merciful kindness and working of God with my Soul: I could also have stept into a stile much higher then this in which I have here discoursed, and could have adorned all things more then here I have seemed to do: but I dare not: God did not play in convincing of me; the Devil did not play in tempting of me; neither did I play when I sunk as into a bottomless pit, when the pangs of hell caught hold upon me: wherefore I may not play in my relating of them, but be plain and simple, and lay

---

[23] Bunyan, *Grace Abounding to the Chief of Sinners*, 1666; facsimile repr. Menston, 1970, para. 190. In the whole of the first edition I noticed only one old-fashioned unsyntactic period, where the break between paras. 221 and 222 comes within a compound sentence. Semi-colons are usually used much as we use them.

[24] *Ibid.*, para. 270. The compositor was running short of *w*s.

down the thing as it was: He that liketh it, let him receive it; and he that does not, let him produce a better. Farewel.[25]

What seems to the author to follow naturally from the avoidance of 'play', the transparent expression of experience, is actually a great compliment to the secure establishment of a style. There is, of course, no such thing as direct recording of experience without style, and not every style would be capable of doing justice to Bunyan's agonies and ecstasies. His style gives the impression that *anything* can be said in it. J. A. Froude rather looks down on Bunyan's puritan phraseology. 'In the language of the time, he became convinced of sin,' says Froude, who reports the experience in the language of the late nineteenth century, when such talk was 'cant'.[26] Bunyan made 'the language of the time' sufficient to express, in prose, exultations, agonies and love, which is more than can be said either for the language of Froude's paraphrases[27] or for Bunyan's trend-setting contemporaries of the Royal Society.

The early-twentieth-century notion of 'stream of consciousness' neglects the difference between experience and the sense we make of it in language, but can perhaps be used of conversations (Miss Bates's stream of consciousness *is* her flow of talk), soliloquies, or some uses of quotation. It may be argued that when the texts of the Bible fill Bunyan's mind he does give us his consciousness by quoting them. This is still tricky not least because isolated texts evidently meant much more to him than to the ordinary reader. They depend on the narrative prose framework; but within it they convey the terrors and comforts that the Bible was to Bunyan.

Nobody would compare Bunyan with Marvell as a poet: at best Bunyan's verse is ruggedly sufficient (though his best-known hymn does not deserve the crude enfeeblement it has received from the editors of the *English Hymnal*). But though the prose of both Bunyan and Marvell attains a level of (to invoke the Leavis word) *life* never reached by Dryden's prose, Bunyan was more creative in his prose writings than Marvell in his.

---

[25] *Ibid.*, Preface.
[26] J. A. Froude, *Bunyan*, English Men of Letters series, repr. 1885, p. 35.
[27] Hale White made a similar criticism the basis of his excellent *John Bunyan*, Literary Lives series, 1905.

7   The prose world

The word *world* comes from two roots, the *-ld* (from the same origin as *old*), meaning more or less *age*, and *wor* from a root meaning *man* as in modern English *were*wolf, and common in Old English compounds as well as the simple form *wer*. Snorri Sturluson's report of Ragnarøk, the twilight of the gods, quotes a terrible line in which the equivalent of our *world* is *verǫld*:

> Vindǫld, vargǫld,   áðr verǫld steypisk

—very literally: wind-age, wolf-age, before man-age throws itself down. (We certainly live in the first stage of this, the wind-age: no doubt the rest will follow.) I want to appeal to this basic Germanic sense of *aeon-of-mankind*, a sense which allows the Greek *eis tous aionas* and similar phrases to go well in English as *world without end*.

Any bit of language makes its sense in a particular context and a particular situation. A poem or even a novel is the context within which all the parts have sense. 'Lady Bertram was quite talkative.'[1] Coming at page 333 this means something quite different from what it would have meant on page 1, and the difference depends on our keeping in mind Lady Bertram's role throughout the preceding pages.

The ancient topic of *deixis*[2] is still of interest to linguists who look at sentences like 'If you come and stand here you will be able to see the top of the tower', where the meaning will obviously depend on who 'you' is, where 'here' is, when 'now' is, which tower and so on. The essay from which these examples come points out that in Donne's poem 'The Flea' 'thou', 'this flea' and the like 'establish a situation of direct address involving a speaking *persona* and a (silent) addressee.'[3] Here the context of words like *flea* is the same as an imagined context of situation without

---

[1] Jane Austen, *Mansfield Park*, vol. II, ch. 2.
[2] Deixis comes from Apollonius Dyscolus (*Quae Supersunt*, vol. I, pp. 5–6) by way of Priscian.
[3] Elena Semino, 'Building on Keith Green's "Deixis and the Poetic Persona": Further Reflections on Deixis in Poetry', *Language and Literature* I. ii, 1992, pp. 139, 136.

which we shall not understand the poem. 'Shut the door!' will make different senses if said to the little boy who habitually forgets, to the servants in the hall if treason is suspected[4] and, retroactively (for time as well as place can affect sense), if the prelude to smacking a child who turns out to be deaf.[5]

The obvious difficulty for linguists is that neither situations nor large contexts can be brought within grammar. Presuppositions are an even worse problem for the grammarian. Every time we say anything we presuppose a particular situation or context; but many presuppositions quite inaccessible to grammar are unstatedly present in everything we say or think.[6] All science, for instance, depends on an absolute pre-supposition of the invariancy of nature. (It has to be presupposed that the standard metre is the same length this morning as last night. This could not be proved scientifically; the proof would depend on the standard metre.) I presuppose that during that same night I was alive continuously. History would be impossible without the presupposition of the unity of time, but a historian who bothered to say so would be at best eccentric.

Knowledge has in common with presuppositions that we rely on both in thinking. (The reason that knowledge is less interesting than discovery is just that we know it already.) Facts, however, can be looked up, but not presuppositions. Presuppositions only exist as the conditions for what we say, by definition ordinarily unstated. Presuppositions are nevertheless 'swallowed down' with language. This is not, in any straightforward manner, implication; presuppositions need not be implied but are that which the world is consistent with. The widest context of any locution is a language, and the widest situation the world it presupposes.

There is an obvious danger of vagueness if we start talking about the world, and even more so if the article is indefinite. On the other hand, what I am referring to is only what for many years has been current in literary studies under the general heading of *background* and which has recently re-emerged, newly spiced with political *parti-pris*, under the name of *the new historicism*. Works of literature are understood, if at all, in the context of their world. The traditional literary fallacy is to try to get at the relevant world *first*, before slotting the poet in. The more interesting, one might say more wonderful thing, is that in actuality the process works the other way round and we somehow get into a world from what we read, see or hear.

[4] Cf. *Thomas of Woodstock*, I. i.   [5] Mark Twain, *Huckleberry Finn*, ch. 23, end.
[6] Cf. discussions in R. G. Collingwood, *An Essay on Metaphysics*, Oxford, 1940, and L. Wittgenstein, *On Certainty*, Oxford, 1969.

To learn a language is to get one kind of whole context for particular utterances. A whole language makes one context which has, as we say, to be kept in mind. I know Chaucer and his contemporaries well enough to be able to make the claim, bigger than it looks, that I can read them 'in Middle English': i.e. in the context of their language as well as its grammar and lexis. (The only alternative is to read in translation, conscious or not, into some other language.) I acquired this knowledge more by reading Chaucer than by reading the notes and studying the dictionaries, though that has to be done too.

A text, however long, will not contain more than a fraction of its language, even if it is the only surviving fragment of that language; but it may nevertheless by working within the whole language give at least a broad hint about the life of which the language is the form.

This whole historical aspect of literary studies proceeds, of course, from the observation that world changes with language. For instance, a word in Homer comes from a lexicon that is not the same as Plato's or that of New Testament Greek: which is one way of saying that the world of Homer was different from those of Socrates or the early church. There is unlikely ever to be a watertight linguistics of world, but that does not imply any unreality in phrases like 'the world of Homer'. This 'world' is partly a matter of what the experienced reader finds surprising. For instance if Grendel's Mother is unsurprising because in those olden days they expected to find a monster in every mere one has *not* got into the world of *Beowulf*. A fragment may be a misleading example of a world, and of course the more we know the better; but the experience remains that a world can get carried on the shoulders of almost anything except possibly an atlas.

If all utterances depend on presuppositions, if we talk *as if* the world were of such-and-such a kind, *what* kind may be gathered from the *way* we talk. The sense that there undoubtedly is in phrases like 'the world of Homer' is a stylistic sense. The *style* of *The Battle of Maldon* says more about the survival of a Germanic heroic world late in the Anglo-Saxon period than could the brute events the poem records. In this way we may get from the *how* of a style to *what* was presupposed to be the case. As R. W. Southern says, 'There is something to be learnt even about Anselm's theology in observing the form in which he cast his sentences and the linguistic effects at which he aimed.'[7] To read Anselm or Homer or *Njal's Saga* is to become a sort of honorary critical member of a world, the relation with which may range from naturalization to heartfelt rejection. (After all the same is true of one's own world.)

---

[7] Eadmer's *Life of St Anselm*, p. xxviii.

All this may be pointing to mysteries, but is still only a development from the commonsense observation that the way we talk says much about the world we live in.

Often the world just changes, almost as often without anyone noticing; but occasionally a change of style can be deliberately aimed at changing a world, as with contemporary use of fabricated forms of 'inclusive language'. This cannot be said to involve propositions or implications, for even odd forms like *(s)he*—purely, of course, of the written language, for there is no way of saying *(s)he*—do not *assert* that male and female humans are equal. But it will hardly be denied that that is the sense made, or that the intention is to change the world accordingly.

'World' in this sense is Leavis's 'third realm', which belongs only to individual human beings but constitutes what we have in common.

I have been emphasizing prose as a genuine form of *making* in language and therefore poetic, but the belief that prose and poetry are antonyms is not just silly, even if generalized into something true of all prose and all poetry. All the verse traditions confer certain possibilities and powers as well, sometimes, as restrictions, that one does not associate with prose. My leading medieval example is from that amazing literary hothouse, Iceland. The century of the sagas is of course one of the great ages of prose literature, making a very distinctive world. Following a common pattern it succeeds an age of heroic verse that survives, alas! only in fragments. Snorri Sturluson (*d.* 1241), to whom much of that survival is to be credited, narrates in the *Prose Edda* many of the old pre-Christian legends. His account of the affair between Frey and Skirnir does manage to capture something mysterious. It is nevertheless so much more ordinarily sensible than 'Skírnirsmál', the poem on the same subject and presumably his source. It quite often happens that Snorri recognizes the limitations of his prose. He tries to narrate the Twilight of the Gods in prose, and in a rare lapse makes the death of Odin so brisk as to appear an anticlimax; apparently realizing the impossibility of the effort, Snorri then begins to quote verse instead, and it must be acknowledged that the passage in consequence gains enormously in power. Numbers of the sagas from time to time give up the effort to render in prose stories that really need verse. Hamlet's soliloquies demand verse as much as Cædmon's hymn or Bede's death-song. Prose by its nature makes worlds different from Homer's or Virgil's. The trap is to suppose that all prose worlds are prosaic in much the same way.

We cannot even assume that all prose used for what we regard as prose purposes will be businesslike. Of the prose of the Ottoman Empire in the nineteenth century it is written:

The peasant could not understand a Turkish newspaper even when it was read to him . . . Some officials were contemptuous of simplicity; even at the end of the Tanzimat [reforming] period it was possible to write a thirteen-page document in two sentences. Punctuation was almost unknown.[8]

Shades of Milton!

I mentioned the well-known fact that prose tends to appear rather late in the history of cultures. When prose ceases to be precious, prose constitutes a public community. The prose ages do have that much in common. This is true both of classical Greece and Rome and of the more surprising example of Anglo-Saxon England, as well as our great prose age, the Augustan. In the prose of King Alfred's Wessex, equally with that of the age of Queen Anne, we meet the shape of a world. The two worlds are, however, quite different.

Erich Auerbach showed convincingly, by the good old methods of 'close reading', that Latin prose under the Carolingians did not become the ordinary language of thought in the way of Latin prose earlier (or, I would say, later).[9] This is to say either that Charlemagne presided over a kind of nostalgic vision rather than a world, or that his world was without form, or to be created only posthumously in epic poetry. To my not very expert ear Anselm's beautifully lucid Latin prose brings in a new world, in the middle age of which Aquinas writes much more like a tenured academic.

The insufficiency of the Dictionary on prose quoted above is in its confusing a formal linguistic definition with a historical judgement. What we take so for granted that we build it into every sentence we write is nothing like a human universal, but a mark of the distinctly modern phase of history. It is no exaggeration to say that we make the modern world as we make prose. Without the common easy possession, without newspapers, television scripts, exam scripts, advertising and government circulars, it would not be our world run differently, it would be a different world, though if we conducted our affairs in blank verse,[10] that

---

[8] Roderic H. Davison, *Reform in the Ottoman Empire, 1856–1876*, Princeton, 1963, p. 176. Let us not inquire how, if there was no punctuation, anyone knew where the sentences were supposed to end.

[9] Auerbach, *Literary Language*, pp. 117–18.

[10] Writing blank verse is easier than prose—arguably, though not for everyone: as we observed, the drilling in the schools for centuries was aimed at prose not verse, so prose is second nature *in our world*. If verse were taught in the same way as prose, we would make verses easier than prose, as I believe was done in Shakespeare's day. Practice is all that's needed. Once or twice, exasperated by my students' fears, I have extemporized blank verse (no trouble!) for round about a quarter of an hour, without more strain than I would have with prose. This note has taken two minutes to write, and proves my point for anyone who doubts.

too might rapidly grow prosaic, as it did in the eighteenth century. But our modern prose is not all worlds world without end.

In the decade after the restoration of King Charles II a number of things fell together, or were pushed, into our modern prose world.

The large historical perception of a crisis in the second half of the seventeenth century has been the work of the literary critics, often those who assumed a non-Cartesian philosophy of language. The basic perceptions were already made by Johnson.

I had lent him 'An Account of Scotland, in 1702', written by a man of various enquiry, an English chaplain to a regiment stationed there. JOHNSON. 'It is sad stuff, Sir, miserably written, as books in general then were. There is now an elegance of style universally diffused. No man now writes so ill as Martin's Account of the Hebrides is written. A man could not write so ill, if he should try. Set a merchant's clerk now to write, and he'll do better.'[11]

Whether Boswell's narrative here is minute-by-minute chronological I don't know, but the transition to the next topic is almost necessary: 'a certain female friend's "laxity of narration and inattention to truth"': Mrs Thrale's 'romancing' denied the prose sensibility. Boswell records as his own contribution the same day, 'to have clear notions on any subject, we must have recourse to analytick arrangement,' with which Johnson agreed: 'Sir, it is what everybody does, whether they will or no.' That evening they were talking about 'the best English sermons for style', and Johnson said,

All the latter preachers have a good style. Indeed, nobody now talks much of style: every body composes pretty well. There are no such inharmonious periods as there were a hundred years ago.

Two days later Johnson replied to 'Mr Harris of Salisbury''s opinion that 'the chief excellence of our language is numerous prose' by commenting on Sir William Temple, on whose style he once told Boswell (1750) he had founded his own:

Sir William Temple was the first writer who gave cadence to English prose. Before this time they were careless of arrangement and did not mind whether a sentence ended with an important word or an insignificant word, or with what part of speech it was concluded.

The author Johnson uses as a contrast with Temple will not surprise us.

Mr Langton, who had now joined us, commended Clarendon. JOHNSON. 'He is objected to for his parentheses, his involved clauses, and his want of harmony. But he is supported by his matter. It is, indeed, owing to a plethora of matter that his style is so faulty . . . —To be distinct, we must talk *analytically*. If we

11 Boswell, *Life of Johnson*, 7 April 1778.

analyse language, we must speak of it grammatically; if we analyse argument, we must speak of it logically.'

As well as being analytick, clear, truthful, eighteenth-century prose is also 'numerous' and periodic, and the emphasis here is on the latter rhetorical qualities, conflated with syntax in the remark on Temple. *But* Johnson concluded the discussion of sermon style with, 'We have no sermons addressed to the passions, that are good for anything.'

Together, these make a recognition of a changed world that later critics have elaborated. Matthew Arnold's characterizations of eight-eenth-century prose, which he contrasts with Milton's, are one of my *points de repère*, and I take the chance of recommending his Preface to *The Six Chief Lives from Johnson's 'Lives of the Poets'*,[12] as just about his best discussion of what he means by 'prose and reason' and why what the phrase points to is both necessary to civilized life and limiting. I have already appealed to the remarkable historical insight expressed in Eliot's phrase 'the dissociation of sensibility'. F. R. Leavis was absorbed life-long with the subject of the great change brought about in the 1660s, perhaps his most important treatment being in his Clark Lectures, for instance:

When we ask how it was that modern prose appeared so decisively in the first decade of the Restoration, with an effect of having prevailed over-night, the answer is an account of the total movement of civilization.[13]

This 'total movement' is just what I mean by the changed world.

Why scholastic philosophy in general and Aristotle in particular came in for so much abuse in the seventeenth century is a mystery. Hobbes's account of language is very Aristotelian at places like 'The generall use of Speech, is to transferre our Mentall Discourse, into Verbal'[14]: 'Words, which are but Pictures of the Thought', as Cowley puts it in 'To the Royal Society'. The members of the Royal Society and the Modists are first cousins in the same philosophical family.[15] Aristotle could at least as plausibly have been taken as patron.

---

[12] Matthew Arnold, Preface to *The Six Chief Lives from Johnson's 'Lives of the Poets'*, 1878, repr. in the 3rd series of *Essays in Criticism*, 1910.

[13] F. R. Leavis, *English Literature in Our Time and the University*, 1969, pp. 93–4. Leavis specifically identifies his theme with Eliot's phrase 'dissociation of sensibility' (*Ibid.*, p. 96).

[14] Thomas Hobbes, 'Of Speech', *Leviathan* I. iv; introd. A. D. Lindsay, 1914; repr. 1957, p. 13. This Everyman has a text much less heavily edited than Michael Oakeshott's, Oxford, 1945.

[15] Cf. Vivian Salmon, '"Philosophical" Grammar in John Wilkins's "Essay"', repr. in Subbiondo, *John Wilkins and 17th-Century British Linguistics*, pp. 206–37. Salmon notices Wilkins's similarity to the Modists.

The development of the modern grammar of the sentence and the final establishment of the newer syntactic punctuation are part of the same 'total movement' as the refurbished and newly confident but still Aristotelian conception of the relation of thought, sense and expression. The new grammar provided the equipment for defining linguistically the form of language that can make truthful statements. The linguists and philosophers of the seventeenth century actually made a better shot at putting Aristotle's programme into operation than Aristotle and his medieval disciples were able, for at last the well-formed sentence, understood grammatically, became (amongst other things) the same as a single thought, capable of making a proposition about the external world. So, as Collingwood said,

The logician's proposition seemed to me a kind of ghostly double of the grammarian's sentence . . . Grammar recognizes a form of discourse called the sentence, and among sentences . . . one kind which express statements. In grammatical phraseology, these are indicative sentences; and logicians have almost always tried to conceive the 'unit of thought', or that which is either true or false, as a kind of logical 'soul' whose linguistic 'body' is the indicative sentence.[16]

Since well before Locke, the predominant tradition of Western thought has been to sneer at disputes about words and to try to concentrate instead on things, as when Robert Greville Lord Brooke begins his redoubtable *Discourse opening the nature of that episcopacie, which is exercised in England*: 'I Ayme not at *Words*, but *Things*; not loving to fight with *Shadowes*.'[17] Words are 'shadows' because only signs of ideas which in turn are only mental representations of things. This part of the traditional picture surely got its come-uppance once and for all in Book III of *Gulliver's Travels*, with the philosopher who carried round with him a set of things, at some of which he pointed rather than utter well-formed sentences. It is not superfluous to notice that *thing* is a word not a thing. But to the extent that this odd idea of the duty of language was ever workable, it was made to work in the late seventeenth century. The primacy of the indicative was reaffirmed.

The syntactically well-formed third person present or past indicative active sentence, making propositions about objects in the external world, suggests what, with great refinement, goes on in physics. The birth of modern science was not accidentally contemporary with the new style and the new grammar. But still, it was not quite the same thing.

[16] R. G. Collingwood, *An Autobiography*, Oxford, 1939, p. 34.
[17] Haller, *Tracts on Liberty*, II, p. 45.

In the controversies about seventeenth-century prose I am generally speaking with R. F. Jones, and in particular with his follower Robert Adolph, and against Morris Croll (with all due gratitude for Croll's erudition) because Jones shares, and Croll quite astonishingly stands out against, the basic perception of the critics that in the decade beginning in 1660 there was a great change in prose and world. Jones's thesis that the new prose is a product of the new science is, all the same, too simple.

The Royal Society of London for the Improving of Natural Knowledge naturally figures in any account of our prose age. Science seems to me much more than the 'marriage of convenience' between nature and thinking that Stillman would make it. Science is of course a human construction: science may be one of the fruits of the tree of knowledge but is not itself found growing on any tree. This still seems to me a love match between partners meant for each other. The world is so, we discover that it is so; the knowledge is a construct but of, let's hope, what really is the case, or what if it is not the case will be contradicted by nature's answer to experiment. The human and social nature of science need not deny that science can observe (rather than invent) what really happens and formulate (rather than invent) laws to explain it. In the right place the Royal Society programme is irrefutable. The right place is, generally speaking, the lab.

What happened, however, was that great efforts were made to generalize the scientific modes of language to all forms of thought. When Bishop Wilkins not only invented a very Aristotelian artificial language but offered its frame of categories and operations (he will not admit verbs) as *universal*, not just scientific, he was trying to impose the scientific as universally valid. Wilkins's universal language is a way of insisting that the making of true propositions about the external world is *the* mode of discourse, an insistence that has of course been repeated on a large scale since the end of the seventeenth century. It is still too much of a simplification to think of the new prose as just generalized science.

Scientists certainly had an obsessive consciousness of the importance of prose style. Adolph has a bibliography four pages long of works 'in which the . . . plain style of the seventeenth century is defended or at least described'.[18] Sprat's doctrine of style in his *History of the Royal Society* is explicit, and its connection with a world clear, though Sprat's stylistics is paradoxical and in a tradition of paradox. He wants an unrhetorical language, restricted to the proper making of propositions, and a dictionary modelled on that of the Académie Française. He warns

---

[18] Adolph, *The Rise of Modern Prose Style*, p. 359.

against 'this vicious abundance of *Phrase*, this trick of *Metaphors*', these 'seeming Mysteries; upon which *we Writers*, and *Speakers*, look so bigg'. The ancients 'had tir'd out the *Sun*, and *Moon*, and *Stars* with their similitudes.'[19] (Cf. Bunyan's epigraph to *The Pilgrim's Progress*, actually a couple of years later, 'I have used similitudes.') The paradox is that Sprat's language is itself imaginative and rhetorical: the sun is not *literally* worn out, any more than the table in the philosophy department groaning under the weight of ostensive definitions. The imagination is denounced in a quite strongly imaginative way.

In this Sprat is but following the philosopher who became in old age a sort of court jester to King Charles II, for Hobbes too denounced metaphor with Elizabethan metaphorical exuberance. Some of Hobbes's best things are metaphorical. Leviathan itself is a metaphor, represented in the famous frontispiece as an emblem. When Hobbes says that the Papacy 'is no other, than the *Ghost* of the deceased *Romane Empire*, sitting crowned upon the grave thereof',[20] the 'no other than' is part of the fun, not a deliberate denial that figurative language is being employed, which could hardly be plausible in the middle of the saucy and magnificent epic simile that Oakeshott calls '*Comparison of the papacy with the kingdom of fairies*'. This is the work of a rhetorician. The archaic *thereof* produces just the sort of cadence the same word is often used for in the Bible.

Even Wilkins writes metaphorically. (Wilkins's artificial language does allow metaphor, but only if explicitly signalled: which seems to me to make it a kind of simile.) In the very paragraph in which he remarks the regrettable impossibility of translating idiomatic expressions straight from one language to another, Wilkins complains that 'this grand imposture of Phrases hath almost eaten out solid knowledge in all professions.'[21] Sprat's paradoxically rhetorical anti-rhetoric also anticipated the great philosopher of sense, John Locke, whose own writing is a distinguished and lively body of the new prose.[22] The zenith of this paradox came two centuries after Locke in imagist poetics, when T. E. Hulme argued in prose of real trenchancy and imaginative life that prose is necessarily opposed to poetry.

[19] Sprat, *The History of the Royal Society*, pp. 112, 416. For Wilkins's contribution, see Francis Christensen, 'John Wilkins and the Royal Society's Reform of Prose Style', in Subbiondo, *John Wilkins and 17th-Century British Linguistics*, pp. 135–52, and Stillman, *The New Philosophy*.

[20] Hobbes, *Leviathan*, ch. 47, p. 381.

[21] Quoted in R. F. Jones, 'Science and Language in England of the Mid-Seventeenth Century', repr. in Fish, *Seventeenth-Century Prose*, p. 103.

[22] Cf. a good commentary in Harding, *Words into Rhythm*, pp. 125 ff. Cf. also Roger Elliott, '*Discourses that Pretend to Inform or Instruct*', Gringley-on-the-Hill, 1987. Take the trouble to find this excellent short account of Locke's style!

And so to the famous culmination of the Royal Society programme: 'a constant Resolution, to reject all the amplification, digressions and swellings of style: to return back to the primitive purity and shortness, when men delivered so many *things*, almost in an equal number of *words*'. (Cf. the already mentioned improvement adopted by Swift's Professor who applied Occam's razor to the words and carried around the things.)

They have exacted from all their members, a close, naked, natural way of speaking; positive expressions; clear senses; a native easiness: bringing all things as near the Mathematical plainness as they can.[23]

This is still quite metaphorical, unless it is just muddled, for how is speaking naked and how is language natural?

I agree with a recent critic's remark that 'The tension between the figural action of the text and its frequently expressed hostility to figuration needs to be explained, not explained away.'[24] My purpose, however, demands only that we notice the strangeness. 'An unmetaphorical style you shall in vain seek for.'[25] It must be very strange that intelligent men in the act of trying to write unmetaphorically did not notice this, but I think the paradox gives us a clue to the success of the Royal Society programme and prose, which are not to be explained altogether by a disinterested love of science.

Jones is rightly corrected by later scholars who point out that many parsons were as attached to 'the plain style' as the scientists, even when they were not one and the same person. The members of the Royal Society of course had an influence out of all proportion to their number, but even Sprat and Wilkins reached more people by way of sermons. Science belongs to the new world, but so do manners. For Boyle, civility and science are more or less inseparable and jointly constitute a rebuke to the rule of the saints. The emotional and imaginative charge of 'natural philosophy', without which the new style would not have got far, is not itself ascribable to 'natural philosophy'. There is a quasi religious fervour about it that belongs more to a whole world than to science.

'Natural' is used obsessively, and so persuasively that some people still think natural what the seventeenth-century philosophers tell us to be so. This is the generation that establishes as 'natural' a view of language which Wittgenstein demonstrated to be just *wrong*. This

---

[23] Sprat, *The History of the Royal Society*, p. 113.
[24] Stillman, *The New Philosophy*, p. 36. Richard W. Kroll argues (*The Material Word*, Baltimore, 1991) that the Restoration and Royal Society writers did not think of language as transparent; he makes much of their use of Epicurus. I am not persuaded.
[25] Thomas Carlyle, *Sartor Resartus*, I. xi, 'Prospective'.

natural is certainly not a product of nature or simply of that disciplined kind of thinking about nature we have come to call science. *Reason, truth* and a noticeably artificial *nature* that go together into a rather reductive *good sense* make the sensibility of one particular age, one that may still seem natural to us to the extent that we still live in that age.

The *History of the Royal Society* itself had, amongst more strictly scientific aims, some that could be equally called political or rhetorical. The *History* of a society only 'Royal' since the year of the revised Prayer Book, 1662, and only about twenty years old, was completed in haste, to combat the recrudescence of fanaticism which was making use of the Plague of 1665 and Fire of 1666. The religious maniacs Defoe later reported stalking the plague-stricken streets were to be deflated by sense in its scientific aspect. The *History* presents itself as anti-fanaticism. 'Many fantastical terms' have been 'introduc'd by our *Religious Sects*'[26] but now 'mens minds are somewhat settled, their Passions allai'd.'[27] The newly refined plain language is to seal the settlement of passion and the recession of fanaticism. Much more than a disinterested love of science went into this: it was a policy for saving a new-made world which, after all, was a literary world as well.

Cope and Jones speculate that Dryden may have seen the *History* before publication and that his *Essay of Dramatick Poesy* may owe something to it, or that the influence may have been of Dryden on Sprat.[28] Either way, there is more than a coincidence of spirit between the two.

The world-view of the dominant spirits of the Restoration, though much opposed to the rule of the saints, and devoted to moderation, was not always held moderately, nor is it moderate in its realism. Aristotelian extremism must be a paradox, but that is what the Restoration world offers, and the modern world still to a large extent accepts, as 'natural'.

'At the end of the seventeenth century reason, commonsense, moderation, was seized upon with passionate intensity . . . Men abandoned themselves to "reason" as in the immediately preceding age they had fought "like mad or drunk / For dame Religion as for punk".'[29] How else could such a significant movement of the human spirit have succeeded?

The climax of Sprat's prophecy to his age, after the times of the 'wild amazing mens minds, with *Prodigies*, and conceits of *Providence*' which 'has been one of the most considerable causes of those spiritual distractions, of which our Country has long bin the *Theater*', is that

---

[26] Sprat, *The History of the Royal Society*, p. 42.   [27] *Ibid.*, p. xxvi.
[28] *Ibid.*, p. xxv n. 36.
[29] Robinson, 'Prose and the Dissociation of Sensibility', p. 269.

it is now the fittest season for *Experiments* to arise, to teach us a Wisdome, which springs from the depths of *Knowledge*, to shake off the shadows, and to scatter the mists, which fill the minds of men with a vain consternation.[30]

This is not only very metaphorical and rhetorical indeed (look at the alliteration and the repetition of amphibracers leading to an orthodox *cursus planus*!): one might well call it an evangel. 'Universal light' seems to 'have overspread this age' (compare Pope's 'God said, Let Newton be, and all was light'), replacing what Dryden called 'all those credulous and doting ages from Aristotle to us'.[31] Set a thief to catch a thief: this itself expresses a kind of credulity, preparing the way for the profound scepticism of Hume.

Dryden became literary dictator partly by intrinsic merit, partly because, expressing so confidently what the dominant party wanted to hear, he was pushed—giving the push the impetus of his own astute self-promotion—by the very small group that then controlled taste as a self-conscious expression of power. 'Sunk to the dregs of a democracy' is of course a Dryden phrase, but his style is much more important than his political opinions, and it is the style of the modern democratic world.

What Dryden gives us in his prose is good sense: that consummately, but nothing else. Dryden's good sense is not as restricted as its successors became after Bentham and it never loses touch with human life as one feels so much modern prose has done; it nevertheless deliberately excludes much of life.

Dryden excludes the spirit of the preceding age. He does with less verve but more effect what Butler essayed in *Hudibras*: *every word* of Dryden's prose and every non-raving word of his non-satirical verse suggests, whatever is being said, that there is nothing in the world that cannot be sorted out between gentlemen of good will, without rancour, intensity of belief or extravagance of feeling. In Dryden's prose there is not only no need to fight for Dame Religion as for punk; the idea just makes no sense. Sense always judges imagination, not *vice versa*. Sense can start civilization again after the twenty years of ridiculous fights about religion and after the millennium of *monkish and doting ignorance*. (And yet he recognized and helped to establish Shakespeare and deferred to Milton!)

The greatest art of the Restoration period was not consonant with the new world. Even Dryden's few poems of real genius, like *MacFlecknoe*, must appear minor beside *Grace Abounding to the Chief of Sinners* or *Paradise Lost*. Moreover, I think that it is in the England of the 1680s

---

[30] Sprat, *The History of the Royal Society*, p. 362.   [31] Cited *ibid.*, p. xviii.

and 1690s that we see for the first time an artistic development that foreshadows the whole eighteenth century in Europe. Passion, tragedy, ecstasy, great beauty, became inexpressible in the styles of language approved by the arbiters of taste. Mozart, the inventor of the operatic equivalent of Shakespeare's mixed play, is one of the great tragic creators, which could not be said for any of the poets contemporary with him. But he was half-anticipated by Purcell, in *Dido and Aeneas*. Dryden did attempt the heroic and tragic, with results that varied between the ridiculous and the outright mad, but the real thing belongs to Purcell, including his settings of Dryden. The things in the world undreamable in Dryden's philosophy had to find expression in music.

Outside music, and excluding satire, the eighteenth century is more homogeneous than any other age of our civilization before television. Johnson's remark that bad eighteenth-century prose is hard to find means at the same time that it is hard to get away from the newly standardized culture, the ancestor of our own *system*.

To say that Dryden's prose is a lesser achievement than either Cranmer's or Bunyan's is less a technical observation than one about Dryden's world: so urbane, but without what Lawrence called the 'depth of vital consciousness' to be found in Cranmer, or in Bunyan, or in Shakespeare.

But yet the very decade of Dryden established the Prayer Book in the form in which it went on through the eighteenth century; and the Age of Reason made no serious effort to supersede the 1611 Bible.

Why could not Dryden make more of the Cranmer tradition? Formally there is less difference between Dryden and Cranmer than similarity. Both are masters of syntactic complication and at the same time of periodic construction. Both are at once rhythmic and close to speech. There is nevertheless a world of difference, literally. Dryden's prose brought in a world quite different from Cranmer's. Dryden was, of course, a very witty man and not without emotion; but it is not unfair to say that his world aspires towards the condition of Swift's Houyhnhnms, the rational horses who drove Gulliver mad.

1660, the date of the beginning of the most resolute reaction in English history, with a powerful government determined that everything should be as it was before the outbreak of 1640, is the date since when nothing has ever been the same again.

Given a culture in which plain statements of fact are the central object of worship and fiction itself is subversive, we catch a glimpse of what the post-enlightenment novelists have been up against: also, perhaps, why their most secure achievements have been comic. To use language comically, ironically, not straight, is itself to subvert the doctrine though not the practice of Sprat and Locke. The comic novel has to be within prose but to redeem prose from the prosaic, by showing the imaginative possibilities of the explicitly anti-imaginative medium. The most interesting question arising is how, then, prose managed to become the medium for the predominant literary form of the modern age, the novel. But that is another and very various set of stories.

Appendix 1   The history of the sentence

To some considerable extent, our readiness to see the modern sentence in older grammatical theory is due to anachronism in translation. R. H. Robins offers the useful caveat 'The translation of *ónoma* and *rhêma* by *noun* and *verb* at this stage [Aristotle's] in the development of Greek grammatical theory may be misleading'; but that comes at the end of the same paragraph in which he has translated Aristotle's *logos* as *sentence*.[1] Robins accurately reports that both Plato and Aristotle include within the *rhema*, often translated predicate *or* verb, some uses of what we call adjectives, and also that the original sense was no more grammatically specialized than *saying* or *proverb*. 'Plato speaks of sentences (lógoi) being composed of nouns and verbs,' says even the brilliantly lucid Michael, still translating the same two words, but later in the same paragraph, 'In the reference of Plato and Aristotle to language *lógos* can seldom be more precisely rendered than by "form of speech".'[2] If *rhema* is so unlike the modern verb should we not think twice before calling a *logos* a sentence? Covington, who is consciously on guard against anachronism, boldly states that *oratio* is 'literally' *sentence* even in Priscian. He also reports Priscian as thinking that 'words are put together to form sentences (*orationes*).'[3] Householder similarly mentions 'what we mistranslate as "parts of speech", which should be "parts of the sentence".'[4] This all seems to me rather like saying that when Priestley defended the phlogiston theory he was *literally* talking about oxygen.

Dionysius of Halicarnassus declines to spend time on the dispute about how many parts of speech there are and says, in Roberts's translation, 'Enough to say that the combination or juxtaposition of these primary parts, be they three, or four, or whatever may be their number, forms the

---

[1] R. H. Robins, *A Short History of Linguistics*, 1967, p. 27.
[2] Michael, *English Grammatical Categories*, p. 39.
[3] Covington, *Syntactic Theory*, pp. 2 and 6, quoting in support a phrase I use in support of the view that Priscian did *not* think of sentences.
[4] *The Syntax of Apollonius Dyscolus*, p. 8.

so-called "members" (or clauses) of a sentence.[5] The Greek here, though, expresses no such confident notion of the sentence as the English, and Dionysius immediately proceeds to periods. We have seen why Roberts's assimilation of the rhetorical terms *period* and *member* to our grammar of the syntactic *clause* and *sentence* is very misleading. Hovdhaugen frequently gives literal translations then modern grammatical equivalents, but the latter cannot but be anachronistic. In R. H. Robins's otherwise illuminating little book *Ancient & Mediaeval Grammatical Theory in Europe* (1951), there is a kind of riot of anachronism, for there Robins uses modern grammatical terms like *sentence*, without any apologies or inverted commas, in the very act of trying to show how modern conceptions developed without a technical terminology.

Fred W. Householder's version of Apollonius the Difficult is of course an immensely useful book and well says, 'The goal of this, as of any translation, is to say in contemporary English exactly what the author said in Greek, but, in this case, without allowing him the knowledge of any linguistic theory more recent than his own,' and

Suppose we consider some of the simplest and most basic of grammatical notions: phrase, (subordinate) clause, noun phrase, verb phrase or predicate (phrase), subject, direct object, indirect object, adverbial phrase, prepositional phrase. Not one of these rudimentary notions was available to A.D. . . .

Although some sort of subject-predicate contrast seems to have been behind the initial development of the idea of noun and verb, and eventually the whole part-of-speech system, a notion such as S → NP + VP is completely absent from A.D.

Householder nevertheless, as we saw, joins Covington in positively insisting on using *sentence* for translating Apollonius Dyscolus's *logos*. He says, however, 'As for "clause", the best A.D. can do is use his word for "sentence", *logos*, but he never clearly grasps the idea of subordination.' Whatever kind of understanding of a *sentence* can it be that uses the same word for *clause* and that has no rudimentary notion of grammatical subject or direct object? 'So whenever you see any of these, or any other English grammatical or linguistic terms in this translation, it should be borne in mind that Apollonius may not have had exactly our categories in mind.'[6] Yes. But the reader of a translation will be prevented from bearing any such thing in mind if it simply uses the modern categories.

---

[5] Dionysius of Halicarnassus, *On Literary Composition being the Greek Text of De Compositione Verborum*, ed. W. Rhys Roberts, 1910, p. 73.

[6] *The Syntax of Apollonius Dyscolus* transl. Householder; quotations in this paragraph from pp. 1–4. I had a stroke of well-disguised luck with this translation, a kind of reverse serendipity, for in the small university in which I worked I did not come upon Householder until I had very laboriously picked my own way through Apollonius in the original. This enabled me to be on guard.

Logos notoriously means something like *language* and *reason* as well as being equated with the Second Person of the Trinity. (Has anyone translated the opening of the Fourth Gospel as 'In the beginning was the well-formed sentence'?) Latin *oratio* has to double up for *oratory*, *speech*, *a speech* (in the oratorical sense) as well as *unit of discourse*. It is possible that, like English *letter*, Greek *logos* and Latin *oratio* may have had a range including general or literary senses but also something syntactically precise. One of the ways in which sciences progress is for a common word to acquire a theoretical sense and become a technical term. It would be pedantic to insist on keeping in mind that *stoicheion*, the word used by Greek grammarians for *a letter*, had earlier meant *the stick on a sundial*. In Ælfric's grammar, good plain Anglo-Saxonate words are made to represent the grammatical abstractions of Donatus. But the Greeks were not acclimatizing in their language conceptions already current in a learned language, they were pushing their language towards grammatical discoveries. It clouds the whole issue to translate the old grammarians as if the discoveries had already been made. The question *when* they were made is extraordinarily hard to settle just because of this obscurity in terminology.

Priscian himself remarks on the different uses of the word *oratio* in order to distinguish the one whose meaning we are investigating. After the definition quoted above (p. 14) he continues:

est autem haec definitio orationis eius, quae est generalis, id est quae in species sive partes dividitur. nam oratio dicitur etiam liber rhetoricus nec non unaqaeque dictio hoc saepe nomine nuncupatur, cum plenam ostendit sententiam, ut verba imperativa et responsiva, quae saepe una dictione complentur, ut si dicam 'quid est summum bonum in vita?' et respondeat quis 'honestas', dico 'bona oratione respondit.'[7]

This definition of *oratio*, however, is of that which is general, which is divided into species or parts. For a rhetorical book is also called *oratio* and some single word is often called by this name, when it shows a complete meaning, as imperative and responsive words (?), which are often completed by one word, as if I shall say 'What is the greatest good in life?' and someone replies 'Integrity', I say 'He replies with good *oratio*.'

As Dinneen wisely observes, 'Technical terms are to be interpreted within their own systems.'[8] If our grammatical system is not the same as that of Apollonius Dyscolus, it may be quite deeply, if subtly, misleading to use our modern terms to translate him. I think *every time* the word *sentence* is used in these translations it should be within 'scare quotes'.

[7] Keil, *Grammatici Latini*, II, pp. 53–4.
[8] Francis P. Dinneen, SJ, '*Suppositio* in Petrus Hispanus', in Bursill-Hall, *de Ortu Grammaticae*, p. 69.

The relevant history is dominated by Aristotle; but first, naturally, came Plato. In the *Sophist* Plato not only distinguishes names from *rhema* (which I would gloss in a preliminary way as 'what is done', still its ordinary often non-linguistic sense in the New Testament) but observes that locutions demand combinations of both and cannot consist only of names or only of what we would call predicates. But as Vorlat observes, 'When Plato opposed the *onoma* and the *rhema*, he was dealing with logical, not with grammatical categories.'[9]

In the *Cratylus* the doctrine appears to be that names can in themselves be either true or false,[10] though that dialogue is so evidently comic that one is not quite sure when the tongue is in the Socratic cheek. The contrary belief that truth and falsity belong to propositions, not to words, which turned out to have far reaching consequences for linguistics as well as for logic, was the contribution of Aristotle.

Aristotle's interest in the forms of language that could be either true or false did not lead him towards syntactic studies. 'A noun or a verb by itself much resembles a concept or thought which is neither combined nor disjoined. Such is "man," for example, or "white," if pronounced without any addition. As yet it is not true nor false.' *Noun* and *verb* translate *onoma* and *rhema*; 'man' appears to be the first and 'white', the second, a 'verb'. This is why Aristotle is accused of the absurdity of making adjectives a kind of verb. He didn't: he took *rhema* in the sense of 'what is said about something', which could cover both what we call verbs and what we call adjectives. Rather similarly, 'Verbs by themselves, then, are nouns': no, still names: of the action named.

It is only when whiteness is truly or falsely predicated of a man that Aristotle gets interested. In the same passage he allows that a prayer is a *logos* but not that it is propositional (*apophantikos*); prayer is not true or false therefore not the province of logic therefore not the province of grammar. Propositional *logoi* must have a word or group of words of doing because that is what makes the true or false proposition about a name.[11] But in grammar 'The **subject**', as Jespersen says, 'cannot be defined by means of such words as active or agent.'[12]

In the *Poetics*, however, the interest is different, and *logos*, without the logical presuppositions of *de Interpretatione*, gets much further away

---

[9] E. Vorlat, *Development of English Grammatical Theory, 1586–1737*, Leuven, 1975, p. 257.

[10] Plato, *Cratylus*, 385c.

[11] Aristotle, *de Interpretatione*, 16a–17a; *The Organon* transl. Harold P. Cooke, Loeb series 1938, pp. 117, 119, 121, 123.

[12] Jespersen, *Essentials of English Grammar*, p. 107; his examples are 'He suffered torture' (where *suffer* is an active verb and *torture* its direct object) and 'He lost his father in the war.'

from our *sentence*. *Logos* is there translated by Hamilton Fyfe as 'phrase': 'a composite sound with a meaning, some parts of which mean something by themselves'.

It is not true to say that every 'phrase' [*logos*] is made up of nouns and verbs, *e.g.* the definition of man; but although it is possible to have a 'phrase' without verbs, yet some part of it will always have a meaning of its own, for example Cleon in 'Cleon walks.' A 'phrase' may be a unit in two ways: either it signifies one thing or it is a combination of several 'phrases'.[13]

Bywater's translation of *logos* here is Speech. A definition (a phrase that does not make a proposition) qualifies as a *logos* here though not as *apophantikos* in the *Organon* because *logos* is now being looked at from a different point of view.

These *logoi* are only coincidentally well-formed sentences. At one extreme the *Iliad* is not a well-formed syntactic structure, and neither at the other is the definition of a man, both of which count as *logoi* in the *Poetics*. To call *The Iliad* one *logos* (where neither *phrase* nor *sentence* will render the sense in English) is a bold assertion of artistic not grammatical unity: 'Thus the *Iliad* is one Speech [*logos*] by conjunction of several; and the definition of man is one through signifying one thing.'[14] The first is recognized as a *logos* for a rhythmic reason, the second for a logical reason. The word rendered 'conjunction' is more literally 'tying together'; Aristotle seems to have most of the available notions of tying together in language *except* the syntax of the well-formed sentence.

Cicero is reported by the Dictionary to use the phrase 'ut sententiae verbis finiantur', which we might unwarily translate: 'as sentences are finished by verbs'. But the Loeb rightly translates the phrase 'to make the thoughts end up with the words'; which takes us back to 'the expression of a single thought'.[15]

In the popular grammar of the Roman Empire and of medieval Christendom syntax was ignored. Dionysius Thrax doesn't mention syntax at all, nor does Donatus.[16] Apollonius Dyscolus is of course the great (though never popular) exception.

Priscian, explicitly and copiously indebted to Apollonius Dyscolus, took syntax seriously and devotes his last two books to the subject, though they, the *Priscianus Minor*, were often not copied with the rest

---

[13] Aristotle, *Poetics*, 1457a; transl. W. Hamilton Fyfe, Loeb edn 1927, repr. 1939, p. 79.
[14] *Aristotle on the Art of Poetry*, transl. Ingram Bywater, Oxford, 1909, p. 61.
[15] Cicero, *De Oratore*, III. xlix. 191, transl. H. Rackham, 1950, II, p. 153. The remark comes in a discussion of feet in periods.
[16] Hovdhaugen says of Dionysius Thrax, 'As we see, there is no place for syntax here' (*Foundations of Western Linguistics*, p. 56). Could that be said of any modern grammar?

and occur far less frequently. Priscian renders the *suntaxis* of Apollonius Dyscolus by *constructio*. But it is not at all clear that he means anything like the modern syntax of the sentence by the Latin word, or that Apollonius means it by the Greek term which means amongst other things the marshalling of soldiers. The *Priscianus Minor* treats the linking of groups of words as a series of separate topics without ever raising *syntactically* the question what unit if any they are linked within. Syntax can, of course, still be so treated,[17] but if so the sentence is just assumed. Whether Priscian made any comparable assumption is the question under discussion. For Priscian, *oratio* or *sententia* is the unit, but what sort of unit has yet to be settled.

Michael observes,

Priscian uses *sententia* similarly as a rhetorical term, but his discussion of it is conducted partly in grammatical terms, and illustrates one step in the development of *sententia* into sentence, for in describing how *usus* differs from *sententia* he says that *sententia* is always a statement (*indicative profertur*) whereas *usus* often takes the form of a question.[18]

With some misgivings at my temerity in disagreeing with so learned and intelligent an authority, I have to say that this seems to me mistaken, much in the way that Aristotle would have been mistaken if he had said that prayers are not well-formed sentences. Questions can be sentences as well-formed as statements. Priscian was reasserting *sententia* as a (logical) statement, not moving towards the modern conception that what makes a grammatical sentence is syntactic well-formedness.

Similarly, the nearest Priscian comes to the grammatical notions of subject and object is by way of logic. 'It is beyond doubt that Priscian used the term suppositum in a purely grammatical sense and without any metaphysical implication,' says the eminently learned Bursill-Hall.[19] Long experience of the groves of academe teaches me that *beyond doubt* normally expresses a lurking doubt, in this case well-founded and supported by a very considerable opinion. Bursill-Hall's quoted certainty immediately follows: 'Thurot claims that the classical grammarians do not seem to have understood the distinction between subject . . . and predicate.' I don't believe anybody ever uses any term without metaphysical implications. Priscian's are the ones of Aristotelian logic as mediated by the Stoics. If *suppositum* is assumed to be the verbal

---

[17] E.g. in Tauno F. Mustanoja, *A Middle English Syntax*, Helsinki, 1960.
[18] Michael, *English Grammatical Categories*, p. 41. Michael also says, 'Priscian does in one passage [XVII. 23, Keil, III, p. 122] suggest a distinction between the logical subject (*suppositum*) and the grammatical subject' (p. 134). I think *suggest* is the right word; Priscian did not follow his own hint.
[19] Bursill-Hall, *Speculative Grammars*, p. 290.

representation of the idea of a substance on which some operation, signified by a verb, is carried out, the logical expectation that a proposition will be made may well defeat any grammatical concern there may be with syntactic structure: I am with Thurot in believing that this happened in the case of Priscian on subject and predicate, and I even believe that something similar happened to the much more subtle and grammatical thinkers, the Modistae.

The classical grammarians frequently give lists of the different elements of discourse, the smaller ones making the larger. Donatus, imitated hundreds of times, gives a descending series. I quote Ælfric's Old English version, because it will be less likely than Latin to distract us with syntactic suggestions.

Littera is stæf on englisc and is se læsta dæl on bocum and untodæledlic. we todælath tha boc to cwydum and syththan tha cwydas to dælum, eft tha dælas to stæfgefegum and syththan tha stæfgefegu to stafum: thonne beoth tha stafas untodæledlice; forthan the nan stæf ne byth naht, gif he gæth on twa.

Littera is letter in English and is the smallest part in books and indivisible. We divide books into *cwydas* and then the *cwydas* into parts (members), then the members into syllables and then the syllables into letters. Then the letters are indivisible, because no letter is anything if it goes in two.[20]

Aristotle's version that started it all goes, in the Loeb translation, 'the series of "parts of speech" [*ta mere . . . lexeos*]: letter, syllable, conjunction, *arthron*, noun, verb [*onoma, rhema*], case [*ptosis*] phrase [*sic: logos*].'[21] A letter is 'an indivisible sound'.

I refrain from translating Ælfric's *cwide* immediately because the question is precisely whether it should be *sentence*.[22] The reason for not bringing in *sentence* is that there is no hint of syntactic structure in these series. The *cwide* is divided into parts, not clauses, and these in turn are made of syllables not syntactic phrases.

Word is not represented in Ælfric's list but is found often enough in Latin; interestingly, it does not *displace* syllable. From the modern point of view syllable is the odd man out because it has no syntactic function. If, however, we are thinking of a structure of sound, and if prosody is a necessary part of grammar, syllable takes its place naturally in the series. Words themselves can be understood as units of sound, perhaps as I advocated.

Much later, the Modistae treated the matter differently, and Radul-

---

[20] *Ælfrics Grammatik und Glossar*, ed. Julius Zupitza, Berlin, 1880, pp. 4–5.
[21] Aristotle 1456b; *Poetics* xx, ed. and transl. W. Hamilton Fyfe, 1927 repr. 1939.
[22] Cf. above, p. 16. *Cwidboc* is not a work of grammar but the Book of Proverbs.

phus Brito denies that *vox* is properly the concern of the grammarian at all.[23]

The old grammarians certainly also discuss units of discourse in the sense of word-classes rather than sound elements when, making different lists, they ask what constitutes *oratio perfecta*. Priscian, as usual imitating Apollonius Dyscolus, asks what *partes* are necessary for a complete *oratio*. This must surely look like a question about well-formed sentences. Both grammarians conduct the experiment of making a *logos/ oratio* containing one each of all but one of the *partes* (not, as reported by Covington, a 'long, elaborate sentence', Priscian's being six words long).[24] What Priscian demonstrates is that a propositional sense can remain after all the parts except noun and verb are removed.

primo loco nomen, secundo verbum posuerunt, quippe cum nulla oratione sine iis completur, quod licet ostendere a constructione, quae continet paene omnes partes orationis. a qua si tollas nomen aut verbum, imperfecta fit oratio; sin autem cetera subtrahas omnia, non necesse est orationem deficere, ut si dicas 'idem homo lapsus heu hodie concidit', en omnes insunt partes orationis absque coniunctione, quae si addatur, aliam orationem exigit. ergo si tollas nomen aut verbum, deficiet oratio, desiderans vel nomen vel verbum, ut si dicam 'idem lapsus heu hodie concidit' vel 'idem homo lapsus heu hodie'; sin subtrahas adverbium, non omnino deficiet oratio, ut 'idem homo lapsus heu concidit'. nec non etiam participium si adimas, neque sic deficiet, ut: 'idem homo heu hodie concidit', nec si praepositionem et interiectionem: 'idem homo cecidit [*sic*]', nec si etiam pronomen: 'homo cecidit'.

In the first place they [the most learned rhetoricians] put the noun, in the second the verb, since with no *oratio* is [the sense] complete without them, which can be shown from a construction which contains nearly all the parts of *oratio*. If you take the noun or the verb from it the *oratio* is made incomplete, but if you take away all the rest, the *oratio* is not necessarily made defective, as if you shall say 'the same man [or, the man himself] fallen alas! today died', in it are present all the parts of *oratio* except the conjunction, which if it is added demands another *oratio*. Therefore if you take away the noun or verb, the *oratio* will become deficient, needing either the noun or the verb, as if I shall say 'the same, fallen, alas! today died.' or 'the same man fallen alas! today'; whereas [if] you take away the adverb, the *oratio* is not altogether defective, as 'the same man, fallen, alas! died'. Nor even if you take away the participle is it yet deficient, as 'the same man alas! today died', nor if the preposition and the interjection: 'the same man died', nor yet if even the pronoun: 'the man died'.[25]

---

[23] Radulphus Brito, *Quaestiones super Priscianum Minorem*, Quaestio 4.1, p. 104.

[24] 'Priscian's observation that a long, elaborate sentence can be shortened word by word and will remain a sentence as long as the main noun and verb are left in (xvii.13)' (Covington, *Syntactic Theory*, p. 58). There's only one noun and one verb. Priscian uses one word fewer than Apollonius Dyscolus because of the absence from Latin of the article.

[25] Keil, *Grammatici Latini*, iii, p. 116. 'Lapsus heu hodie concidit' is actually grammatical

Parts are removed in turn from the *logos/oratio*, and we still have a *perfecta oratio*; but at last with only noun and verb left nothing more can be taken away. (He goes on to allow that the *vis* of a noun can be given by a pronoun and that the noun can be subsumed in the verb, as in *fulminat, tonat*.) Priscian's experiment, however, omits the conjunction, because he says that to bring it in would make another *oratio*, which makes far better sense if he is thinking of propositions than if he is trying to think about complex, compound, simple or text sentences. The whole argument, indeed, is valid if he is thinking of logical propositions, but false if applied to our sentence.

If we are playing hunt-the-sentence, *of course* Priscian is getting warm. The distance from our modes of thought is still equally remarkable. Priscian's demonstration actually *differentiates* what he is discussing from anything we could see as syntactic structure. The formation of imperative plus accusative can be as well-formed a sentence as the noun-subject plus indicative verb. 'Shut the door!' will give a command, not say anything about anything, and therefore does not count as a complete thought in Priscian's discussion, any more than prayers in Aristotle's. We have seen that Priscian allows some one-word locutions as *bonae orationes*; there, when he *is* using *bona oratio* in the sense of grammatical or well-formed, he is *not* talking about sentences. These are not *sententiae* because they make no propositions.

The so-called 'insular grammarians' of the early Middle Ages, who had to present Latin grammar to cultures where Latin was much more alien than in Italy or Gaul, still made hardly any move towards the well-formed sentence. I have no idea how many early medieval grammars and commentaries on grammar are extant (the Irish of the dark ages seem to have been particularly copious[26]) but the number is certainly large; all the ones I have been able to sample are much the same in following the lines of the classical grammarians. They did not suppose that any increased attention to syntax would make their task easier. As Michael observes, 'The earlier grammarians of the medieval period, Bede, Alcuin, Ælfric, do not discuss syntax.'[27]

I think the minimum sufficient condition to be met before we recognize thought about sentences is a *syntactic* understanding of the

---

in Latin as in English, the adjectival participle *lapsus* acting as noun and subject like the English *fallen*.

[26] Cf. lists in Donatus Ortigraphus, *Ars Grammatica*, ed. John Chittenden, Turnholt, Brepols, 1982.

[27] Michael, *English Grammatical Categories*, p. 123. Vivien Law's index has a total of three entries under *syntax* (Vivien Law, *The Insular Grammarians*, Woodbridge, 1982).

subject–verb relation and a clear conception of the syntactic domain of a finite verb.

The movements in this direction came later in the Middle Ages. Priscian has no one word for *government*, and the gradual establishment of *regere* as a necessary word in syntax is important, leading to *regimen* as almost a synonym of *constructio*. Thurot dates this development from the eighth century.[28] Explanations were offered of why one word governs another by the definitions of force (*ex vi*) of different kinds. Dissatisfaction with the apparently unprincipled multiplication of 'forces' *ad hoc* seems to have been one of the goads to the Modistae, who did try hard to give a proper autonomous theory to grammar.

As reported by Covington, by the early eleventh century there were three competing theories of *regimen*, but

> The doctrine expressed in the didactic grammars of Hugh of St Victor (well before 1141), Alexander de Villa Dei (1199?), and Eberhardus Bethuniensis (1212?) is simple: *regere* means 'require a noun to be in a particular case.' For example, most verbs govern (*regunt*) a nominative subject and an accusative object.[29]

It is important that the verbs are now thought to do the governing, but the whole *ex vi* terminology is still firmly within the assumption that syntax is about pairs of words (like noun and verb, noun and adjective). There is still no conception of a *grammatical* unit within which all the governments are explained. *Regimen* is not about the well-formed sentence.

Regimen can, however, be purely grammatical in the sense of attending to relations of words rather than of conceptions (which must have raised difficulties for the severely realist Modistae) in for instance Peter Helias: 'dictionem regere dictionem nihil aliud est quam trahere secum eam in constructione ad constructionis perfectionem, non autem dico ad significationis determinationem.' ('For a word to govern a word is nothing other than to draw it into construction with itself for the completing of the construction, but not, I say, for the determining of meaning.')[30] This does make syntax independent of mental concepts.

Covington says that

> With the revival of logic [beginning late in the tenth century] came a restoration of the link between logic and grammar that had existed in Stoic times but had been broken long before the time of Priscian . . . The re-establishment of the connection resulted in a period of rapid progress in both fields.[31]

---

[28] Thurot, *Extraits*, pp. 82, 244–5; perhaps still the best account.
[29] Covington, *Syntactic Theory*, p. 13.
[30] Cited *ibid.*, p. 16.   [31] *Ibid.*, p. 9.

I will not pause to argue my opinion that the link was never broken. The connection, new or old, meant that grammar was approached again from an Aristotelian philosophy less challengeable than it had ever been. For the schoolmen Aristotle is just *philosophus*. Covington cites a definition of grammar from Dominicus Gundissalinus, from the mid twelfth century: 'scientia ordinandi singulas dictiones in oratione ad significandum conceptiones animae', the science of ordering single words in an *oratio* to signify the conceptions of the mind.[32] Abelard thought logic close to *physica* because it investigates 'the "properties of things" which the mind uses words to signify'.[33] The duty of an *oratio* is to express *conceptus compositi*, compound concepts like Aristotle's 'the man is white'; all of which is familiar.

Covington goes on to quote 'a twelfth-century logical work': 'Et dicitur subiectum in logica id quod dicitur suppositum in grammatica, scilicet quod construitur cum verbo ex parte ante, ex vi personae. Praedicatum est quod in grammatica dicitur appositum.' 'That which is called *suppositum* in grammar is called the subject in logic—namely the thing that is prior to the verb in construction, by the power of person. The predicate [in logic] is what in grammar is called the *appositum*.' I don't recognize this as an account of the (syntactic) subject and predicate. Anything grammatical is still understood by way of logic.

Anyone with an hypothesis runs the risk of growing attached to it and clinging on to it even when contrary evidence turns up. I am fond of the notion that in the Middle Ages they neither wrote nor had any grammar of sentences, but I will let it go if it is refuted. The evidence most likely to do this comes from the Modistae, who certainly took syntactical thought much further, and who definitely pre-echo some modern positions. 'The great achievement of the Modistae with regard to syntactic theory was the development of a formal model of sentence structure,' says Covington.[34] Perhaps it was. There are still some questions about how they understood *sentence*.

The Modistae certainly did raise seriously the question whether there can be a pure grammar, or as I would say whether grammar can be an autonomous discipline, and answered it positively.[35]

They had naturally to recur to the old question what constitutes *oratio perfecta*. Modistic doctrine is that there are three matters to be consid-

---

[32] *Ibid.*, p. 20.
[33] Martin M. Tweedale, 'Abelard and the Culmination of the Old Logic', *The Cambridge History of Later Medieval Philosophy*, p. 143.
[34] Covington, *Syntactic Theory*, p. 41.
[35] E.g. Radulphus Brito, *Quaestiones super Priscianum Minorem*, 1 . 11.

ered: *constructio*, *congruitas* and *perfectio*. Construction is putting words together, congruity making sure that the rules of concord and government are obeyed (though why this is not included in *constructio* is not *grammatically* clear), and that the linked words are proper for each other; but how are we to understand *perfectio*?

Covington takes *perfectio* to be a well-formedness condition, in a modern sense. In his account, Thomas of Erfurt lists three 'conditions for *perfectio*' in addition to the presence of *suppositum* and *appositum*:

(1) The subject and the predicate must be linked in a *constructio intransitiva actuum* (a subject–verb construction) [more literally one in which the action flows from substantive to predicate],
(2) There must be *congruitas* throughout.
(3) There must be no unterminated dependencies. For example, *si Socrates currit*, 'if Socrates runs', is not a complete sentence because the 'if' implies a dependency on something in another clause.[36]

This brings us, of course, very close to the modern sentence, and Radulphus Brito comes even closer when he adds a fourth condition, 'the predicate has to be a finite verb, not an infinitive, since Socratem currere, "for Socrates to run", is not a sentence.'[37]

If I nevertheless 'venture to disagree' with scholars such as Covington I am not just being polite. But there are still a few considerations that make me wonder whether we have got to the sentence.

I notice, in the first place, that *constructio* itself is not thought to be of well-formed sentences. *Si Socrates currit* satisfies condition 1. Why, then, must there be no unterminated dependencies? 'Socrates currit' is a perfect *oratio*, but if *si* is added the resultant phrase, though correctly constructed, is incomplete, because as a conditional clause it derives from a larger sentence. This is *not* the kind of reason given by any of the Modists I have seen. They never say simply that if there are unterminated dependencies the syntactic structure is not well-formed. Bursill-Hall's statements of the matter are significantly different from Covington's He agrees that in Modistic grammar the *sermo* (the meaning waiting in the mind to be signified by the right modes) has to undergo the three *passiones* of construction, congruity and completion, but he paraphrases Thomas of Erfurt on *perfectio* like this:

Perfectio: Completion is the third and final stage of Thomas's syntactic theory and states the requirements necessary to complete a congruent combination of the constructibles in order to express a mental concept in the form of a favourite sentence-type of Latin and thereby create perfect understanding in the mind of the hearer. It is appropriate to use the term 'favourite sentence-type' in this

---

[36] Covington, *Syntactic Theory*, p. 61.
[37] *Ibid.*, p. 70; Raduphus Brito, *Quaestiones super Priscianum Minorem*, I. 75, p. 343.

context, since Thomas insists, as a first requirement of a complete construction, on the presence of a *suppositum* and *appositum*, so that the complete expression of a mental concept can be achieved only by means of an SP construction.[38]

The SP construction is necessary not for syntactic reasons but as the mode of signifying the compound concept. The Modists at this point always appeal to the mind not to syntax: if there are unterminated dependencies the compound concept of the mind is not signified. Cf. Peter of Spain:

A word-group [Dinneen's intelligent rendering of *oratio*] is either complete or incomplete. A perfect or complete word-group generates complete sense in the mind of the hearer, like 'the man is white'; incomplete or imperfect is one that generates incomplete sense in the mind of the hearer, like 'white man'.[39]

We wouldn't say 'white man' is an imperfect sentence, but as noun phrase a possible part of a sentence. For Peter of Spain the (logical) completeness or incompleteness of the sense, not syntactic well-formedness, decides whether the *oratio* is *perfecta*. *Perfectio*, then, is not a grammatical test.

We have seen that Covington has no qualms about reporting Modistic syntax as straightforwardly that of sentence structure. But he says himself:

One point on which all the Modistae agree is that the completeness of the sentence is defined by its ability to carry out its communicative function, which is to express a compound concept and thereby convey a complete thought to the hearer; that is, for them, the concept 'complete sentence' has a functional basis rather than being defined by an arbitrary formation rule like Chomsky's S → NP, VP.[40]

Perfectio, the demand for the existence of a proposition in the mind, itself illustrates the *absence* of an autonomous grammar of the sentence from Modist thinking.

It must be remembered that the Modistae were not 'pure' grammarians in the sense that certain modern linguists are, and a major achievement of modern linguistics has been the creation of a technical language free from association with other disciplines; the Modistae were logicians and philosophers . . . which will perhaps account for the intricacy and wealth of their grammatical terminology.

Yes. And 'The restraints that logic placed on his concept of grammatical structure show visibly through his syntactic theory.'[41]

---

[38] Thomas of Erfurt, *Grammatica Speculativa*, p. 104; cf. p. 30 and Bursill-Hall, *Speculative Grammars*, pp. 301–9.

[39] Peter of Spain, *Language in Dispute*, transl. Francis P. Dinneen, SJ, Amsterdam, 1990, p. 3.

[40] Covington, *Syntactic Theory*, p. 71.

[41] Bursill-Hall, Introduction to Thomas of Erfurt, *Grammatica Speculativa*, pp. 31, 97.

Everything looks different if *oratio* is sense or proposition not sentence. The curious form of the demand for *perfectio* becomes comprehensible if the perfection is that of the thought in the mind, not that of the syntactic structure.

Aristotle's most imitated fictional character, the white man, usually wears a black cloak. Thomas of Erfurt raises the possibility that the *cappa* might be *categorica* not *nigra*.[42] I asserted that there can be well-formed constructions that make no sense; Thomas and I agree about that. But for him an *oratio* cannot be nonsense if by Aristotelian definition the *logos* only comes into being in the first place to signify the compound concept in the mind, which in turn reflects the real world. There is no such thing as a categorical cloak, therefore we can have no conception of such a nonentity, therefore *cappa categorica*, though congruous in the sense of joining noun and adjective correctly as to case, number and gender, will not be proper language. Bertrand Russell and the Wittgenstein of the *Tractatus* would have been thoroughly at home with the family of arguments, but they are not grammatical ones. In this view of things, grammaticality must be determined by the nature of the world, as Abelard saw.

The Modists differ markedly amongst themselves about case; it is one important matter about which they have no group doctrine. But none of them I have seen begins to discuss case in relation to sentence structure. Similarly, sound is not of the first importance either to Chomsky or to Radulphus Brito, but for different reasons. In the Chomskyan scheme sound is notoriously the 'surface' in which the deep structures which are the central concern of grammar are only indirectly and misleadingly 'mapped'. For Radulphus too *vox* is an accident; it signifies, however, not deep structures but signs and modes of signifying. Nothing like 'deep structure' appears in his model; its place is still occupied by the (logical) compound concepts which the modes of signifying signify.

To come down for a moment to the classroom: some of the texts in Thomson's collection of grammars of Latin written in English by Oxford-influenced fifteenth-century masters translate *partes orationis* as one would expect, 'partys of speche', but others as 'partys of reson';[43] and *oratio* in English can be 'a reson'. In the background is the folk-etymology of *oratio* as *mouth-reason*, but the word takes us further than that. It shows that these grammarians were thinking of the unit of meaning before the unit of syntax; where we would say *sentence* they would say *reson*, still having in mind something more like our *proposition*.

---

42 Thomas of Erfurt, *Grammatica Speculativa*, para. 111; p. 308.
43 Thomson, *Grammatical Texts*, A line 1, p. 1, &c.; Text D, line 1, p. 32, &c.

Practical questions are usefully answered by these grammars, but the answer to 'How knouest thou the principall verbe in a reson when thou hast many verbys in yt?' is still conspicuously unsyntactic.

'Euermore my fyrst verbe schall be my principall verbe except he cum ny after ony off thes sygnys: 'that', 'whom' or 'the wyche', or ony off thes: 'but', 'whan', 'after that', 'before that', 'alltho', 'sinthe' 'except' or other like.[44]

At this point Text LL drops the matter without raising awkward questions about subordinate clauses. A *reson* then is, as *oratio* for the much more theoretically rarified Modists, the verbal signification of something predicated of something else in the real world.

One sign that a *reson* is not quite the same as a sentence is given by the splendid phrase *a hangyng resun*, for the use of 'the ablatyff case absolute' ('a partycipull of a verbe impersonall sett by hymsylfe and no word in the reson sett owt or understonde of the wheche he may be gouernd'[45]). It is assumed that the ordinary state of a *reson* is not to be 'hanging'; but it will still be a kind of *reson* if it hangs. (This too conforms to Modist doctrine: they also recognize ablative absolutes as *sermones*.)

Nicholas Orme reports what he calls 'a genre of Latin and English sentences in school treatises and exercise books: sometimes in Latin alone, and sometimes in Latin with English translations'. His examples include 'Far fro the ee, far fro the hart', a non-sentence proverb translated into the equally proverbial but well-formed Latin sentence 'Non ocula nota, res est a corde remota.' The same thing happens when the nonsentence 'Sittyng, standyng, rawf, richard, fals to pos wyt wantyng' gets translated as 'Sedentis standi radulfi ricardo inest opponere carenti ingenio.'[46] In fact the master seems indifferent about whether his English examples are well-formed sentences or not, but he does seem to require that they be translated into a Latin 'reson'.

It remains my opinion that in the ordinary school understanding of the middle ages our concept of the sentence is not found, and that Latin was somehow taught without it.

The Modistae, as whole-hogging Realists, thought that *all* parts of speech are modes of signifying which by way of concepts in the mind must ultimately reflect a real order in the universe. 'The sentence' for

---

[44] *Ibid.*, Text LL, lines 35–40. Cf. a discussion in Text FF, p. 186, which also relies on word order, e.g. 'The nowne that folowyth the verbe shal be the accusatyue case for the more parte' (lines 17–18) and Text X, p. 116.

[45] Cf. *Ibid.*, Text X, lines 223–30, p. 116.

[46] Nicholas Orme, 'Latin and English Sentences in Fifteenth-Century Schoolbooks', *Yale University Library Gazette*, October 1985, pp. 56–7.

the Modistae is as much a matter of the *logos apophantikos* as it was for Aristotle.[47] Radulphus Brito was a principled linguistic universalist, and when he discusses the differences between Greek and Latin he takes it for granted that both languages are expressing the same mental operations, universal to mankind. The differences between Greek and Latin are merely accidental. The grammarian's business is to explain the modes by which language signfies these mental operations.

The Modistae much developed the notion of transitivity from its origins in Apollonius Dyscolus.[48] According to the Modistae *all* constructions are transitive or intransitive. Action is thought to move from one substance to another; this is represented in language by the verb's signifying the movement of action from suppositum to appositum. The accusative signifies the recipient of an action: as it was put in an English grammar of the fifteenth century:

How knowest accusatyf case? Whenne I haue noun, pronoun or participle comyng in a reson aftur a verbe, gerundyf, participle or supyn and the dede of any of hem passe into hym, hit schall be accusatyf case.[49]

This was an advance on Priscian but cannot be seen as autonomously grammatical.

In the Modist way of putting it, the verb signifies *distance* between two concepts, made by a transitive or intransitive suffering of the suppositum. *Distantia* is sometimes simply translated by *verb*; but it could only be a grammatical conception by way of the logical understanding of the proposition.

Bursill-Hall gives an interesting comparative table of the definition of key terms in grammar by three of the Modistae, Martin of Dacia, Siger of Courtrai and Thomas of Erfurt. They all agree that the verb is the *pars orationis* which (in Martin of Dacia's version) 'significat per modum fieri distantis a substantia', in our lingo, signifies by making propositions about something real. *Oratio* does not appear in the list at all! nor in Appendix B of the Thomas of Erfurt edition, 'Definitions of the Modes and Technical Terms'.

Covington cites from Thurot, 'Simplicis orationis duae sunt partes, scilicet suppositum et appositum,' and translates, 'A simple sentence has

---

[47] Pinborg makes the Aristotelian link in the other direction, between Radulphus Brito and Saussure: cf. his diagram, Radulphus Brito, *Quaestiones super Priscianum Minorem*, p. 63.
[48] Cf. 'Apollonius Dyscolus uses "metabasis" or "diabasis" to distinguish between the two basic kinds of relationship that exist in a sentence between the several participants and the predicate or verb' (C. H. Kneepkens, 'Transitivity, Intransitivity and Related Concepts in Twelfth-Century Grammar: an Explorative Study', in Bursill-Hall, *de Ortu Grammaticae*, p. 162).
[49] Thomson, *Grammatical Texts*, Text D, lines 140–3, p. 35.

two parts, a subject and a predicate.'[50] 'Simplex oratio', however, is not the *simple sentence* it must sound like to us, but a single proposition, relating topic and (logical) predicate. The modes of signifying are entrusted with the task of translating this into language, but the singleness is that of the proposition.

In the long term, Aristotelian philosophy of language cannot be reconciled with the ambition to make grammar a speculative science. Pinborg refers to 'the theory's serious intrinsic difficulties, particularly in connection with the analysis of the relationship between language and reality', and says,

The aim of speculative grammar was to describe intra-linguistic relationships, but the Modistae could not accomplish what they wanted without invoking to some degree the structure of reality. This actually was their warrant for believing that their results were scientific and universal.[51]

As Aristotelians, they had to rest their grammar at last outside language. Radulphus Brito seems philosophically the boldest of the Modists I have read, trying hard to make grammar really the study of the *modes* not the *significata*. If so, the only reason why *perfectio* did not trigger *the well-formed sentence* and lead straight to Port Royal, or even to the later Wittgenstein, was the confinement within Aristotelian realism, which was beyond challenge. For if *perfectio* is syntactic, what is to stop us from saying that the completion of the unit of language is the same as the completion of the thought? The Philosopher prevented the Modists from taking this Wittgensteinian step. But the inability to do so made them vulnerable to an ultra-Aristotelian retort.

Pinborg reports the decisive attack by Johannes Aurifaber (Jean Orfèvre? John Goldsmith?): the whole conception of *modes of signifying* was argued to be unnecessary. As Covington puts it,

The Modistae, as moderate realists, had assumed that reality had a definite structure that was mirrored in cognition and in language; the objectors challenged this assumption, arguing that words were purely arbitrary representations of thoughts, and hence that the modistic theory of the cognitive and ontological basis of language was untenable.[52]

Take care of the thoughts and the words will take care of themselves. 'It suffices to know the distinctions of objects and concepts in order to describe how language works.'[53] The modes of signifying then became obvious candidates for the Razor, Ockham being apparently the most

[50] Covington, *Syntactic Theory*, p. 69; Thurot, *Extraits*, p. 218.
[51] Pinborg in *The Cambridge History of Later Medieval Philosophy*, pp. 256, 261.
[52] Covington, *Syntactic Theory*, p. 120.
[53] Pinborg in *The Cambridge History of Later Medieval Philosophy*, p. 267.

influential opponent of the Modistae. Covington reports Aurifaber (whom I have not read) as thinking that 'mental language is crucially different from vocal language, and that only mental language is of scientific interest.' Grammar cannot then be a serious science. Then came Ockham, who according to Covington thinks the operations of the mind very like those of language (premonitions of Foucault!) but did not reach the Wittgensteinian conclusion that if so we may as well after all look at language, which unlike mental operations is available for us to look at.[54]

I agree that the Modistae came close to defining the well-formed sentence. Let us keep in mind, though, that they were not quite men in the street or even average Latin-reading *clerkes*. 'Modism was normally quite absent from the elementary classroom,' and 'There were many places, such as Oxford and Cambridge, where modistic grammar scarcely caught on even among the theoreticians.'[55]

Almost anyone beginning to learn Latin in medieval Europe would have done so in the literary tradition of Donatus, grammar being the first humble step towards reading Virgil.

Sixteenth-century English grammarians still seem to have little more idea of the sentence than Donatus. (See Michael's discussions, *passim*.) Jonson in the *English Grammar*, posthumously published in 1640, still follows ancient tradition in distinguishing nouns and verbs without regarding their relative functions within the sentence. As to punctuation, 'The distinction of a *perfect* sentence,' he says, 'hath a more full stay, and doth rest the spirit, which is a *pause* or a *period*.' A rest for the spirit would never do for Chomsky. It is still unclear whether the perfection of the sentence includes syntactic perfection. Jonson just calls what we know as the colon a *pause*: 'A *pause* is a distinction of a sentence, though perfect in itself, yet joined to another.' Here the perfection in itself may seem to be in a modern sense syntactic, as the joining; possibly a move towards the 'text' sentence—but in Jonson these matters are still unclear.

We have to wait for the French seventeenth century to see *construction* clearly and consistently distinguished from *sentence*. 'For example, the three sentences *accepi litteras tuas*, *tuas accepi litteras*, and *litteras accepi tuas* exhibit three different constructions, but they have the same

---

54 Covington, *Syntactic Theory*, pp. 123 ff.
55 *Ibid.*, pp. 131, 132. The *scarcity* of syntax! Bursill-Hall reports that there are forty-five extant manuscripts of Thomas of Erfurt's treatise and of these only six are known to contain the section on syntax.

syntax.'[56] The older grammarian would have been more interested in the 'construction' than the syntax.

Full grammatical explicitness about sentences is not achieved in English until around the turn of the seventeenth and eighteenth centuries, when a grammarian can still be found apologizing for using modern syntactic terminology. Michael quotes [A.] Lane, 1700:

I hope the Learned will forgive me, if I be forc'd to make use of some terms not usual in Grammar, as *Subject, Predicate, Object*, and such like . . . If I have borrowed these Terms from Logick, I am perswaded that Aristotle borrowed them first from Grammar.[57]

There are *thousands* of medieval manuscripts extant that have never been read since the Middle Ages, and tens of thousands with long marginal glosses that, like so many modern academic works, have probably never been read at all. Who can be sure that in a neglected corner (Modist scholia somewhere on the maverick Virgilius Maro Grammaticus?) some prophetic thinker may not have invented TG grammar? If so, the mansucript remained obscure and uncopied. Such a grammar could not have belonged to the history of thought. Nobody would have understood it.

The first great step in our understanding of the relations of grammar and thought after Aristotle and his classical and medieval refiners was taken by the grammarians of the seventeenth century; and then, I seriously believe, the next one was by Wittgenstein, who did the relevant work in Cambridge and knew Leavis.

---

[56] Chomsky's report of Du Marsais, *Cartesian Linguistics*, p. 47.
[57] Michael, *English Grammatical Categories*, p. 480.

Appendix 2   Medieval punctuation theory

Walter Ong was referring to the whole tradition from the classical age to the end of the Middle Ages when he wrote 'So far as I have been able to find, these grammarians *never* refer to the position of a punctuation mark in terms of grammatical structure.'[1] The classical grammarians treat punctuation as part of eloquence, the art of phrasing and pausing.[2] As usual Donatus was widely followed. He distinguishes three punctuation marks:

Tres sunt omnino positurae vel distinctiones, quas Graeci *theseis* vocant, distinctio, subdistinctio, media distinctio. distinctio est, ubi finitur plena sententia: huius punctum ad summam litteram ponimus. subdistinctio est, ubi non multum superest de sententia, quod tamen necessario separatum mox inferendum sit: huius punctum ad imam litteram ponimus. media distinctio est, ubi fere tantum de sententia superest, quantum iam diximus, cum tamen respirandum sit: huius punctum ad mediam litteram ponimus. in lectione tota sententia periodus dicitur, cuius partes sunt cola et commata [id est membra et caesa].

The points or divisions which the Greeks call *theses* are just three in number: the division, the sub-division and the mid-division. The division is used when the full meaning is finished; we place the sign for this on a level with the top of the letters. The subdivision is used when not much is left of the sense, which yet has to be separated from what is soon to be put in place; we place the sign of this at the bottom of the line of letters. The mid-division is used when as much of the sense remains [to be said] as we have said already, but when breathing is necessary; we place the sign of this at the mid level of the line of letters. In reading, the whole [unit of] meaning is called the period, the parts of which are *cola* and *commata*, that is the members and phrases.[3]

If my translation of *sententia* is right, it is plain that this expresses an idea of punctuation as something oral, not syntactic.

---

[1] Walter J. Ong, 'Historical Backgrounds of Elizabethan and Jacobean Punctuation Theory', *PMLA* 59, 1944, p. 351; cited Graham-White, *Punctuation*, p. 36.

[2] Medieval treatments of punctuation are collected in the oddly titled *Corpus Stigmatologicum Minus*, ed. Hubert and by the masterly Ch. Thurot, *Extraits*.

[3] Donatus, *Ars Grammatica* i. v; Keil, *Grammatici Latini*, IV, p. 372.

Dositheus agrees with Donatus about the *distinctio* and *subdistinctio* and where to put them.[4] Dositheus says that the *distinctio* is a mark of silence at the end of a unit of meaning (*silentii nota cum sensu terminato*); the *subdistinctio* 'est diuturnitas quaedam temporis differens orationem ad sententiae qualitatem.' I think this is especially interesting, as being intelligently directed to *quality* (no doubt understood as a term in Stoic philosophy): 'a certain duration of time varying the speech to the quality of the thought'. This goes well with the following opinion that through punctuation discourse should be made convincing and lucid and should express emotion well: 'ut actus verborum emineat et luceat, qui ex aliquo venit affectu vel indignatione seu miseratione conlata' 'so that the movement of the words should stand out (or be given light and shade) and shine forth, which comes from some feeling or disdain or pity brought together.' Dositheus also discusses the medial pause in verse, of which he says,

hoc solum servat officium, ut legentis spiritum levissima respiratione refoveat et nutriat. sic enim pronuntiando reticere quis debet, quoad spirat, quia spiritus ipse a defectione vincatur, deinde vires resumat.

This performs one service alone: to refresh and feed the spirit/breath of the reader with the lightest possible breath. For thus anyone who has to be silent while articulating, until he breathes, because the very spirit/breath is conquered by failure [of breath], then resumes his forces.[5]

Like Donatus, Dositheus clearly directs the discussion towards vocal performance, not to the distinguishing of syntactic units. The regaining of strength may be something really experienced by the reader, but need not be grammatical. Dositheus does argue that the wrong phrasing will give the wrong sense, and he gives some verse examples, but no syntactic explanations. He goes on to list the places in which punctuation should be introduced, and they include one possibly syntactic context[6] but otherwise before 'similitudines', or the vocative case, or before 'sed' or 'quoniam' or 'interrogativa'.[7]

Cassiodorius agrees in thinking that punctuation is needed *legere . . . competenter*; without it we shall not be understood. He says the

---

[4] Wingo rightly complains that it is impossible to know from Keil, who does not reproduce manuscript punctuation, whether the examples Dositheus gives follow his own prescriptions (Wingo, *Latin Punctuation*, p. 24).

[5] Keil, *Grammatici Latini*, VII, pp. 428, 429. Keil's footnote shows that Diomedes used almost identical phrasing.

[6] 'et siquando *a persona* ad personam transitus erit factus', which *may* mean: 'when the transitivity has been accomplished from one person to another', i.e. in modern terms when a transitive construction is complete.

[7] Wingo notes that Dositheus may mean our interrogatives here or may mean 'a vocative apostrophe or interjection' (*Latin Punctuation*, p. 24).

subdistinctio should be used *cum nullus sermo deest, sed gradatim tendit ad plenam* ('when no expression(?) is missing, but it is tending a step at a time toward fulfilment')[8] and instances 'arma virumque cano'. This too is only vaguely syntactic, if that.

The *point of interrogation* is the most ancient of the marks that could be taken as purely syntactic,[9] but in medieval texts they do not have quite their modern function. Clemoes discusses the *punctus interrogativus* as 'the inflection of an interrogative sentence'.[10] Unlike our question mark, however, it was used for phrases other than questions, but also on the other hand for the indirect questions at the end of which it would be incorrect for us to use a question mark. The older way is to mark pauses or intonations, from which, if anyone wants, the syntax can be inferred. But it is always this indirect route, by way of phrasing.

For later medieval accounts of punctuation see Clemoes, Parkes and Levinson. I do not think there was any development from Donatus significant enough to need much discussion here, though for instance the Beneventan school is of interest.[11]

I will give just one example, an already cited Carthusian text, of the old punctuation still intact in the fifteenth century and here uniting the rhythmic understanding of verse and period with the logical under-standing of *sententia*:

Et sciendum quod in ordine carthusiensi habentur tres pausationes, siue positure, in lectura diuini officii. Quarum prima sic figurata *?* ; uocatur punctus circumflexus. Secunda sic figurata ✓ ; uocatur punctus eleuatus. Tertia, que est in fine orationis, uocatur uersus ; . . . Primus punctus *?* uocatur a gramaticis media distinctio, metrum siue coma. Secundus punctus ✓ uocatur subdistinctio, punctus siue colum, id est membrum. Tertius punctus ; uocatur plena distinctio, uersus et periodus. Primus debet fieri quando sensus orationis est incompletus; secundus fit quando sensus orationis est satis completus sed aliquid bene potest addi; tertius fit quando oratio est totaliter completa . . . sed facienda sunt puncta sicut sunt signata in libris diuini officii correctis in ordine; et non secundum uoluntatem legentis. Item nota quod coma fit quando sentencia est dependens et suspensiua; colum, siue cola, quando sentencia est stans et perfecta sed adhuc dependere uidetur; periodus uero dicitur distinctio finitiua quando amplius sentencia non dependet.

---

[8] Keil, *Grammatici Latini*, VII, p. 146.
[9] According to Parkes the *puncti interrogativi* date from the second half of the eighth century. They actually arise at one moment when the rhetorical divisions of the *period* were in the ascendant over the logical divisions of the *sententia*.
[10] Clemoes, *Liturgical Influence*, p. 13.
[11] Cf. Levinson, *Punctuation*, p. 35, who quotes Wright as saying of the Beneventan school, 'Punctuation was not placed at junctures that appear to be syntactically indistinguishable from others where punctuation is used.' She comments, 'The explanation is clear when the marks are understood as guides to the oral reader, not as grammatical signals.'

You should know that in Carthusian practice three pauses or punctuation marks are used in the reading of the divine Office. The first, written [in the present work] *?*, is called the circumflex point. The second, written ✓ , is called the raised point. The third, which comes at the end of the unit of sense, is called the verse *;*. The first point *?* is called by grammarians the small division, foot (?) or *comma*. The second point ✓ is called the middle division, point or *colon*: that is the *member*. The third point *;* is called the full division, the verse and the period. The first must be used when the sense of the *oratio* is incomplete; the second is used when the sense of the *oratio* is complete enough but when something can well be added; the third is used when the *oratio* is absolutely complete. These pauses are to be made as indicated in the books of the divine Office corrected according to these uses, and not at the will of the reader. Note that the *comma* is made when the sense is hanging, the *colon* or *cola* when the sense is free-standing and finished but still seems to hang [= ask for completion?]; the terminal division is called *period* when the sense does not hang more fully.[12]

The first clear discussion I have found of punctuation as a syntactic matter comes, unsurprisingly, from fifteenth-century Italy, complete with an example:

Coma . . . poniturque post uniuscuiusque uerbi suas constructiones: qua demonstratur uel precedens a sequenti uel sequens a precedenti uerbo dependere . . . Virgula . . . ponitur inter duo substantiua, uel duo adiectiua, ne faciant confusionem, et inter duo uerba quando eorum constructiones non distincte sed mixte sunt, et ubicumque distinguendum est.

The *comma* is placed after every construction of a verb in which either the preceding depends on the following or the following from the preceding on the verb . . . The virgule . . . is put between two nouns, or two adjectives, so that they should not make confusion, and between two verbs when their constructions are not [as we would say] in two main clauses but [as we would say] compound, and when they must be distinguished.[13]

The criteria here are remarkably syntactic, not voice-directed. The sentence used to illustrate the principles is a genuine text sentence; it could have been punctuated otherwise to make more than one sentence. It seems to me even more remarkable that even in Renascence Italy this way of treating the matter was far from standard.

Virgulae convexae, called by Erasmus *lunulae* (half moons), were recommended by Gasparino Barzizza (1359–1431). 'Humanist scribes had introduced parentheses to isolate interpolated expressions which were grammatically independent of their immediate contexts,' says Parkes.[14] Yes: the *grammaticality* of the practice is very informative. But as a matter of fact the original explanations of it were still not

[12] Hubert, *Corpus Stigmatologicum Minus*, p. 163.
[13] *Ibid.*, pp. 166–7, citing Thurot, *Extraits*, p. 416.
[14] Parkes, *Pause and Effect*, pp. 48, 87.

grammatical. Parentheses are discussed in the earliest grammar printed in England, the *Opus Grammaticum* of 1494, along with virgule, colon and period which appear to belong to the older system; parentheses were adapted to it not *vice versa*. The use of parentheses is a good example of practice anticipating theory. Early uses of parentheses naturally varied, and included, according to Lennard, the marking of *sententiae*.[15] But in the sixteenth century, when many round brackets appear to be doing little else than display syntax, this was still not how the grammarians explained them. Mulcaster still does not appeal to any syntactic notion of the unity of the sentence, but accounts for parenthesis as one bit of sense inserted into another:

Parentheses is expressed by two half circles, which in writing enclose some perfit branch, as not mere impertinent, so not fully concident to the sentence, which it breaketh, and warneth us, that the words inclosed by them, ar to be pronounced with a lower and quikker voice, then the words either before or after them.[16]

As we saw, a clearly syntactic understanding of punctuation does not appear in England until the later seventeenth century.

15 John Lennard, *But I Digress*, Oxford, 1991, p. 23.
16 Cited Graham-White, *Punctuation*, p. 38.

Appendix 3   Punctuation in a few manuscripts

This could easily become very voluminous. I only want to quote enough medieval manuscripts to demonstrate that prose punctuation, if any, may be expected (1) to be *per cola et commata*, (2) to vary within limits and (3) to be independent of the syntax of the well-formed sentence. The main evidence must be the Bible, because thousands of medieval Bibles are extant, and they can be quoted almost at random to establish these three points.

All the medieval bibles I have seen from the twelfth century onwards are written out as prose, not in verses as was the older and newer practice. Verse divisions are indicated if at all by punctuation not lineation.

I mentioned 1 Corinthians xiv. 33: 'For God is not *the author* of confusion, but of peace, as in all churches of the saints,' and the question whether the last clause should really go with the following 'Let your women keep silence.' The modern Vulgate agrees with the English 1611:

33 Non enim est dissensionis Deus, sed pacis: sicut et in omnibus Ecclesiis sanctorum doceo.
34 Mulieres in Ecclesiis taceant, non enim permittitur eis loqui, sed subditas esse, sicut et lex dicit.

Medieval bibles, however, are sometimes vaguer:

· Non enim dissensionis & [*sic*] deus sed pacis sicut et in omnibus ecclesiis sanctorum doceo · mulieres in ecclesiis taceant non enim permittitur eis loqui sed subditas esse sicut lex dicit · Si[. . .][1]

· Non est enim discensionis deus sed pacis sicut doceo in omnibus sanctorum ecclesiis [line end no punctuation] Mulieres in ecclesiis taceant. Non enim permittitur eis loquised subditas esse · sicut et lex dicit · Si[. . .][2]

---

[1] Cambridge University Library Dd. xv. 35, f. 402 v. a; fifteenth-century pocket volume, microscopic hand; let anyone check this reading who will!
[2] Cambridge University Library Mm. iii. 2, f. 340 v. b; thirteenth century.

· Non enim est dissensionis Deus sed pacis ⸝ sicut in omnibus ecclesiis sanctorum doceo. ¶[paragraph and illuminated capital] Mulieres in ecclesiis taceant. Non enim permittitur eis loqui ⸝ sed subditas esse. sicut et lex dicit.[3]

; Non enim est dissensionis deus ⸝ sed pacis in omnibus ecclesiis sicut [scribal transposition marks] sanctorum doceo ; Mulieres in ecclesiis taceant. non enim permittitur eis loqui ⸝ sed subiectas esse sicut et lex dicit ; Siquid [. . .][4]

. non enim dissensionis est deus. sed pacis ⸝ sicut et in omnibus ecclesiis sanctorum doceo Mulieres in ecclesiis taceant. non enim permittitur eis loqui sed subditas esse. sicut&lex dicit. s[. . .][5]

. non est dissensionis deus ⸝ sed pacis. sicut in omnibus ecclesiis sanctorum doceo. Mulieres in ecclesiis taceant. Enim non permittitur eis loqui. sed subditas esse ⸝ sicut et lex dicit. S[. . .][6]

Non enim est dissensionis deus sed pacis · sicut in omnibus Ecclesiis sanctorum doceo. Mulieres in Ecclesiis taceant · Non enim permittitur eis loqui sed subditas esse . sicut et lex dicit · S[. . .][7]

English:

for whi god is not of discencioun ⸝ but of pees as in al the chirchis of hooli men J teche ¶ wimmen in chirchis be stille for it is not suffrid to hem to speke ⸝ but to be suget as the lawe seith [no punctuation][8]

/ ffor whi. god is not of disencion but of pees as in alle chirches of holi men I teche // wymmen in chirches be stille for it is not suffred to hem to speke but to be suget as the lawe seith//[9]

for whi god is not of discensioun ⸝ but of pees / as in alle chirchis of hooli men I teche / wommen in chirchis be stille / for it is not suffrid to hem to speke ⸝ but to be suget as the lawe seith/[10]

for whi god is not of discencioun : but of pees as I teche in alle chirches of hooli men / wymmen in chirches be stille / for it is not suffred to hem to speke : but to be suget as the lawe seith/[11]

---

[3] Cambridge University Library Dd. viii. 12, f. 413 v. b; thirteenth century, very neat small hand, capitals red and blue alternately to indicate periods or paragraphs. This manuscript uses very many contractions, the expansion of some of which is debatable, but the punctuation is clear.

[4] Cambridge University Library Dd. i. 14, f. 365 v. b; fourteenth century.

[5] Cambridge University Library Dd. v. 52, f. 326 r. a. No punctuation after *doceo* but alternate capitals in red and blue, blue for the M of *Mulieres*; a tiny fourteenth-century hand.

[6] Cambridge University Library Mm. i. 2, f. 506 r. a. Red dab on M; fourteenth century or older; nice bookhand.

[7] Cambridge University Library Dd. xii. 47, f. 434 v. a. Red dabs on M and second N; fourteenth-century *tiny* but legible hand.

[8] Hereford Cathedral Library O.vii. i, f. 334 r. b.

[9] Cambridge University Library Ll. i. 13, f. 231 r.

[10] Cambridge University Library Mm. ii. 15, f. 329 v. a.

[11] Cambridge University Library Dd. i. 27 (2), f. 484 r. b.

/ forwhi god is not of dissencioun ⫽ but of pees / as in alle chirchis of hooli men I teche / women in chirchis be stille / for it is not suffrid to hem to speke ⫽ but to be suget as the lawe seith/[12]

On the other hand all the texts I have looked at that use punctuation at all have the 'fiat voluntas tua sicut in celo & in terra'[13] of the Lord's Prayer without punctuation, taking 'in earth as it is in heaven' to go only with 'thy will be done', not with all the first three members.

How to treat what looks to us a complex sentence?

8 Then Peter filled with the holy Ghost, said vnto them, Ye rulers of the people, and Elders of Israel,
9 If we this day be examined of the good deed done to the impotent man, by what meanes he is made whole,
10 Be it knowen vnto you all, and to all the people of Israel, that by the Name of Jesus Christ of Nazareth, whom ye crucified, whome God raised from the dead, euen by him, doeth this man stand here before you, whole.[14]

8 Tunc repletus Spiritu sancto Petrus, dixit ad eos: Principes populi, et seniores, audite:
9 Si nos hodie dijudicamur in benefacto hominis infirmi, in quo iste salvus factus est,
10 Notum sit omnibus vobis, et omni plebi Israel: quia in nomine Domini nostri Jesu Christi Nazareni, quem vos crucifixistis, quem Deus suscitavit a mortuis, in hoc iste astat coram vobis sanus.[15]

⫽ Tunc petrus repletus spiritu sancto ⫽ dixit ad eos. Principes populi et seniores. si nos hodie iudicamur in benefacto hominis infirmi in quo iste saluus factus est ⫽ notum sit omnibus uobis et omni plebi Israel. quia in nomine ihesu christi nazareni. quem uos crucifixistis. quem deus suscitauit á mortuis. in quo hoc iste astat coram uobis sanus. hic est lapis [. . .]¹⁶

. Tunc petrus repletus spiritu sancto ⫽ dixit ad eos · Principes populi et seniores israel ⫽ audite · Si nos hodie diudicamur in benefacto hominis infirmi in quo iste saluus factus est ⫽ notum sit omnibus uobis et omni plebiisrael [sic] quod in nomine ihesu christi nazareni quem uos crucifixistis. quem deus suscitauit a mortuis. in iste astat coram uobis sanus · Hic est lapis [. . .]¹⁷

. Tunc petrus repletus spiritu sancto dixit ad eos principes popli & seniores audite · Si nos hodie diiudicamur in benefacto hominis infirmi in quo iste sanus factus est notum sit omnibus uobis · & omni plebi Israel quia in nomine iesu

---

¹² Cambridge University Library Gg. vi. 8, f. 96 r. a.
¹³ Cambridge University Library Mm. iii. 2, f. 296 v. a.
¹⁴ Acts iv, 1611; noticeable variations from the punctuation of modern editions.
¹⁵ Biblia Sacra Latina ex Biblia Sacra Vulgatæ Editionis Sixti V et Clementis VIII, repr. 1977.
¹⁶ Cambridge University Library Dd. viii. 12, f. 427 r. a.
¹⁷ Cambridge University Library Dd. x. 29, f. 489 v. b; fourteenth century.

christi nazareni quem uos crucifixistis · quem Deus suscitavit a mortuis · in hoc
iste astat coram uobis sanus hic est [no punctuation][18]

⸓ Tunc petrus repletus spiritu sancto dixit ad eos · principes populi . et seniores
audite · Si nos hodie diudicamur inbenefacto hominis infirmi in quo iste saluus
factus est ⸓ notum sit omnibus uobis et omni [?]plebi israel. quod in nomine
ihesu christi nazareni quem uos crucifixistis · quem deus suscitauit a mortuis ·
In iste [?] astat coram uobis sanus Hic [no punctuation][19]

· tunc repletus spiritu sancto petrus dixit ad eos · principes populi et seniores
audite · si nos hodie iudicamur in benefacto hominis infirmi in quo iste salvus
factus est · Notum sit omnibus uobis & omni plebi Israel quia in nomine domini
nostri jesu christi nazareni quem vos crucifixistis quem Deus suscitavit a
mortuis · in hoc iste astat coram vobis sanus · Hic [. . .][20]

Tunc petrus repletus spiritu sancto Petrus dixit ad eos; Principes popli &
seniores audite; Si nos hodie diiudicamur in benefacto hominis infirmi inquo
iste salvus factus est. notum sit omnibus uobis. & omni plebi Israel. quia [or
quod] in nomine domini nostri iesu christi nazareni quem uos crucifixistis quem
deus suscitauit a mortuis. in hoc ipse[?] stat coram vobis sanus: hic [. . .][21]

? Tunc repletus spiritu sancto petrus ⸓ dixit ad eos. Principes populi & seniores
audite. Si nos hodie diiudicamur in benefacto hominis infirmi in quo iste saluus
factus est ⸓ notum sit omnibus uobis et omni plebi israel quia [or quod] in
nomine ihesu christi nazareni quem uos crucifixistis quem deus suscitauit a
mortuis ⸓ in hoc iste astat coram uobis sanus. H[. . .][22]

. Tunc repletus Spiritu Sancto Petrus dixit ad eos principes populi & seniores.
Audite. Si nos hodie diiudicamur in beneficio hominis infirmi in quo iste saluus
est · Notum sit omnibus uobis et omni plebi israel · quia in nomine domini
nostri iesu christi nazareni quem uos crucifixistis quem deus suscitauit a mortuis
in hoc iste astat coram vobis sanus · Hic [. . .][23]

⸓ tunc repletus spiritu sancto petrus dixit ad eos, Principes populi & seniores
audite, sinos hodie iudicamur in benefacto hominis infirmi / inquo iste saluus
factus est ⸓ notum sit omnibus uobis & omni plebi israel. quod innomine
domini nostri ihesu christi nazareni quem uos crucifixistis quemdeus suscitaui-
tamortuis ⸓ in hoc iste astatcoram uobis sanus, Hic [. . .][24]

? Tunc Petrus repletus spiritu sancto, dixit ad eos. Principes populi & seniores
Israel, si nos hodie diiudicamur de eo quod bene fecerimus homini infirmo, in
quo iste saluus factus est ⸓ notum sit omnibus uobis & omni plebi Israel, quod
in nomine Iesu Christi nazareni quem uos crucifixistis quem deus suscitauit a
mortuis in hoc iste astat coram uobis sanus. Hic [. . .][25]

[18] Cambridge University Library Mm. iii. 2, f. 359 r. b.
[19] Cambridge University Library Dd. xii. 47, f. 454 v.
[20] Cambridge University Library Dd. xv. 35, f. 421 r. a.
[21] Cambridge University Library Dd. i. 14, f. 382 v. a.
[22] Cambridge University Library Mm. i. 2, f. 528 v. b.
[23] Cambridge University Library Dd. v. 6, f. 326 v. a; huge fourteenth-century folio.
[24] Cambridge University Library Dd. v. 52, f. 341 r. b.
[25] *New Testament*, ed. Erasmus, Basle, 1516, p. 255.

Wyclyffite:

in what name ✓ han ye do this thing ✓/ thanne petir was fillid with the hooli goost ✓ & seide to hem / ye princis of the puple & ye eldere men ✓ heere ye / if we todai be demid in the good dede of a syk man in whom this man is maad saaf ✓ be it knowun to you alle & to alle the puple of israel / that in the name of ihesu crist of nazareth whom ye crucifieden. whom god reiside fro deeth ✓ in this this man stondith hool bifore you / this [. . .]²⁶

in what name ✓ han ye don this thing ? thanne petir was fillid with the hooli gost ✓ & seide to hem / ye pryncis of the peple ✓ & ye elder men heere / if we to dai ben deemed in the good deede of a syc man / In whom this man is maad saaf ✓ be it knowun to you alle & to al the peple of israel that in the name of ihesu crist of nazareth . whom ye crucifieden . whom god reiside from deeth . in this . this man stondith hool bifore you / this is the stoon ✓²⁷

in what name han ye don this thing / than petir was fulled with the holi gost [end of page] & seide to hem ye prynces of the puple & ye elder men: here ye yif we to dai ben demed in the good deede of a seek [sic] in whom this man is man is [sic] maad saaf be it knowen to you alle & to alle the puple of israel that in the name of ihesu crist of nazareth whom ye crucefyeden . whom god reised fro deeth : in this this man stondith hool bifore you [line end] this is the ston [. . .]²⁸

In what name han ye doon this thing? / thanne petir was fillid with the hooli goost ✓ & seide to hem / ye prynces of the peple & ye eldere men ✓ heere ye / if we todai be demed in the good dede of a sijk man in whom this man is maad saaf ✓ be it knowun to you alle & to al the peple of israel / that in the name of ihesu crist of nazareth whom ye crucifieden whom god reiside fro deeth ✓ in this this man stondith hool bifore you / this is the stoon ✓ which was reproued [. . .]²⁹

A fourteenth-century English version of Acts *not* Wycliffite:

¶Thanne Peter fulfilled of tho holygoste · saide vnto hem [line end] Princes of pople and olde men here and vndurstondes·/ If we to daye ben demed in tho gode dede of this seke man in tho whiche ho this is[?] made saufe ¶ knowne thinge be hit vnto yowe ✓ ande to alle tho folke of Israel [end of line] ffor in tho name of Ihesu criste of nazareth the whiche yhe crucified whom god raysed agayn fro dethe · and that he this stondes before yow hole. he this Jhesus es tho stone that of yowe was reproued [. . .]³⁰

Tyndale 1534:

Then Peter full of the holy goost sayd vnto them: ye rulars of the people / & elders of Israel / Yf we this daye are examined of the good dede done to the sycke man / by what meanes he is made whoale: be yt knowen vnto you all / and

²⁶ Cambridge University Library Mm. ii. 15, f. 343 v. b.
²⁷ Hereford Cathedral Library O. VII. 1, f. 347 v. a. I had to use a microfilm of this manuscript and will not vouch for all the virgules, though the manuscript certainly employs virgules.
²⁸ Cambridge University Library Ll. i. 13, f. 232 v.
²⁹ Cambridge University Library Gg. vi. 8, f. 130 v.
³⁰ Cambridge University Library Dd. xii. 39, f. 22 v.–23 r.

to the people of Israel / that in the name of Jesus Christ of Nazareth / whom ye crucified / and whom God raysed agayne from deeth: even by him doth this man stonde here present before you whoale. This [. . .][31]

'Hollybush':

Than Peter fylled wyth the holy goost sayde vnto them: Ye rulers of the people, and elders of Israell, herken, yf we thys daye be examined in the good dede of the sycke man, whereby he is made whole: be it knowen vnto you, and vnto all the people of Israell, that in the name of our LORD Jesus Christe of Nazareth, whom ye haue crucifyed, whome God hath raysed from the deade, in the same standeth he here before you whole.[32]

Coverdale:

Peter full of the holy goost, sayde vnto them: Ye rulers of the people, and ye Elders of Israel, Yf we this daye be examyned concernynge this good dede vpon the sicke man, by what meanes he is made whole, be it knowne then vnto you and to all the people of Israel, that in the name of Jesus Christ of Nazareth, whom ye crucified, whom God hath raysed vp from the deed, stondeth this man here before you whole. This [. . .][33]

Cicero may fairly be thought a distinguished composer of long complex sentences, as in this modern text:

At multi ita sunt imbecilli senes, ut nullum offici aut omnino vitae munus exsequi possint. At id quidem non proprium senectutis vitium est, sed commune valetudinis. Quam fuit imbecillus P. Africani filius, is qui te adoptavit, quam tenui aut nulla potius valetudine! Quod ni ita fuisset, alterum illud exstitisset lumen civitatis; ad paternam enim magnitudinem animi doctrina uberior accesserat. Quid mirum igitur in senibus, si infirmi sunt aliquando, cum id ne adulescentes quidem effugere possint?

Yet, it may be urged, many old men are so feeble that they can perform no function that duty or indeed any position in life demands. True, but that is not peculiar to old age; generally it is a characteristic of ill-health. Note how weak, Scipio, was your adoptive father, the son of Publius Africanus! What feeble health he had, or rather no health at all! But for this he would have shone forth as the second luminary of the state; for to his father's greatness of intellect he had added a more abundant learning. What wonder, then, that the aged are sometimes weak, when even the young cannot escape the same fate?[34]

Parkes quotes a Carolingian manuscript that punctuates this passage much as some old copies of the Latin Bible, with a new line extended

[31] Tyndale 1534, Martin Emperowr edn, f. clxi r.
[32] *The newe testament both in Latine and Englyshe* . . . faythfully translated by Johan Hollybushe, Southwarke, 1538, f. 160 r.
[33] Coverdale's Bible 1535; New Testament, f. liii r. b.
[34] Cicero, *de Senectute, de Amicitia, de Divinatione*, with transl. by William Armistead Falconer, Loeb edn, 1922, pp. 42–5. This text agrees with the Badius edn, Paris, 1527, about where the sentence boundaries come.

into the margin for every period, here reproduced as conventional paragraph indentions:

At multi ita sunt inbecilli senes . ut nullum officii aut omnino uitae munus exequi possint ·
At id quidem non proprium senectutis uitium est . sed commune ualitudinis ·
Quam fuit inbecillus P. africanus filius is qui te adoptauit . quam tenui aut nulla potius ualitudine/
Quod ni ita fuisset . alterum illud extitisset lumen ciuitatis ·
Ad paternam enim magnitudinem . animi doctrina uberior accesserat ·
Quid mirum igitur in senibus si infirmi sint aliquando . cum id ne adulescentes quidem effugere possint/³⁵

Here are a few examples of what later medieval scribes made of the passage:

At multa ita sunt imbecilli senes ut nullum officium aut omnino uite munus exequi possint · At id quidem non proprium senectutis uitium est · Sed commune ualitudinis · Quam fuit imbecillus p scipio affricani filius is qui te adoptauit · quam tenui aut nulla potnus [*sic*] ualitudine · Quod nisi ita fuisset alterum illud extitisset lumen ciuitatis ¶ Ad paternam enim animi magnitudinem doctrina uberior accesserat · Quid mirum igitur in senibus si infirmi sint aliquando cum id ne adolescentes quidem effugere possunt ·³⁶

· At multi ita imbecilles senes sunt ut nullum officii aut omnino vite munus exequi possint · ¶ At id quidem proprium [*sic* no *non*] senectutis vicium est / sed commune valitudinis Quam fuit imbecillus p affricani filius is qui te adoptauit [no punctuation but line end] Quam tenui aut nulla potius valitudine Quod ni ita fuisset alterum illud extitisset lumen ciuitatis · Ad paternam enim magnitudinem animi doctrina veberior accesserat [no punctuation but end of column] Quid mirum igitur in senibus si infirmi sint aliquando · cum id ne adolescentes quidem effugere possint [no punctuation but line-end]³⁷

At multi ita sunt imbeccilles senes / ut nullum offici/ aut omnino uite munus exequi possint. At id quidem non proprium senectutis uitium est / sed comune ualetudinis. quam fuit imbecillus P. affricani filius is qui te adoptauit / quam tenui / aut nulla potius ualetudine/ quod ni ita fuisset. alterum illud extitisset lumen ciuitatis. ad paternam enim magnitudinem animi doctrina uberior accesserat. Quid mirum igitur in senibus si infirmi sint aliquando cum id ne adolescentes quidem effugere possint?³⁸

There is some general agreement about where the phrase-boundaries come, but none about their degree of importance.

---

³⁵ Parkes, *Pause and Effect*, Plate 14.
³⁶ Cambridge University Library Dd. xiii. 2, f. 13 v.; ?fifteenth century.
³⁷ Cambridge University Library Mm. ii. 4, f. 137 r. a–b; fifteenth century.
³⁸ Cambridge University Library Mm. v. 18, f. 129 v.; fifteenth century.

An example of what seems to me a well-written if fierce piece of medieval Latin, a passage of St Bernard's *de Gradibus Humilitatis* which appears like this in the Paris edition of 1640:

Mvltis verò modis fiunt excusationes in peccatis. Aut enim dicit qui se excusat, non feci: aut feci quidem sed benè feci: aut si malè, non multum malè: aut si multum malè, non mala intentione. Si autem & de illa sicut Adam vel Eua conuincitur aliena suasione excusare se nititur. Sed qui procaciter etiam aperta defendit, quando occultas, & malas cogitationes cordi suo aduenientes humiliter reuelaret Abbati?

In many ways, truly, do they make their excuses about sins. For he who excuses himself either says, 'I did not': or, 'I did indeed but I did well': or 'if ill, not very ill': or 'if very ill, not with bad intention'. But so also he depends on excusing himself about that as Adam or Eve was overcome by the persuasion of another. But whoever defends himself shamelessly or openly, when he shall humbly reveal to the Abbot the hidden and ill cogitations coming into his heart?[39]

A Hereford Cathedral Library manuscript of the thirteenth century gives the passage like this:

Mvltis uero modis fuerint excusaciones in peccatis · Aut enim dicte [?] quise excusat · non feci · Aut feci quidem sed bene feci · aut si male ⸓ non multum male · aut si male multum ⸓ si [*sic*] male[abbreviation] intencione · Sienim & de illa sic adam & eua conuincitur ⸓ aliena suasione excusare se nititur · Sed qui procaciter & aperta defendit ⸓ qu[abbreviation] occultas & malas cogitaciones cordi suo aduenientes humiliter reuelaret abbati?[40]

To make this a little more reader-friendly I have regularized the spelling in the three following texts of the same passage from the same library to follow the 1640 edition, recording only variants of wording and punctuation:

Mvltis vero modis fiunt excusationes in peccatis . Aut enim dicit qui se excusat . non feci aut feci quidem · sed bene feci · aut si male ⸓ non multum male . aut si multum male ⸓ non mala intentione · Si autem & de illa sicut Adam vel Eua conuincitur ⸓ aliena suasione excusare se nititur . Sed qui procaciter & aperta defendit quando occultas & malas cogitationes cordi suo aduenientes Humiliter reuelaret Abbati?[41]

Mvltis vero modis · peccatorum · fiunt excusationes in peccatis · Aut enim dicit qui se excusat non feci · aut feci quidem sed bene feci · aut simale non multum male · aut si multum male non mala intentione · Si autem & de illa sicut Adam vel Eua conuincitur · Aliena suasione excusare nititur · Sed qui procaciter etiam aperta defendit ⸓ quando occultas & malas cogitationes cordi suo aduenientes humiliter reuelaret Abbati?[42]

[39] *Opera Omnia Sancti Bernardi Clarævallensis*, Paris, 1640; *De Gradibus Humilitatis*, col. 978.
[40] Hereford Cathedral Library P. III. xii, ff. 150 v. b–151 r. a.
[41] Hereford Cathedral Library O. I. iv, f. 94 r. b.
[42] Hereford Cathedral Library O. v. xii, ff. 43 v. b–44 r. a.

Mvltis vero modis fiunt excusationes in peccatis · Aut enim dicit qui se excusat non feci · aut feci quidem sed bene feci · aut si male non multum male. aut si multum male · non mala intentione · Si autem & de illa sicut Adam vel Eua conuincitur · aliena suasione se excusare nititur · Sed qui procaciter etiam aperta defendit quando occultas & malas cogitationes cordi suo aduenientes humiliter reuelaret Abbati ·[43]

Two put a major pause, perhaps as we would end a text sentence, after 'convincitur'. This gives a better sense than the 1640 edition: 'And so he excuses himself about that like Adam or Eve: he was overcome by the persuasion of another.'

A little later in the same work the 1640 edition has:

Post decimum itaque gradum qui rebellio dictus est, expulsus vel egressus de monasterio statim excipitur ab vndecimo. Et tunc ingreditur vias quæ videntur hominibus bonæ, quarum finis (nisi fortè Deus eas illi sepierit) demerget eum in profundum inferni, id est, in contemptum Dei. Impius [. . .]

Thus after the tenth step which is called rebellion, the man expelled or going out of the monastery immediately is received by the eleventh. And then he follows ways which seem good to men, of which the end (unless perchance God keep them from him) drowns him in deep hell, that is, in contempt of God. Impious . . .[44]

In the same four Hereford mss this appears as:

Post ximum [? — x + a number of minims] itaque gradum qui rebellio dictus est expulsus uel egressus de monasterio statim excipitur ab ·ximo & tunc ingreditur uias que uidentur hominibus bone quarum finis nisi deus eas forte illi sepierto [sic] ∫ demerget eum in profundum inferni ·id est incontemptum dei · Impius [. . .][45]

Again with regularized spelling in the three following:

Post decimum itaque gradum qui rebellio dictus est · expulsus vel egressus de monasterio. statim excipitur ab vndecimo · Et tunc ingreditur vias quae videntur hominibus bonae ∫ quarum finis nisi forte deus eas illi sepierit demergit eum in profundum inferni id est in contemptum Dei. Impius [. . .][46]

Post decimum itaque· gradum qui rebellio dictus est expulsus vel egressus de monasterio statim excipitur ab vndecimo · Et tunc ingreditur vias quae videntur hominibus bonae quarum finis nisi deus eas forte sepierit demerget eum in profundum inferni id est in contemptum Dei · Impius [. . .][47]

---

[43] Hereford Cathedral Library P. I. i, f. 7 r. a. This manuscript does also use an occasional ∫.

[44] *Opera Omnia Sancti Bernardi*; *De Gradibus Humilitatis*, col. 979.

[45] Hereford Cathedral Library P. III. xii, f. 151 v. a. The mid puncti precede a numeral and abbreviation and are not punctuation.

[46] Hereford Cathedral Library O. v. xii, f. 44 v. a.

[47] Hereford Cathedral Library P. I. i, f. 7 v. a. The punctus after *itaque* may be an abbreviation sign.

Post decimum itaque gradum qui rebellio dictus est expulsus vel egressus de monasterio statim ab undecimo suscipitur. Et tunc ingreditur vias quae videntur hominibus bonae quarum finis nisi forte deus eas sibi sepierit demerget eum inprofundum inferni id est in contemptum Dei. Impius [. . .][48]

Ready-made examples of variant punctuation in an English prose work, in manuscripts much closer in time and place than the Bible manuscripts I have quoted, can be found in the Early English Text Society's series of printings of manuscripts of the *Ancrene Wisse*.

[48] Hereford Cathedral Library O. 1. iv, f. 94 v. b.

Appendix 4 Cranmer and the *cursus*

Cranmer's use of the *cursus* was the subject of a series of scholarly discussions beginning about a century ago[1] which strangely petered out as theoretical stylistics developed. The subject, however, is not exhausted.

The *cursus* gave from the heyday of Greek oratory onwards approved ways of rounding off clauses and periods. These were beautifully and extensively practised for instance in the Collects of western masses, and there thoroughly familiar to any pre-Reformation priest or *clerk*. In the *cursus curie romane* they were made obligatory for letters from the Roman curia during the papal zenith from the early years of the twelfth century to about the middle of the fourteenth, and the practice spread through many of the (Latin-writing) chanceries of Europe in that period. Special officers supervised the *cursitores* to ensure the proper rhetoric, and the approved forms of *cursus* were thought of as an insurance against forgery—a danger to which the papacy was indeed exposed.

Following the doctrines of Quintilian and Cicero, the beginnings of periods were important, and it is no accident that bulls often begin with a real bang, like the famous *Unam Sanctam Ecclesiam*. A member beginning with a run of dactyls was frowned upon as tending to levity.[2] But the main emphasis was on ending members and periods with the correct rhythmical units.

The ordinary and original description of the *cursus* cadences is metrical. With some variations three endings were approved: *planus* (dactyl plus trochee); *tardus*, (two dactyls); and *velox* (dactyl plus two trochees the stress of the first trochee being subordinate). *Velox* was supposed to be reserved for the end of the period. Later, rival schools of theory developed in France and Italy. The French stuck to foot-descriptions, but Guido Faba and others refined the matter so that 'The rule in its most concise form stated that if the last word were trisyllabic the preceding word must have a similarly placed stress, and that if it

[1] For full bibliography, see editorial footnotes in Croll, *Style, Rhetoric and Rhythm*.
[2] Cf. Denholm-Young, *Collected Papers*, ch. 2, 'The *Cursus* in England'.

were quadrisyllabic the preceding word must have an opposite stress.'[3] So on both accounts *univérsi fidéles* would be *planus*, *máter ecclésia* would be *tardus* and *firmiter iniungéntes* would be *velox*. There is considerable complication and dispute about the possible exemplification of the forms. Albertus de Morra, later Pope Gregory VIII, insisted that the last word in a period should be preceded by a dactyl.[4] Whether and under what circumstances monosyllables and disyllables were permissible was discussed, but the norm was to make the *clausula* a trisyllable or quadrisyllable; further rules concerned the avoidance of cacophony. Two or more *cursus* together were *compound* and not to be overdone.

The *cursus* endings descended from the classical rhetors, by way of much more fluid earlier medieval practice. Thrasymachus was 'the first person who deliberately introduced metrical cadences into prose for rhetorical effect'.[5] Originally the *cursus* would be understood as successions of *quantitative* feet. This goes some way to explain the oddity to us of names like *tardus* and *velox*, for to anyone accustomed to accentual rhythms, two dactyls are unlikely to sound slow or dactyl plus two trochees fast. Albert C. Clark gives an attractively clear account of how and why the change to accentual patterns came about.[6] Jerome furnishes plenty of examples of accentual *cursus* endings.

Tempest cites the report in Longinus that 'knowing beforehand the endings as they become due, people actually beat time with the speakers, and get before them, and render the movement too soon as though in a dance.'[7] This raises not for the first time the question whether the Greek metres were entirely quantitative: dance steps may well be in time but have an essential beat as well. Cicero frequently uses the term *percussio* in his discussions of rhythm.[8] I don't see how we can avoid understanding this as to do with *beat*, which may have something to do with the fact noticed by Clark that Cicero himself often rounds off the *ambitus* with an *accentual cursus*-form. Howbeit, by the twelfth century the rhythms were certainly accentual and are so read in both correspondence and liturgical texts.[9]

---

[3] *Ibid.*, p. 45.
[4] Clark, *The Cursus in Medieval and Vulgar Latin*, p. 15.
[5] *Ibid.*, p. 5.   [6] *Ibid.*, p. 10.
[7] Norton R. Tempest, *The Rhythm of English Prose*, Cambridge, 1930, p. 74. This is a good short account of the *cursus*.
[8] E.g. Cicero, *De Oratore*, III. xlvii, 182, xlviii, 186.
[9] A leafing through the Sarum Missal confirms that the Collects normally though not always do use the *cursus* forms, though often without strict adherence to the rules reported about secondary stress and polysyllables. The practice is common enough to form a metre-like expectation. But the phrases that do not end with the *cursus* forms often come very near them, which may suggest that the expectation is not quite metrical (for a miss in metre is often as good as a mile) but a less precise instinct about the proper

The *cursus* forms naturally spread to the vernaculars, where the discussion of them runs into difficulties. Cicero and the Papal curialists have in common that they are working in a language whose members or clauses will ordinarily end in polysyllables, and there will not be much doubt as to whether a *cursus* form was intended.

What is much commoner in English, however, as an analytic language, is the rhythmic pattern of a *cursus* form made by the use of more monosyllabic words than any theorist of Latin would approve. If we accept these as naturalized *cursus* it may seem that the rule is getting very elastic. I think, however, that it is fair enough to assume that the patterns ´ ˘ ˘ ´ ˘ , ´ ˘ ˘ ´ ˘ ˘ and especially ´ ˘ ˘ ˘ ´ ˘ are at least noticeable, and shall recognize as *cursus* in English any phrase that so ends. The Roman *cursus* was a rigid codification of freer cadences found all over the place in earlier Latin. If we see similar patterns in the vernaculars they probably have some significance.

way to end a *member*. The *secreta*, the prayers offered *sotto voce* by the priest, to which ordinary rhetorical considerations of audibility and sound effect cannot apply, appear to be as bound by the *cursus* as the other prayers, though oddly enough the Postcommunion possibly less so. It is also noticeable that the employment of the *cursus* seems to be bounded by the text of the prayers themselves, not including the *qui tecum* or *per eundem*. This may give a hint about the comparable English endings.

Examples going through only three consecutive days of the Sarum Missal:

In uigilia natalis domini Collect 'expectacione letificas' (*tardus*), 'leti suscipimus' (*tardus*), 'securi uideamus' (*velox* but only if *securi* can be accented on first syllable), Secretum 'omnipotens deus' (*planus* but disyllable ending), 'natalicia preuenimus' (Croll *planus* 2), 'sempiterna gaudentes' (*planus*), Postcommunion 'natiuitate respirare' (*anomalous*), 'pascimur et potamur' (*anomalous* or just possibly *velox*); Missa in die natalis domini, Missa in gallicantu Collect 'illustracione clarescere' (*tardus*), 'in terra cognouimus' (*tardus* but with incorrect number of syllables in penultimate), 'in celo perfruamur' (Croll *planus* 2 *ditto*), Secretum festiuitatis oblacio' (*tardus*), 'inueniamur forma' (*velox* if *in* can be accented and with disyllabic end), 'nostra substancia' (*tardus*), Postcommunion 'domine deus noster' (*velox* but syllabically irregular), 'frequentare gaudemus' (*planus*), 'pertinere consorcium' (*tardus*); Missa in mane Collect 'omnipotens deus', 'luce perfundimur' (*tardus* with disyllable penultimate), 'resplendeat opere' (*tardus*), 'fulget in mente' (*planus* but with short words), the Collect in memory of St Anastasia 'omnipotens deus', 'sollempnia colimus' (*tardus*), 'patrocinia senciamus' (*velox*), Secretum 'apta proueniant' (*tardus*, disyllabic penult.), 'conferat quod diuinum est' (*anomalous*), Second Secretum 'dignanter oblata' (*planus*), 'prouenire concede (*planus*), Postcommunion 'natalis instauret' (*planus*), 'reppulit uetustatem' (not quite *velox*); Magna Missa Collect 'omnipotens deus', 'natiuitas liberet' (*tardus*), 'seruitus tenet' (*planus* with short last word), Secretum 'maculis emunda' (Croll *planus* 2), Postcommunion 'omnipotens deus', 'generacionis est auctor' (*planus* but with unpolysyllabic last foot), 'sit ipse largitor' (*anomalous*): St Stephen's Day Collect 'imitari quod colimus' (*tardus* using a monosyllable), 'natalicia celebramus' (*velox*), 'filium tuum' (*planus* using disyllable), Secretum 'martyris stephani' (*tardus* depending on the accentuation of the proper name), 'reddat innocuos' (*tardus*, disyllabic penult.), Postcommunion 'sumpta misteria' (*tardus*, ditto), 'protectione confirment' (*planus*). Etc. etc. (*The Sarum Missal* edited from Three Early Manuscripts by J. Wickham Legg, Oxford, 1916).

The interest in the *cursus* in English arose when it was noticed that the Prayer Book Collects often use *cursus* rhythms. Cranmer certainly knew, extremely well, Latin Collects that employed the *cursus*-forms, though there is no effort, as Croll observes, to reproduce exactly the forms of any Latin original in its English translation.

In the brief account that follows I shall ignore Croll's considerable extension of the *cursus* as he observes it in English, even including his extemely common Planus-2, ´ ˘ ˘ ˘ ´ ˘ (i. e. *planus* but with an extra unstressed syllable before the trochee, as in 'supplications of thy people'), and his *extended* forms with additional trochees at the end, but I shall follow Croll in ignoring for English the Papal rules about ending with tri- or quadrisyllables.

Some *cursus* forms are found in English, even by the rules of Guido Faba. 'Perspicacious inquiry' is *planus*; 'respectable burial'[10] is a *tardus*, and a phrase I saw used of the BBC, 'terrible corporation', is a perfect *velox*, as is 'marital disillusion'.[11] If unlike the *cursitores* we allow single words to form a *cursus*, the placename *Abergavenny* makes a *planus*, though it seems so odd to hear it as such that I wonder whether, as there may well have been some element of accent in classical Latin *cursus*, there may be some hangover of quantity into English: the two stressed syllables here are so short that they may fail of the true *cursus* effect. At the end of the same railway line out of Cardiff, however, *Manchester Piccadilly* (though not the train) is surely a perfect *velox*. The haunting phrases *early retirement* and *terminal cancer* are both *planus*, as is 'question and answer' and the names Samuel Johnson and William Wordsworth.

Many English *clausulae* are, anyway, quite unambiguous (including that one, *tardus*). A statistical investigation into the probability of *cursus* forms appearing by pure chance would be useful. My opinion is that even in modern texts they are too frequent for chance to be a likely explanation. I happen to be re-reading *Under Western Eyes* and so, naturally, notice the *cursus*-forms in Conrad. They are frequent, even if the strict Latin rules are applied, as in the first two examples. These are more or less at random:

profound satisfaction (*planus*), envious ecstasy (*tardus*), I am not a heroic person (*velox*), thoughts than from evil fortune (*velox*), not disappointed (*planus*), moments of waiting (*planus*), grounds of the Château Borel (*velox*), invisible interference (*velox*), funeral aspect (*planus*), feminine intuition (*velox*), effective and universal (*velox*), weary sagacity (*tardus*), middle-class order (*planus*),

---

[10] T. F. Powys, *Mock's Curse*, Denton, 1995, p. 17.
[11] Evelyn Waugh, *Brideshead Revisited*, 3rd edn, 1945, p. 9.

inexpressible dreariness (*tardus*), frightful tranquillity (*tardus*), commonplace definitions (*velox*), doubt on the verge of terror (*velox*), etc. etc.[12]

The suggestion is not that Conrad had studied the medieval papal bulls, but that his sense of English rhythm was much indebted to Cranmer, both directly and by way of other authors and of the spoken language.

The titles of three of D. H. Lawrence's travel books take the form of *tardus* (*Twilight in Italy, Sea and Sardinia, Mornings in Mexico*). Chapter titles of *The Rainbow* include several instances of *velox*: 'How Tom Brangwen Married a Polish Lady', 'Childhood of Anna Lensky', 'Girlhood of Anna Brangwen'.

James Hogg, the *bona fide* Ettrick Shepherd, was surely never drilled in *cursus* forms, but equally surely he was orally well educated in Lowland Scots and well read in English. I noticed in *The Brownie of Bodsbeck* (a title which itself forms a *planus*) a sentence that ends with a no less than three *cursus* forms nearly one after the other, not quite a compound because two superfluous syllables come before the final *velox*: 'he be|took him to his old expedient [*velox* if *to his* and *-ient* are slurred into one metrical syllable]—fled with precipitation [*velox*], and re|turned to the Muchrah [*planus* if I have got the accentuation of the proper noun right, taking it to be the Gaelic equivalent of a name which in Welsh means *pig-plain*]'.[13]

The William Hickey column of the *Daily Express* of 12 June 1937 yields the *velox* 'murder from Brixton prison', *ditto* 'director but no conductor', *ditto* 'gala at Covent Garden', the *planus* 'committee said lawyers', *ditto* 'conductors weren't mentioned'; but I found no instance of *tardus*. Lord Beaverbrook had strong views about prose style, which are said to have been pasted up on the wall; but I never heard that he pontificated about the *cursus*.

I must avoid extending this into a ramble through what I happen to have read lately. So, to come back to Cranmer: Croll concentrated his attention on some of the Collects, but the *cursus* forms are also found all over the place in the most commonly used liturgical and biblical texts. If we ignore Latin rules about polysyllables, the Lord's Prayer begins with a *velox*:

> Fáther which àrt in héaven

and the version with a doxology ends with no less then three *plani* one after another:

---

[12] Joseph Conrad, *Under Western Eyes*, phrases from pp. 134 ff in the Cheap Form edn, 1924 repr.

[13] James Hogg, *The Brownie of Bodsbeck*, ed. Douglas S. Mack, Edinburgh, 1976, p. 42.

For thíne is the kíngdom
The pówer and the glóry
For éver and éver

The *cursus* forms are so frequent in the more formal passages of the English Bible ('wounded for our transgressions', *velox*) and Cranmer's liturgical writing that accident is an implausible explanation (*velox*). Need it follow that Cranmer deliberately employed the *cursus*?[14]

Why does the Apostles' Creed end not with 'and the everlasting life' but 'and the life everlasting'? Perhaps because of an instinct for the *cursus*, here a *planus*, like the one that ends the first clause, 'father almighty'. In the Alternative Service Book 1980 Rite B the phrase 'heavenly blessing' (*planus*) occurs, but it is a paraphrase of the even more rhetorical *velox* of Cranmer, perfect by the strictest Latin rules provided only that the -*ion* ending can be monosyllabic, 'heavenly benediction'. Perhaps it was again the *cursus* instinct that guided Cranmer.

The Responses at Morning and Evening Prayer, amongst the most commonly used phrases in English, yield 'mercy upon us' (*planus*), 'bless thine inheritance' (*tardus*) and 'take not thy holy spirit from us' (strictly not *cursus* but *velox* extended in the Croll-approved manner by an additional trochee). Naturally there are plenty of *cursus* forms in Cranmer's first important piece of liturgical writing, the Litany. The repeated *miserable sinners* only misses *planus* by having one unstressed syllable too many. 'The world, the flesh and the devil' ends in *planus*.

Latin, as an inflected language in which stress never falls on the last syllable of inflected endings unless recited as paradigms, naturally has *cola* and periods that end in unstressed syllables. Latin monosyllables can effectively end clauses, as in the repeated *te* of the Gloria in Excelsis: 'Adoramus te, benedicamus te' and so on. But in Latin it is much rarer for a stressed monosyllable to end a phrase than in English. The main objection to attributing the *cursus* forms in English to a deliberate rhetoric is just that they are all trochaic or dactyllic, and the Bible's and Cranmer's sentences, like everyone else's, frequently end on a stress. *In the beginning was the Word.* The *cursus* forms, naturally for Latin, are all 'falling rhythms', in which the stress comes first: not with a bang but a whimper (*planus*). But English prose writers as well as poets do often

[14] I have not been able to verify 'Cranmer's conscious use of the *cursus* which he mentioned in his letter to the king' (Vivian Green, 'Thomas Cranmer, the Prayer Book and the English Language', *Essays by Divers Hands*, new series vol. XLVI, ed. Raleigh Trevelyan, 1990, p. 64). It seems that the letter about the Litany of 7 October 1544 is meant (cf. *ibid.*, p. 57), but the Parker Society edition does not mention the *cursus* (Cranmer, *Miscellaneous Writings*, p. 412).

want to end with a bang. Large amounts of work on rising and falling rhythms in Engish were done mainly by Germans over a century ago, but nobody ever suggested that the former are infrequent in English prose.

I suppose that the general principle is to make a period ending in a stress rather emphatic, and Cranmer often does this, for instance in the repeated 'world without end', which is perhaps best taken (amongst the obvious alternatives) as trochee followed by strong iamb. All the alternatives lead up to a stress. The commonest Collect ending is 'Through Jesus Christ our lord', and the simplest way of taking that is as iambic trimeter. It would be quite unnatural to force it into anything like *cursus* form or to do anything to disguise the rising, not falling, movement. (The *Amen* would not produce a *cursus* pattern if included.) The sentences ending in a stress need not, moreover, be either the upward movement looking to a reply ending with a *cursus* or particularly emphatic or introductory. The psalms, we noticed, habitually go in verses of two halves, but the second half in Coverdale is as likely to end in a stress as the first. Psalm xxiii, for instance, in the versions of both Coverdale and 1611, ends its *cola* mainly by ˘ ´ ´ ˘ or ˘ ˘ ´ ˘.

I don't think one can say more than that in the whole music of Cranmer's prose there are audible echoes of the *cursus*, but not anything systematic (perfect *velox*). Systematic use of the *cursus* would surely create more of a quasi-metrical expectation of *cursus* forms, so that we might even object to not finding them, as in papal correspondence where a failure might suggest forgery. But there are plenty of excellent non-*cursus* endings in Cranmer, also of not-quite-*cursus* forms, like ´ ˘ ´ ˘. In metre, a near miss can be worse than a mile, for it suggests a mistake or that the writer is trying for and missing a metrical pattern. At least the *cursus* was not being used strictly, and if consciously at all, much more in the spirit of the vaguer rhetoric that preceded Papal regularization.

The question is whether our making of *cursus* forms is ever metrical in the sense of choosing a pattern from more than one possibility because (even if we don't know it) it makes a cadence. I think this does sometimes occur.

Thánksgiving is the stress recorded by the Fowlers' Pocket Oxford, but I think the word is that English rarity, a trisyllable of alternative accentuation. The first *colon* of the second verse of the Venite (Psalm xcv, the first of the canticles daily said or sung at Morning Prayer) goes 'Let us come before his presence with thánksgiving', ending with the Dictionary stress so as to make a *tardus*. *Thanksgíving* there would make a rather clumsy non-*cursus* series of trochees. The 1662 Eucharist, however, prescribes words at the delivery of bread ending 'feed on him in thy heart by faith with thanksgiving.' This is ordinarily *thanksgíving*, making a *planus* rather than the not-*cursus* cadence that would be made there by *thánksgiving*. The suggestion must be that there is enough of a sense left even of the forms of approved *cursus* for this one to be chosen.

Polyphiloprogenitive as the opening line of 'Mr. Eliot's Sunday Morning Service' is iambic tetrameter, the first two feet trochaically substituted; as the last word of a period it could probably be phrased as a *tardus*.

The *cursus* patterns are frequent enough to invite the reader to fall gladly into them, other things being equal (English *velox*), but that's about as far as it goes.

As far as I can judge, then, Croll is right to think of the makers of the Prayer Book as writing the *cursus*-forms out of their common sense of English and liturgical rhythm, rather than deliberately. But this may mean we are looking at a bigger thing than an isolated rhetorical habit of sixteenth-century English.

Cursus forms need not be restricted to prose.

> Lily O'Grady
> Silly and shady

turns *plani* into a metre. Fijn van Draat investigated the *cursus* in alliterative verse. (I think his work deserves much more attention than it gets.) *Most* of the lines in *Piers Plowman* end with *cursus* rhythms! Nobody supposes that these cadences were prescribed by Latin prose habit to the verse of the Germanic languages. The explanation is presumably that the *cursus* forms themselves derive from rhythmic patterns common in many Indo-European languages.

In modern English the one exception I might have to make to the generalization that authors fall into the *cursus* because of the habit of the language is the verse of T. S. Eliot: I would not put it past Old Possum to be doing it on purpose. So many of his most characteristic line-endings follow a *cursus* pattern!—'go south in the winter' (*planus*), 'And the camels galled, sore-footed, refractory' (*tardus*), 'the night-fires going out, and the lack of shelters' (*velox*), 'living and partly living' (*velox*). Eleven of the twenty lines of the first paragraph of 'The Journey of the Magi' end in *cursus* forms that are not at all doubtful (*planus*), and a majority here must be significant (*tardus*). There are still the other nine, most of which are not doubtful either. Even Eliot making *cursus* forms was probably just following the grain of a language in which something that comes naturally in many languages is particularly prominent, rather than being deliberately archaic.

Eliot's influence may nonetheless help to keep the *cursus* going. I mentioned Evelyn Waugh's education into the prose world. The Prologue to *Brideshead Revisited* is of course in very competent modern prose. At the same time it is quite obviously indebted to the rhythmic movement of poems like 'The Journey of the Magi', and it is very periodic. I offer the following as a final example of a *tetracolon* as well as of *cursus* forms, and I have punctuated it so as to need no further demonstration:

The camp stood where, until quite lately, had been pasture and ploughland [*planus*]: the farm house still stood, in a fold of the hill, and had served us, for battalion offices [*tardus*]: ivy still supported, part of what had once been, the walls of a fruit-garden [*tardus*]: half an acre, of mutilated old trees, behind the wash-houses, survived of an orchard. [*planus*].

It need not follow that this is the best Waugh. The plangency these *cursus* cadences express may be an omen of the consequent sentimentality.

There are plenty of places in the relevant Papal correspondence where *cursus*-forms do not mark the ends of (modern) sentences.[15] The practice of the *cursus curie romane* is nevertheless a nudge in the direction of modern well-formed sentences. The *cursus* endings are likely to be those of main clauses, which may then be pulled together into a period, ending with a *velox*, that will also commonly be a text sentence. But the impulsion towards syntax was from rhetoric. If many of these documents can be given modern punctuation without the sense of strain I often notice in medieval English texts, that is because the periodic rhetoric was carrying complex syntax much in the way we saw verse doing.

[15] Examples in H. Denifle and G. Palmieri, (eds.), *Specimina Palaeographica Regestorum Romanorum Pontificum . . . ab Innocentio III ad Urbanum V*, Rome, 1888; papal letters sometimes have to go into long lists of names, which can be punctuated but not syntactically, e.g. plate II, 14 May 1198.

Texts frequently cited

References to texts mentioned only once or twice will be found in the notes. Except where otherwise stated the Book of Common Prayer and the Authorized Version of the Bible are quoted from ordinary modern reprints. When the 1549 and 1552 versions of the Book of Common Prayer are quoted without further note the text is that of *The First and Second Prayer Books of King Edward the Sixth*, Everyman, n.d. Shakespeare is quoted from *Mr William Shakespeares Comedies, Histories, & Tragedies*, a facsimile edition prepared by Helge Kökeritz, Oxford, 1955; abbreviated as Folio.

London is the place of publication, except of periodicals, when none is stated. The following are abbreviated when cited.

Abercrombie, David, *Studies in Phonetics and Linguistics*, Oxford, 1965
Adolph, Robert, *The Rise of Modern Prose Style*, Cambridge, Mass., 1968
Apollonius Dyscolus, *Quae Supersunt*, ed. R. Schneider and G. Uhlig, 3 vols., Leipzig, 1910.
The Syntax of Apollonius Dyscolus, transl. Fred W. Householder, Amsterdam, 1981
Auerbach, Erich, *Literary Language and its Public in Late Latin Antiquity and in the Middle Ages*, 1965
Ayris, Paul and David Selwyn (eds.), *Thomas Cranmer, Churchman and Scholar*, Woodbridge, 1993
Barish, Jonas A., *Ben Jonson and the Language of Prose Comedy*, Cambridge, Mass., 1960
Bunyan, John, *The Works of John Bunyan*, ed. George Offor, 3 vols., 1856
Bursill-Hall, G. L., *Speculative Grammars of the Middle Ages*, The Hague, 1971
et al., (eds.), *de Ortu Grammaticae*, Amsterdam, 1990
The Cambridge History of Later Medieval Philosophy, ed. Norman Kretzmann, Anthony Kenny and Jan Pinborg, Cambridge, 1982
Chambers, R. W., *On the Continuity of English Prose from Alfred to More and his School*, Oxford, Early English Text Society, separate repr., 1950
Chronicle: *Two of the Saxon Chronicles Parallel*, ed. Charles Plummer on the basis of an edition by John Earle, 2 vols., Oxford, repr. 1929
Clark, Albert C., *The Cursus in Medieval and Vulgar Latin*, Oxford, 1910
Clemoes, Peter, *Liturgical Influence on Punctuation in Late Old English and Early Middle English Manuscripts*, The Department of Anglo-Saxon, Occasional Papers no. 1, Cambridge, 1952

Covington, Michael A., *Syntactic Theory in the High Middle Ages: Modistic Models of Sentence Structure*, Cambridge, 1984

Cranmer, Thomas, *Miscellaneous Writings and Letters*, ed. John Edmund Cox, Parker Society, Cambridge, 1846

Writings and Disputations of Thomas Cranmer . . . Relative to the Sacrament of the Lord's Supper, ed. John Edmund Cox, Parker Society, Cambridge, 1844

Croll, Morris W. *Style, Rhetoric and Rhythm*, ed. J. Max Patrick and Robert O. Evans, with John M. Wallace and R. J. Schoeck, Princeton, 1966

Cureton, Richard D., *Rhythmic Phrasing in English Verse*, 1992

Daniell, David, (ed.), *Tyndale's New Testament*, New Haven, 1989

Tyndale's Old Testament, New Haven, 1991

Denholm-Young, N., *Collected Papers*, Cardiff, 1969

Dionysius Thrax, 'The *Tekhne Grammatike* of Dionysius Thrax', transl. Alan Kemp, in Daniel J. Taylor, (ed.), *The History of Linguistics in the Classical Period*, Amsterdam, 1987

Donatus, *Ars Grammatica* and *Ars Minor*, in Keil, vol. IV

Eadmer, *The Life of St Anselm*, ed. with transl. by R. W. Southern, Oxford, 1962

Fijn van Draat, P., *Rhythm in English Prose*, Heidelberg, 1910

Fish, Stanley E., (ed.), *Seventeenth-Century Prose: Modern Essays in Criticism*, New York, 1971

Gordon, E. V., *An Introduction to Old Norse*, rev. A. R. Taylor, Oxford, 1957, repr. 1988

Graham-White, Anthony, *Punctuation and its Dramatic Value in Shakespearean Drama*, Newark, Delaware, 1995

The Greek New Testament, ed. Kurt Aland *et al.*, 1968

Haller, William, (ed.), *Tracts on Liberty in the Puritan Revolution 1638–1647*, 3 vols., New York, 1934, repr. 1965

Harding, D. W., 'Rhythmical Intention in Wyatt's Poetry', *Scrutiny* vol. XIV, 1946

Words into Rhythm, Cambridge, 1976

Hovdhaugen, Even, *Foundations of Western Linguistics*, Oslo, 1982

Hubert, M., (ed.), *Corpus Stigmatologicum Minus*, ALMA (*Archivum Latinitatis Medii Aevi*), *Bulletin du Cange*, XXXVII, Brussels, 1970, 5–224; XXXIX, 1974, 55–84

Jespersen, Otto, *Essentials of English Grammar*, 1933

Johnson, Samuel, *A Dictionary of the English Language*, repr. 1786

Keil, H., (general ed.), *Grammatici Latini*, 7 vols and supplement, Leipzig, 1855 onwards

Levinson, Joan Persily, *Punctuation and the Orthographic Sentence, a Linguistic Analysis*, PhD dissertation, City University of New York, 1985

Lewis, C. S., *English Literature in the Sixteenth Century excluding Drama*, Oxford, 1954, repr. 1959

Locke, John, *An Essay Concerning Human Understanding*, abridged and ed. Raymond Wilburn, 1947

MacCulloch, Diarmaid, *Thomas Cranmer: a Life*, New Haven, 1996

Michael, Ian, *English Grammatical Categories and the Tradition to 1800*, Cambridge, 1970

Mitchell, Bruce, *Old English Syntax: vol. 1, Concord, the Parts of Speech, the Sentence*, Oxford, 1985

More, Sir Thomas, *The workes of Sir Thomas More . . . wrytten by him in the Englysh tonge*, 1557

Mueller, Janel L., *The Native Tongue and the Word*, Chicago, 1984

Muir, Kenneth, *Life and Letters of Sir Thomas Wyatt*, Liverpool, 1963

Murphy, James, *Rhetoric in the Middle Ages*, Berkeley, 1974

Nunberg, Geoffrey, *The Linguistics of Punctuation*, Stanford, 1990

The Oxford English Dictionary, prepared by J. A. Simpson and E. S. C. Weiner, 2nd edn, Oxford, 1989; 1st edn referred to as the *New English Dictionary*

Parkes, M. B., *Pause and Effect, an Introduction to the History of Punctuation in the West*, Aldershot, 1992

Parry, David, (ed.), *Excerpts from Old English Literature*, Swansea, 2nd edn 1995

Priscian, *Institutionum Grammaticarum*, in Keil, vols. II–III

Procter, Francis, rev. Walter Howard Frere, *A New History of the Book of Common Prayer*, 1901, repr. 1902

Radulphus Brito, *Quaestiones super Priscianum Minorem*, ed. Heinz W. Enders and Jan Pinborg, 2 vols. paginated consecutively, Stuttgart, 1980

Rhetores Latini Minores, ed. K. Halm, Leipzig, 1843, repr. Frankfurt, 1964

Robinson, Ian, *Chaucer's Prosody*, Cambridge, 1971

   The New Grammarians' Funeral, Cambridge, 1975

   Prayers for the New Babel, Retford, 1983

   'Prose and the Dissociation of Sensibility', *The New Pelican Guide to English Literature*, ed. Boris Ford, vol. 3, 1982

   'Reconstruction', in Roger Knight and Ian Robinson, (eds.), *'My Native English': Criticisms of an Unnecessary Crisis in English Studies*, Gringley-on-the-Hill, 1988, pp. 171–202

   Review of Roy Harris, *Language, Saussure and Wittgenstein*, *Philosophical Investigations* xv. 1, January 1992, pp. 83–9

   'Richard II' and 'Woodstock', Gringley-on-the-Hill, 1988

   The Survival of English, repr. Gringley-on-the-Hill, 1989

   'Thomas Cranmer on the Real Presence', *Faith and Worship*, 43, Advent 1997, pp. 2–10

Saintsbury, George, *A History of English Prose Rhythm*, 1912

Simpson, Percy, *Shakespearian Punctuation*, Oxford 1911, repr. 1969

Sprat, Thomas, *The History of the Royal Society of London for the Improving of Natural Knowledge*, photographic repr. ed. Jackson I. Cope and Harold Whitmore Jones, Washington and London, 1959

Stillman, Robert E., *The New Philosophy and Universal Languages in Seventeenth-Century England*, Lewisburg, 1995

Subbiondo, Joseph L., (ed.), *John Wilkins and 17th-Century British Linguistics*, Amsterdam, 1992

Tempest, Norton R., *The Rhythm of English Prose*, Cambridge, 1930

Thomas of Erfurt, *Grammatica Speculativa*, ed. and transl. G. L. Bursill-Hall, 1972

Thomson, David, (ed.), *An Edition of the Middle English Grammatical Texts*, New York, 1984

Thurot, Ch., *Extraits de Divers Manuscrits Latins pour Servir à l'Étude des Doctrines*

Grammaticales du Moyen Age, Notices et Extraits des Manuscrits de la Bibliothèque Impériale, xxii, Paris, 1868, pt 2, repr. Frankfurt-am-Main, 1964

Tyndale, William, *The Beginning of the New Testament Translated by William Tyndale 1525*, facsimile edn introd. Alfred W. Pollard, Oxford, 1926

Wingo, E. Otha, *Latin Punctuation in the Classical Age*, The Hague, 1972

Wittgenstein, Ludwig, *Philosophical Investigations*, transl. G. E. M. Anscombe, Oxford, 2nd edn 1958, repr. 1963

Index